PRIVACY AND IDENTITY PROTECTION SERIES

PRIVACY: AN OVERVIEW OF FEDERAL LAW GOVERNING WIRETAPPING AND ELECTRONIC EAVESDROPPING

PRIVACY AND IDENTITY PROTECTION SERIES

Social Security Numbers and ID Theft
Felipe D. Sorrells (Editor)
2010. ISBN: 978-1-60741-604-3

Privacy: An Overview of Federal Law Governing Wiretapping and Electronic Eavesdropping
Alderic Jimenez (Editor)
2010. ISBN: 978-1-60741-654-8

PRIVACY AND IDENTITY PROTECTION SERIES

PRIVACY: AN OVERVIEW OF FEDERAL LAW GOVERNING WIRETAPPING AND ELECTRONIC EAVESDROPPING

ALDERIC JIMENEZ
EDITOR

Nova Science Publishers, Inc.
New York

For permission to use material from this book please contact us:
Telephone 631-231-7269; Fax 631-231-8175
Web Site: http://www.novapublishers.com

LIBRARY OF CONGRESS CATALOGING-IN-PUBLICATION DATA
Privacy : an overview of federal law governing wiretapping and electronic eavesdropping / editor, Alderic Jimenez. p. cm.

Includes bibliographical references and index.
ISBN 978-1-60741-654-8 (hardcover : alk. paper)
1. Wiretapping--United States. 2. Eavesdropping--United States.
3. Privacy, Right of--United States. I. Jimenez, Alderic.
KF9670.P75 2009
345.73'052--dc22

2009035607

Published by Nova Science Publishers, Inc. ✦ New York

CONTENTS

PREFACE

This report provides an overview of federal law governing wiretapping and electronic eavesdropping. It also appends citations to state law in the area and contains a bibliography of legal commentary as well as the text of the Electronic Communications Privacy Act (ECPA) and the Foreign Intelligence Surveillance Act (FISA).

It is a federal crime to wiretap or to use a machine to capture the communications of others without court approval, unless one of the parties has given their prior consent. It is likewise a federal crime to use or disclose any information acquired by illegal wiretapping or electronic eavesdropping. Violations can result in imprisonment for not more than five years; fines up to $250,000 (up to $500,000 for organizations); in civil liability for damages, attorneys' fees and possibly punitive damages; in disciplinary action against any attorneys involved; and in suppression of any derivative evidence. Congress has created separate but comparable protective schemes for electronic communications (e.g., e-mail) and against the surreptitious use of telephone call monitoring practices such as pen registers and trap and trace devices.

Each of these protective schemes comes with a procedural mechanism to afford limited law enforcement access to private communications and communications records under conditions consistent with the dictates of the Fourth Amendment. The government has been given even more narrowly confined authority to engage in electronic surveillance, conduct physical searches, install and use pen registers and trap and trace devices for law enforcement purposes under the Electronic Communications Privacy Act and for purposes of foreign intelligence gathering under the Foreign Intelligence Surveillance Act.

This report includes a brief summary of the recently expired Protect America Act, P.L. 110-55 and of the Foreign Intelligence Surveillance Act of 1978 Amendments Act of 2008, P.L. 110-261 (H.R. 6304).

This book consists of public domain documents which have been located, gathered, combined, reformatted, and enhanced with a subject index, selectively edited and bound to provide easy access. It is available in an abridged form without footnotes, quotations, or appendices as CRS Report 98-327, *Privacy: An Abbreviated Outline of Federal Statutes Governing Wiretapping and Electronic Eavesdropping*, by Gina Marie Stevens and Charles Doyle.

In: Privacy: An Overview of Federal Law...
Editor: Alderic Jimenez
ISBN: 978-1-60741-654-8

Chapter 1

INTRODUCTION

Depending on one's perspective, wiretapping and electronic eavesdropping are either "dirty business," essential law enforcement tools, or both. This is a very general overview of the federal statutes that proscribe wiretapping and electronic eavesdropping and of the procedures they establish for law enforcement and foreign intelligence gathering purposes. Although the specifics of state law are beyond the scope of this report, citations to related state statutory provisions have been appended. The text of pertinent federal statutes and a selected bibliography of legal materials appear as appendices as well.[1]

End Note

[1] Portions of this report draw upon a series of earlier reports, no longer available, entitled: *Wiretapping and Electronic Surveillance: A Brief Discussion of Pertinent Supreme Court Cases, A Summary and Compilation of Federal State Statutes, and a Selected Legal Bibliography* (1970); *Wiretapping and Electronic Surveillance: A Brief Discussion of Pertinent Supreme Court Cases, A Summary and Compilation of Federal State Statutes, and a Selected Legal Bibliography* (1971); *Wiretapping and Electronic Surveillance: Federal and State Statutes (1974); Taps and Bugs: A Compilation of Federal and State Statutes Governing the Interception of Wire and Oral Communications* (1981); *The Interception of Communications: A Legal Overview of Bugs and Taps (1988); Wiretapping & Electronic Surveillance: The Electronic Communications Privacy Act and Related Matters* (1992); *Taps, Bugs & Telephony: An Overview of Federal Statutes Governing Wiretapping and Electronic Eavesdropping* (1998); *Privacy: An Overview of Federal Statutes Governing Wiretapping and Electronic Eavesdropping* (2001); id. (2003); id. (2006).

As used in this report "electronic eavesdropping" refers to the use of hidden microphones, recorders and any other mechanical or electronic means of capturing ongoing communications, other than wiretapping (tapping into telephone conversations). In previous versions of this report and other earlier writings, it was common to use a more neutral, and consequently preferred, term – electronic surveillance – at least when referring to law enforcement use. Unfortunately, continued use of the term "electronic surveillance" rather than "electronic eavesdropping" risks confusion with forms of surveillance that either have individualistic definitions (e.g., "electronic surveillance" under the Foreign Intelligence Surveillance Act, 50 U.S.C. 1801(f)), that involve surveillance that does not capture conversation (e.g., thermal imaging or electronic tracking devices), or that may or may not capture conversation (e.g., video surveillance which when it does capture conversation is covered by the law governing electronic eavesdropping, see *United States v. Williams*, 124 F.3d 411 (3d Cir. 1997)).

Related developments are discussed in CRS Report RL30465, *The Foreign Intelligence Surveillance Act: An Overview of the Statutory Framework and Recent Judicial Decisions*; CRS Report 97-1025, *Cybercrime: An Overview of the Federal Computer Fraud and Abuse Statute and Related Federal Criminal Laws*; CRS Report RL30677, *Digital Surveillance: The Communications Assistance for Law Enforcement Act*; and CRS Report RL34409, *Selected Laws Governing the Disclosure of Customer Phone Records by Telecommunications Carriers.*

In: Privacy: An Overview of Federal Law… ISBN: 978-1-60741-654-8
Editor: Alderic Jimenez

Chapter 2

BACKGROUND

At common law, "eavesdroppers, or such as listen under walls or windows, or the eaves of a house, to hearken after discourse, and thereupon to frame slanderous and mischievous tales, are a common nuisance and presentable at the court-leet; or are indictable at the sessions, and punishable by fine and finding of sureties for [their] good behavior," 4 BLACKSTONE, COMMENTARIES ON THE LAWS OF ENGLAND, 169 (1769).

Although early American law proscribed common law eavesdropping, the crime was little prosecuted and by the late nineteenth century had "nearly faded from the legal horizon."[1] With the invention of the telegraph and telephone, however, state laws outlawing wiretapping or indiscretion by telephone and telegraph operators preserved the spirit of the common law prohibition in this country.

Congress enacted the first federal wiretap statute as a temporary measure to prevent disclosure of government secrets during World War I.[2] Later, it proscribed intercepting and divulging private radio messages in the Radio Act of 1927,[3] but did not immediately reestablish a federal wiretap prohibition. By the time of the landmark Supreme Court decision in *Olmstead*, however, at least forty-one of the forty-eight states had banned wiretapping or forbidden telephone and telegraph employees and officers from disclosing the content of telephone or telegraph messages or both.[4]

Olmstead was a Seattle bootlegger whose Prohibition Act conviction was the product of a federal wiretap. He challenged his conviction on three grounds, arguing unsuccessfully that the wiretap evidence should have been suppressed as a violation of either his Fourth Amendment rights, his Fifth Amendment privilege against self-incrimination, or the rights implicit in the Washington state statute that outlawed wiretapping.

For a majority of the Court, writing through Chief Justice Taft, Olmstead's Fourth Amendment challenge was doomed by the absence of "an official search and seizure of his person, or such a seizure of his papers or his tangible material effects, or an actual physical invasion of his house or curtilage[5] for the purposes of making a seizure," 277 U.S. at 466.[6]

Chief Justice Taft pointed out that Congress was free to provide protection which the Constitution did not.[7] Congress did so in the 1934 Communications Act by expanding the Radio Act's proscription against intercepting and divulging radio communications so as to include intercepting and divulging radio or wire communications.[8]

The Federal Communications Act outlawed wiretapping, but it said nothing about the use of machines to surreptitiously record and transmit face to face conversations.[9] In the absence of a statutory ban the number of surreptitious recording cases decided on Fourth Amendment grounds surged and the results began to erode *Olmstead*'s underpinnings.[10]

Erosion, however, came slowly. Initially the Court applied *Olmstead*'s principles to the electronic eavesdropping cases. Thus, the use of a dictaphone to secretly overhear a private conversation in an adjacent office offended no Fourth Amendment precipes because no physical trespass into the office in which the conversation took place had occurred, *Goldman v. United States*, 316 U.S. 129 (1942). Similarly, the absence of a physical trespass precluded Fourth Amendment coverage of the situation where a federal agent secretly recorded his conversation with a defendant held in a commercial laundry in an area open to the public, *On Lee v. United States*, 343 U.S. 747 (1952). On the other hand, the Fourth Amendment did reach the government's physical intrusion upon private property during an investigation, as for example when they drove a "spike mike" into the common wall of a row house until it made contact with a heating duct for the home in which the conversation occurred, *Silverman v. United States*, 365 U.S. 505 (1961).

Silverman presented something of a technical problem, because there was some question whether the spike mike had actually crossed the property line of the defendant's town house when it made contact with the heating duct. The Court declined to rest its decision on the technicalities of local property law, and instead found that the government's conduct had intruded upon privacy of home and hearth in a manner condemned by the Fourth Amendment, 365 U.S. at 510-12.[11]

Each of these cases focused upon whether a warrantless trespass onto private property had occurred, that is, whether the *means* of conducting a search and seizure had been so unreasonable as to offend the Fourth Amendment. Yet in each case, the object of the search and seizure had been not those tangible papers or effects for which the Fourth Amendment's protection had been traditionally claimed, but an intangible, a conversation. This enlarged view of the Fourth Amendment could hardly be ignored, for "[i]t follows from . . . *Silverman* . . . that the Fourth Amendment may protect against the overhearing of verbal statements as well as against the more traditional seizure of papers and effects," *Wong Sun v. United States*, 371 U.S. 471, 485 (1963).

Soon thereafter the Court repudiated the notion that the Fourth Amendment's protection was contingent upon some trespass to real property, *Katz v. United States*, 389 U.S. 347 (1967). Katz was a bookie convicted on the basis of evidence gathered by an electronic listening and recording device set up outside the public telephone booth that Katz used to take and place bets. The Court held that the gateway for Fourth Amendment purposes stood at that point where an individual should to able to expect that his or her privacy would not be subjected to unwarranted governmental intrusion, 389 U.S. at 353.[12]

One obvious consequence of Fourth Amendment coverage of wiretapping and other forms of electronic eavesdropping is the usual attachment of the Amendment's warrant requirement. To avoid constitutional problems and at the same time preserve wiretapping and other forms of electronic eavesdropping as a law enforcement tool, some of the states established a statutory system under which law enforcement officials could obtain a warrant, or equivalent court order, authorizing wiretapping or electronic eavesdropping.

The Court rejected the constitutional adequacy of one of the more detailed of these state statutory schemes in *Berger v. New York*, 388 U.S. 41 (1967). The statute was found deficient its failure to require:

- a particularized description of the place to be searched;
- a particularized description of the crime to which the search and seizure related;
- a particularized description of the conversation to be seized;
- limitations to prevent general searches;
- termination of the interception when the conversation sought had been seized;
- prompt execution of the order;
- return to the issuing court detailing the items seized; and
- any showing exigent circumstances to overcome the want of prior notice. 388 U.S. at 58-60.

Berger help persuade Congress to enact Title III of the Omnibus Crime Control and Safe Streets Act of 1968, 87 Stat. 197, 18 U.S.C. 2510 - 2520 (1970 ed.), a comprehensive wiretapping and electronic eavesdropping statute that not only outlawed both in general terms but that permitted federal and state law enforcement officers to use them under strict limitations designed to meet the objections in *Berger*.

A decade later another Supreme Court case persuaded Congress to supplement Title III with a judicially supervised procedure for the use of wiretapping and electronic eavesdropping in foreign intelligence gathering situations. When Congress passed Title III there was some question over the extent of the President's inherent powers to authorize wiretaps –without judicial approval –in national security cases. As a consequence, the issue was simply removed from the Title III scheme.[13] After the Court held that the President's inherent powers were insufficient to excuse warrantless electronic eavesdropping on purely domestic threats to national security, *United States v. United States District Court*, 407 U.S. 297 (1972), Congress considered it prudent to augment the foreign intelligence gathering authority of the United States with the Foreign Intelligence Security Act of 1978, 92 Stat. 1783, 50 U.S.C. 1801-1862. The Act provides a procedure for judicial review and authorization or denial of wiretapping and other forms of electronic eavesdropping for purposes of foreign intelligence gathering.

In 1986, Congress recast Title III in the Electronic Communications Privacy Act (ECPA), 100 Stat. 1848, 18 U.S.C. 2510 - 2521. The Act followed the general outline of Title III with adjustments and additions. Like Title III, it sought to strike a balance between the interests of privacy and law enforcement, but it also reflected a Congressional desire to avoid unnecessarily crippling infant industries in the fields of advanced communications technology, H.Rept. 99-647, at 18-9 (1984); S.Rept. 99-541, at 5 (1986).

ECPA also included new protection and law enforcement access provisions for stored wire and electronic communications and transactional records access (e-mail and phone records), 18 U.S.C. 2701 - 2710, and for pen registers as well as trap and trace devices (devices for recording the calls placed to or from a particular telephone), 18 U.S.C. 3121 - 3126.[14]

Over the years, Congress has adjusted the components of Title III/ECPA or FISA. Sometimes in the interests of greater privacy; sometimes in the interest of more effective law enforcement or foreign intelligence gathering. The 107th Congress, for instance, amended the basic statutes in the USA PATRIOT Act, P.L. 107-56, 115 Stat. 272 (2001); the Intelligence Authorization Act for Fiscal Year 2002, P.L. 107-108, 115 Stat. 1394 (2001); the 21st Century Department of Justice Appropriations Authorization Act, P.L. 107-273, 116 Stat. 1758

(2002); the Department of Homeland Security Act, P.L. 107-296, 116 Stat. 2135 (2002). The later modifications appear in the USA PATRIOT Improvement and Reauthorization Act, P.L. 109-177, 120 Stat. 192 (2006) and the Foreign Intelligence Surveillance Act of 1978 Amendments Act of 2008, P.L. 110-261, 122 Stat. 2436 (2008).

End Notes

[1] "Eavesdropping is indictable at the common law, not only in England but in our states. It is seldom brought to the attention of the courts, and our books contain too few decisions upon it to enable an author to define it with confidence. . . . It never occupied much space in the law, and it has nearly faded from the legal horizon." 1 BISHOP, COMMENTARIES ON THE CRIMINAL LAW, 670 (1882).

[2] 40 Stat.1017-18 (1918)("whoever during the period of governmental operation of the telephone and telegraph systems of the United States . . . shall, without authority and without the knowledge and consent of the other users thereof, except as may be necessary for operation of the service, tap any telegraph or telephone line . . . or whoever being employed in any such telephone or telegraph service shall divulge the contents of any such telephone or telegraph message to any person not duly authorized or entitled the receive the same, shall be fined not exceeding $1,000 or imprisoned for not more than one year or both"); 56 *Cong.Rec.* 10761-765 (1918).

[3] 44 Stat. 1172 (1927)(". . . no person not being authorized by the sender shall intercept any message and divulge or publish the contents, substance, purpose, effect, or meaning of such intercepted message to any person . . .").

[4] *Olmstead* v. *United States*, 277 U.S. 438, 479-80 n.13 (1928)(Brandeis, J., dissenting). *Olmstead* is remembered most today for the dissents of Holmes and Brandeis, but for four decades it stood for the view that the Fourth Amendment's search and seizure commands did not apply to government wiretapping accomplished without a trespass onto private property.

[5] Curtilage originally meant the land and buildings enclosed by the walls of a castle; in later usage it referred to the barns, stables, garden plots and the like immediately proximate to a dwelling; it is understood in Fourth Amendment parlance to describe that area which "harbors those intimate activities associated with domestic life and the privacies of the home," *United States v. Dunn*, 480 U.S. 294, 301 n.4 (1987).

[6] Olmstead had not been compelled to use his phone and so the Court rejected his Fifth Amendment challenge. 277 U.S.C. at 462. Any violation of the Washington state wiretap statute was thought insufficient to warrant the exclusion of evidence, 277 U.S. at 466-68. Justice Holmes in his dissent tersely characterized the conduct of federal wiretappers as "dirty business," 277 U.S. at 470. The dissent of Justice Brandeis observed that the drafters of the Constitution "conferred as against the Government, the right to be let alone – the most comprehensive of rights and the right most valued by civilized men. To protect that right, every unjustifiable intrusion by the Government against privacy of the individual whatever the means employed, must be deemed in violation of the Fourth Amendment," 277 U.S. at 478-79.

[7] "Congress may of course protect the secrecy of telephone messages by making them, when intercepted inadmissible in evidence in federal criminal trials, by direct legislation," 277 U.S. at 465.

[8] 48 U.S.C. 1103-4 (1934), 47 U.S.C. 605 (1940 ed.). The Act neither expressly condemned law enforcement interceptions nor called for the exclusion of wiretap evidence, but it was read to encompass both, *Nardone v. United States*, 302 U.S. 379 (1937); *Nardone v. United States*, 308 U.S. 321 (1939).

[9] Section 605 did ban the interception and divulgence of radio broadcasts but it did not reach the radio transmission of conversations that were broadcast unbeknownst to all of the parties to the conversation. Late in the game, the FCC supplied a partial solution when it banned the use of licensed radio equipment to overhear or record private conversation without the consent of all the parties involved in the conversation, 31 *Fed.Reg.* 3400 (March 4, 1966), amending then 47 C.F.R. §§2.701, 15.11. The FCC excluded "operations of any law enforcement offices conducted under lawful authority," *id.*

[10] The volume of all Fourth Amendment cases calling for Supreme Court review increased dramatically after *Mapp v. Ohio*, 367 U.S. 643 (1961), acknowledged the application of the Fourth Amendment exclusionary rule to the states.

[11] "The absence of a physical invasion of the petitioner's premises was also a vital factor in the Court's decision in *Olmstead v. United States* . . . . In holding that the wiretapping there did not violate the Fourth Amendment, the Court noted that the insertions were made without trespass upon any property of the defendants. They were made in the basement of the large office building. The taps from house lines were made in the streets near the houses. 277 U.S. at 457. There was no entry of the houses or offices of the defendants. 277 U.S. at 464. Relying upon these circumstances, the Court reasoned that the intervening wires are not part of (the defendant's) house or office any more than are the highways along which they are stretched. 277 U.S. at 465. "Here, by contrast, the officers overheard the petitioners' conversations only by usurping part of the

petitioners' house or office – a heating system which was an integral part of the premises occupied by the petitioners, a usurpation that was effected without their knowledge and without their consent. In these circumstances we need not pause to consider whether or not there was a technical trespass under the local property law relating to party walls. Inherent Fourth Amendment rights are not inevitably measurable in terms of ancient niceties of tort or real property law . . . .

"The Fourth Amendment, and the personal rights which it secures, have a long history. At the very core stands the right of a man to retreat into his own home and there be free from unreasonable governmental intrusion . . . This Court has never held that a federal officer may without warrant and without consent physically entrench into a man's office or home, there secretly observe or listen, and relate at the man's subsequent criminal trial what was seen or heard.

"A distinction between the dictaphone employed in Goldman and the spike mike utilized here seemed to the Court of Appeals too fine a one to draw. The court was unwilling to believe that the respective rights are to be measured in fractions of inches. But decision here does not turn upon the technicality of a trespass upon a party wall as a matter of local law. It is based upon the reality of an actual intrusion into a constitutionally protected area. What the Court said long ago bears repeating now: It may be that it is the obnoxious thing in its mildest and least repulsive form; but illegitimate and unconstitutional practices get their first footing in that way, namely, by silent approaches and slight deviations from legal modes of procedure. *Boyd v. United States*, 116 U.S. 616, 635. We find no occasion to re-examine Goldman here, but we decline to go beyond it, by even a fraction of an inch," 365 U.S. at 510-12 (internal quotation marks omitted).

[12] We conclude that the underpinnings of *Olmstead* and *Goldman* have been so eroded by our subsequent decisions that the trespass doctrine there enunciated can no longer be regarded as controlling. The Government's activities in electronically listening to and recording the petitioner's words violated the privacy upon which he justifiably relied while using the telephone booth and thus constituted a search and seizure within the meaning of the Fourth Amendment. The fact that the electronic device employed to achieve that end did not happen to penetrate the wall of the booth can have no constitutional significance." Later courts seem to prefer the "expectation of privacy" language found in Justice Harlan's concurrence: "My understanding of the rule that has emerged from prior decisions is that there is a twofold requirement, first that a person have exhibited an actual (subjective) expectation of privacy and, second, that the expectation be one that society is prepared to recognize as reasonable," 389 U.S. at 361.

[13] 18 U.S.C. 2511(3)(1970 ed.)("Nothing contained in this chapter or in section 605 of the Communications Act . . . shall limit the constitutional power of the President to take such measures as he deems necessary to protect the Nation against actual or potential attack or other hostile acts of a foreign power, to obtain foreign intelligence information deemed essential to the security of the United States, or to protect national security information against foreign intelligence activities. . .").

[14] These provisions were also grounded in Supreme Court jurisprudence. In *United States v. Miller*, 425 U.S. 435, 441-43 (1976), the Court held that a customer had no Fourth Amendment protected expectation of privacy in the records his bank maintained concerning his transactions with them. These third party records were therefore available to the government under a subpoena duces tecum rather than a more narrowly circumscribed warrant, 425 U.S. 44-45. In *Smith v. Maryland*, 442 U.S. 735, 741-46 (1979), it held that no warrant was required for the state's use of a pen register or trap and trace device which merely identified the telephone numbers for calls made and received from a particular telephone. No Fourth Amendment search or seizure occurred, the Court held, since the customer had no justifiable expectation of privacy in such information which he knew or should know that the telephone company might ordinarily capture for bill or service purposes, *id.*

In: Privacy: An Overview of Federal Law… ISBN: 978-1-60741-654-8
Editor: Alderic Jimenez

Chapter 3

PROHIBITIONS

Unless otherwise provided, Title III/ECPA outlaws wiretapping and electronic eavesdropping, possession of wiretapping or electronic eavesdropping equipment, use or disclosure of information obtained through illegal wiretapping or electronic eavesdropping, and in order to obstruct justice, disclosure of information secured through court-ordered wiretapping or electronic eavesdropping, 18 U.S.C. 2511. Elsewhere ECPA outlaws:

- unlawful access to stored communications, 18 U.S.C. 2701;
- unlawful use of a pen register or a trap and trace device, 18 U.S.C. 3121; and
- abuse of eavesdropping and search authority or unlawful disclosures under the Foreign Intelligence Surveillance Act, 50 U.S.C. 1809, 1827.

In: Privacy: An Overview of Federal Law… ISBN: 978-1-60741-654-8
Editor: Alderic Jimenez

Chapter 4

ILLEGAL WIRETAPPING AND ELECTRONIC EAVESDROPPING

At the heart of Title III/ECPA lies the prohibition against illegal wiretapping and electronic eavesdropping, 18 U.S.C. 2511(1), that proscribes:

- any person from
- intentionally
- intercepting, or endeavoring to intercept,
    - wire, oral or electronic communications
    - by using an electronic, mechanical or other device
    - unless the conduct is specifically authorized or expressly not covered, e.g.

one of the parties to the conversation has consent to the interception

the interception occurs in compliance with a statutorily authorized, (and ordinarily judicially-supervised) law enforcement or foreign intelligence gathering interception,

the interception occurs as part of providing or regulating communication services,

certain radio broadcasts, and

in some places, spousal wiretappers.

PERSON

The prohibition applies to "any employee, or agent of the United States or any State or political subdivision thereof, and any individual, partnership, association, joint stock company, trust, or corporation," 18 U.S.C. 2510(6).[1]

INTENTIONAL

Conduct can only violate Title III/ECPA if it is done "intentionally," inadvertent conduct is no crime; the offender must have done on purpose those things which are outlawed.[2] He need not be shown have known, however, that his conduct was unlawful.[3]

JURISDICTION

Section 2511(1) contains two interception bars – one, 2511(1)(a), simply outlaws intentional interception; the other, 2511(1)(b), outlaws intentional interception when committed under any of five jurisdictional circumstances with either an implicit or explicit nexus to interstate or foreign commerce.[4] Congress adopted the approach because of concern that its constitutional authority might not be sufficient to ban instances of electronic surveillance that bore no discernable connection to interstate commerce or any other of the enumerated powers. So it enacted a general prohibition, and as a safety precaution, a second provision more tightly tethered to specific jurisdictional factors.[5] The Justice Department has honored that caution by employing subparagraph (b) to prosecute the interception of oral communications, while using subparagraph (a) to prosecute other forms of electronic eavesdropping, DEPARTMENT OF JUSTICE CRIMINAL RESOURCE MANUAL at 1050.[6]

INTERCEPTION

Interception "means the aural or other acquisition of the contents" of various kinds of communications by means of electronic, mechanical or other devices.[7] The definition raises questions of where, when, what, and how. Although logic might suggest that interception occurs only in the place where the communication is captured, the cases indicate that interception occurs as well where the communication begins, is transmitted, or is received.[8]

Once limited to aural acquisitions, ECPA enlarged the definition by adding the words "or other acquisition" so that it is no longer limited to interceptions of communications that can be heard.[9] The change complicates the question of whether the wiretap, stored communications, or trap and trace portions of the ECPA govern the legality of various means of capturing information relating to a communication. The analysis might seem to favor wiretap coverage when it begins with an examination of whether an "interception" has occurred. Yet, there is little consensus over when an interception occurs; that is, whether "interception" as used section 2511 contemplates only surreptitious acquisition, contemporaneous with transmission, or whether such acquisition may occur anytime before the initial cognitive receipt of the contents by the intended recipient.[10]

The USA PATRIOT Act resolved some of the uncertainty when it removed voice mail from the wiretap coverage of Title III, 115 Stat. 283 (2001)(striking the phrase "and such term includes any electronic storage of such communication" from the definition of "wire communications" in Title III (18 U.S.C. 2510(1)) and added stored *wire* communications to the stored communications coverage of 18 U.S.C. 2703.

As for the "what," the interceptions proscribed in Title III are confined to those that capture a communication's content. Trap and trace devices and pen registers once captured only information relating to the source and addressee of a communication, not its content. That is no longer the case. The "post-cut-through dialed digit features" of contemporary telephone communications now transmit communications in such a manner that the use of ordinary pen register or trap and trace devices will capture both non-content and content.[11] As a consequence, a few courts have held, either as a matter of statutory construction or constitutional necessity, that the authorities must rely on a Title III wiretap order rather than a pen register/trap and trace order if such information will be captured.[12]

By Electronic, Mechanical, or Other Device

The statute does not cover common law "eavesdropping," but only interceptions "by electronic, mechanical or other device," 18 U.S.C. 2510(4).[13] That phrase is in turn defined so as not to include hearing aids or extension telephones in normal use.[14] Whether an extension phone has been installed and is being used in the ordinary course of business or in the ordinary course of law enforcement duties, so that it no longer constitutes an interception device for purposes of Title III/ECPA and comparable state laws has proven a somewhat vexing question.[15]

Although often intertwined with the consent exception discussed below, the question generally turns on the facts in a given case.[16] When the exemption is claimed as a practice in the ordinary course of business, the interception must be for a legitimate business reason, it must be routinely conducted, and at least in some Circuits employees must be notified that their conversations are being monitored.[17] Similarly, "Congress most likely carved out an exception for law enforcement officials to make clear that the routine and almost universal recording of phone lines by police departments and prisons, as well as other law enforcement institutions, is exempt from the statute," *Adams v. Battle Creek*, 250 F.3d at 984.[18] The exception contemplates administrative rather than investigative monitoring,[19] which must nevertheless be justified by a lawful, valid law enforcement concern.[20]

Wire, Oral, or Electronic Communications

An interception can only be a violation of ECPA if the conversation or other form of communication intercepted is among those kinds which the statute protects, in over simplified terms – telephone (wire), face to face (oral), and computer (electronic). Congress used the definitions of the three forms of communications to describe the communications beyond the Act's reach as well as those within its grasp. For example, "oral communication" by definition includes only those face to face conversations with respect to which the speakers have a justifiable expectation of privacy.[21] Similarly, "wire communications" are limited to those that are at some point involve voice communications (i.e. only aural transfers).[22] Radio and data transmissions are generally "electronic communications." The definition includes other forms of information transfer but excludes certain radio transmissions which can be innocently captured without great difficulty.[23] Although it is not a federal crime to intercept radio communications under any number of conditions, the exclusion is not a matter of definition but of special general exemptions, 18 U.S.C. 2511(2)(g), discussed below.

Endeavoring to Intercept

Although the statute condemns attempted wiretapping and electronic eavesdropping ("endeavoring to intercept"), 18 U.S.C. 2511(1), the provisions appear to have escaped use, interest, or comment heretofore, perhaps because the conduct most likely to constitute preparation for an interception – possession of wiretapping equipment – is already a separate crime, 18 U.S.C. 2512, discussed, *infra*.

Exemptions: Consent Interceptions

Consent interceptions are common, controversial and have a history all their own. The early bans on divulging telegraph or telephone messages had a consent exception. The Supreme Court upheld consent interceptions against Fourth Amendment challenge both before and after the enactment of Title III.[24] The argument in favor of consent interceptions has always been essentially that a speaker risks the indiscretion of his listeners and holds no superior legal position simply because a listener elects to record or transmit his statements rather than subsequently memorializing or repeating them.[25] Wiretapping or electronic eavesdropping by either the police or anyone else with the consent of at least one party to the conversation is not unlawful under the federal statute.[26] These provisions do no more than shield consent interceptions from the sanctions of federal law; they afford no protection from the sanctions of state law. Many of the states recognize comparable exceptions, but some only permit interception with the consent of *all* parties to a communication.[27]

Under federal law, consent may be either explicitly or implicitly given. For instance, someone who uses a telephone other than his or her own and has been told by the subscriber that conversations over the instrument are recorded has been held to have implicitly consented to interception when using the instrument.[28] This is not to say that subscriber consent alone is sufficient, for it is the parties to the conversation whose privacy is designed to protect.[29] Although consent may be given in the hopes of leniency from law enforcement officials or as an election between unpalatable alternatives, it must be freely given and not secured coercively.[30]

Private consent interceptions may not be conducted for a criminal or tortious purpose.[31] At one time, the limitation encompassed interceptions for criminal, tortious, *or* otherwise injurious purposes, but ECPA dropped the reference to injurious purposes for fear that First Amendment values might be threatened should the clause be read to outlaw consent interceptions conducted to embarrass.[32]

Exemptions: Publicly Accessible Radio Communications

Radio communications which can be inadvertently heard or are intended to be heard by the public are likewise exempt. These include not only commercial broadcasts, but ship and aircraft distress signals, tone-only pagers, marine radio and citizen band radio transmissions, and interceptions necessary to identify the source any transmission, radio or otherwise, disrupting communications satellite broadcasts.[33]

Exemptions: Government Officials

Government officials enjoy an exemption when acting under judicial authority, whether that authority is provided for in Title III/ECPA for federal and state law enforcement officers acting under a court order,[34] acting in an emergency situation pending issuance of a court order,[35] or in the case of communications of an intruder in a communications system acting with the approval of the system provider;[36] in the Foreign Intelligence Surveillance Act,[37] or in the separate provisions according them the use of pen registers and trap and trace devices.[38]

Exemptions: Communication Service Providers

There is a general exemption for those associated with supplying communications services, the telephone company, switchboard operators, and the like. The exemption not only permits improved service and lets the telephone company protect itself against fraud,[39] but it allows for assistance to federal and state officials operating under a judicially supervised interception order,[40] and for the regulatory activities of the Federal Communications Commission.[41]

Domestic Exemptions

A few courts recognize a "vicarious consent" exception under which a custodial parent may secretly record the conversations of his or her minor child in the interest of protecting the child.[42] Although rejected by most,[43] a handful of federal courts have held that Title III/ECPA does not preclude one spouse from wiretapping or electronically eavesdropping upon the other,[44] a result other courts have sometimes reached through the telephone extension exception discussed above.[45]

Subject to the same exceptions, section 2511 also protects wire, oral and electronic communications from any person who intentionally:

- discloses or endeavors to disclose information with reason to know it has been unlawfully intercepted, or
- uses or endeavors to use information with reason to know it has been unlawfully intercepted, or

- discloses or endeavors to disclose information with intent to obstruct justice and with reason to know the information was secured through a court-ordered interception.

CONSEQUENCES: CRIMINAL PENALTIES

Interceptions in violation of Title III/ECPA are generally punishable by imprisonment for not more than five years and/or a fine of not more than $250,000 for individuals and not more than $500,000 for organizations.[46] The same penalties apply to the unlawful capture of cell phone and cordless phone conversations, now that the Homeland Security Act, 116 Stat. 2158 (2002), has repealed the reduced penalty provisions that at one time applied to the unlawful interceptions using radio scanners and the like, 18 U.S.C. 2511(4)(b)(2000 ed.). There is a reduced penalty, however, for filching satellite communications as long as the interception is not conducted for criminal, tortious, nor mercenary purposes: unauthorized interceptions are broadly proscribed subject to an exception for unscrambled transmissions[47] and are subject to the general five-year penalty, but interceptions for neither criminal, tortious, nor mercenary purposes subject offenders to only civil punishment.[48] Equipment used to wiretap or eavesdrop in violation of Title III is subject to confiscation by the United States, either in a separate civil proceeding or a part of the prosecution of the offender.[49]

In addition to exemptions previously mentioned, Title III provides a defense to criminal liability based on good faith.[50] As noted below, the defense seems to lack sufficient breadth to shelter any offender other than a government official or some one working at their direction.

CONSEQUENCES: CIVIL LIABILITY

Victims of illegal wiretapping or electronic eavesdropping may be entitled to equitable relief, damages (equal to the greater of actual damages, $100 per day of violation, or $10,000),[51] punitive damages, reasonable attorney's fees and reasonable litigation costs, 18 U.S.C. 2520.[52] A majority of federal courts hold that a court may decline to award damages, attorneys' fees and costs once a violation has been shown, but a few still consider such awards mandatory.[53] In addition, a majority holds that governmental entities other than the United States may be liable for violations of section 2520[54] and that law enforcement officers enjoy a qualified immunity from suit under section 2520.[55]

The cause of action created in section 2520 is subject to a good faith defense, 18 U.S.C. 2520(d). The only apparent efforts to claim the defense by anyone other than a government official or someone working at their direction have been unsuccessful.[56]

CONSEQUENCES: CIVIL LIABILITY OF THE UNITED STATES

The USA PATRIOT Act authorizes a cause of action against the United States for willful violations of Title III, the Foreign Intelligence Surveillance Act or the provisions governing stored communications in 18 U.S.C. 2701-2712, 18 U.S.C. 2712.[57] Successful plaintiffs are entitled to the greater of $10,000 or actual damages, and reasonable litigation costs, 18 U.S.C. 2712(a).

CONSEQUENCES: ADMINISTRATIVE ACTION

Upon a judicial or administrative finding of a Title III violation suggesting possible intentional or willful misconduct on the part of a federal officer or employee, the federal agency or department involved may institute disciplinary action. It is required to explain to its Inspector General's office if declines to do so.[58]

CONSEQUENCES: ATTORNEY DISCIPLINE

At one time, the American Bar Association (ABA) considered it ethical misconduct for an attorney to intercept or record a conversation without the consent of all of the parties to the conversation, ABA Formal Op. 337 (1974). The reaction of state regulatory authorities with the power to discipline professional misconduct was mixed. Some agreed with the ABA.[59] Some agreed with the ABA, but expanded the circumstances under which recording could be conducted within ethical bounds.[60] Some disagreed with the ABA view.[61] The ABA has now repudiated its earlier position, ABA Formal Op. 01-422 (2001). Attorneys who engage in *unlawful* wiretapping or electronic eavesdropping will remain subject to professional discipline in every jurisdiction;[62] in light of the ABA's change of position, courts and bar associations have had varied reactions to *lawful* wiretapping or electronic eavesdropping by members of the bar.[63]

CONSEQUENCES: EXCLUSION OF EVIDENCE

When the federal wiretap statute prohibits disclosure, the information is inadmissible as evidence before any federal, state, or local tribunal or authority, 18 U.S.C. 2515.[64] Individuals whose conversations have been intercepted or against whom the interception was directed[65] have standing to claim the benefits of the section 2515 exclusionary rule through a motion to suppress under 18 U.S.C. 2518(10)(a).[66] Paragraph 2518(10)(a) bars admission as long as the evidence is the product of (1) an unlawful interception, (2) an interception authorized by a facially insufficient court order, or (3) an interception executed in manner contrary to the order authorizing the interception.18 U.S.C. 2518(10)(a). Mere facial insufficiency is not enough; the defect must be of a nature that substantially undermines the regime of court-supervised interception for law enforcement purposes.[67]

Although the Supreme Court has held that section 2515 may require suppression in instances where the Fourth Amendment exclusionary rule would not, *Gelbard v. United States*, 408 U.S. 41, 52 (1972), some of the lower courts have recognized the applicability of the good faith exception to the Fourth Amendment exclusionary rule in section 2515 cases.[68] Other courts have held, moreover, that the fruits of an unlawful wiretapping or electronic eavesdropping may be used for impeachment purposes[69].

The admissibility of tapes or transcripts of tapes of intercepted conversations raise a number of questions quite apart from the legality of the interception. As a consequence of the prerequisites required for admission, privately recorded conversations are more likely to be found inadmissible than those recorded by government officials. Admissibility will require the party moving for admission to show that the tapes or transcripts are accurate, authentic and trustworthy.[70] For some courts this demands a showing that, "(1) the recording device was capable of recording the events offered in evidence; (2) the operator was competent to operate the device; (3) the recording is authentic and correct; (4) changes, additions, or deletions have not been made in the recording; (5) the recording has been preserved in a manner that is shown to the court; (6) the speakers on the tape are identified; and (7) the conversation elicited was made voluntarily and in good faith, without any kind of inducement."[71]

End Notes

[1] Although the governmental entities are not subject to criminal liability, as noted *infra*, some courts believe them subject to civil liability under 18 U.S.C. 2520.

[2] In order to underscore that the inadvertent reception of a protected communication is not a crime, the subcommittee changed the state of mind requirement under Title III of the Omnibus Crime Control and Safe Streets Act of 1968 from 'willful' to 'intentional,'" S.Rept. 541, at. 23 (1986); "This provision makes clear that the inadvertent interception of a protected communication is not unlawful under this Act," H.Rept. 99-647, at 48-9 (1986). *See, e.g., In re Pharmatrak, Inc.*, 329 F.3d 9, 23 (1st Cir. 2003); *Sanders v. Robert Bosch Corp.*, 38 F.3d 736, 742-43 (4th Cir. 1994); *Lonegan v. Hasty*, 436 F.Supp.2d 419, 429 (E.D.N.Y. 2006).

[3] *Narducci v. Village of Bellwood*, 444 F.Supp. 924, (N.D. Ill. 2006).

[4] (1) Except as otherwise specifically provided in this chapter any person who – (a) intentionally intercepts, endeavors to intercept, or procures any other person to intercept or endeavor to intercept, any wire, oral, or electronic communication;

"(b) intentionally uses, endeavors to use, or procures any other person to use or endeavor to use any electronic, mechanical, or other device to intercept any oral communication when – (I) such device is affixed to, or otherwise transmits a signal through, a wire, cable, or other like connection used in wire communication; or (ii) such device transmits communications by radio, or interferes with the transmission of such communication; or (iii) such person knows, or has reason to know, that such device or any component thereof has been sent through the mail or transported in interstate or foreign commerce; or (iv) such use or endeavor to use (A) takes place on the premises of any business or other commercial establishment the operations of which affect interstate or foreign commerce; or (B) obtains or is for the purpose of obtaining information relating to the operations of any business or other commercial establishment the operations of which affect interstate or foreign commerce; or (v) such person acts in the District of Columbia, the Commonwealth of Puerto Rico, or any territory or possession of the United States," 18 U.S.C. 2511(1)(a),(b).

[5] Subparagraph (a) establishes a blanket prohibition against the interception of wire communication. Since the facilities used to transmit wire communications form part of the interstate or foreign communications network, Congress has plenary power under the commerce clause to prohibit all interception of such communications whether by wiretapping or otherwise.

"The broad prohibition of subparagraph (a) is also applicable to the interception of oral communications. The interception of such communications, however, does not necessarily interfere with the interstate or foreign commerce network, and the extent of the constitutional power of Congress to prohibit such interception is less clear than in the case of interception of wire communications. . . .

"Therefore, in addition to the broad prohibitions of subparagraph (a), the committee has included subparagraph (b), which relies on accepted jurisdictional bases under the commerce clause, and other provisions of the Constitution to prohibit the interception of oral communications," S.Rept. 90-1097, at 91-2 (1968).

[6] As will be noted in moment, the statutory definitions of wire and electronic communications contain specific commerce clause elements, but the definition of oral communications does not, *see* notes 29 and 30, *infra.* Subsequent Supreme Court jurisprudence relating to the breadth of Congress' commerce clause powers indicates that the precautions may have been well advised, *United States v. Lopez*, 514 U.S. 549 (1995) and *United States v. Morrison*, 529 U.S. 598 (2000).

[7] The dictionary definition of "aural" is "of or relating to the ear or to the sense of hearing," MERRIAM-WEBSTER'S COLLEGIATE DICTIONARY 76 (10th ed. 1996).

[8] *United States v. Luong*, 471 F.3d 1107, 1109 (9th Cir. 2006)("an interception occurs where the tapped phone is located and where the law enforcement officers first overheard the call . . . *United Stats v. Rodriguez*, 968 F.2d 130, 136 (2d Cir. 1992); *accord United States v. Ramirez*, 112 F.3d 849, 852 (7the Cir. 1997)(concluding that an interception occurs in the jurisdiction where the tapped phone is located, where the second phone in the conversation is located, and where the scanner used to overhear the call is located); *United States v. Denman*, 100 F.3d 399, 403 (5th Cir. 1996)").

[9] S.Rept. 99-541, at 13 (1986)(the "amendment clarifies that it is illegal to intercept the non-voice portion of a wire communication. For example, it is illegal to intercept the data or digitized portion of a voice communication"); *see also* H.Rept. 99-647, at 34 (1986).

[10] *United States v. Smith*, 155 F.3d 1051, 1058 (9th Cir. 1998)(unauthorized retrieval and recording of another's voice mail messages constitutes an "interception"); *Konop v. Hawaiian Airlines, Inc.*, 302 F.3d 868, 878 (9th Cir. 2002)(fraudulent access to stored communication does not constitutes "interception;" interception requires access contemporaneous with transmission); *United States v. Councilman*, 418 F.3d 67, 79-80(1st Cir. 2005)(en banc)(service provider's access to e-mail "during transient storage" constitutes "interception"; without deciding whether "interception is limited to acquisition contemporaneous with transmission"); *United States v. Jones*, 451 F.Supp.2d 71, 75 (D.D.C. 2006)(government's acquisition from the phone company of text messages was no interception because there was no contemporaneous access); *Fraser v. National Mutual Insurance Co.*, 135 F.Supp.2d 623, 634-37 (E.D.Pa. 2001) ("interception" of e-mail occurs with its unauthorized acquisition prior to initial receipt by its addressee); *Steve Jackson Games, Inc. v. United States Secret Service*, 36 F.3d 457, 461-62n.7 (5th Cir. 1994) (Congress did not intend for "interception" to apply to e-mail stored on an electronic bulletin board; stored wire communications (voice mail), however, is protected from "interception"); *United States v. Meriwether*, 917 F.2d 955, 959-60 (6th Cir. 1990)(access to stored information through the use of another's pager does not constitute an "interception"); *United States v. Reyes,* 922 F.Supp. 818, 836-37 (S.D.N.Y. 1996)(same); *Wesley College v. Pitts*, 947 F.Supp. 375, 385 (D.Del. 1997)(no "interception" occurs when the contents of electronic communications are acquired unless contemporaneous with their transmission); *see also, Adams v. Battle Creek*, 250 F.3d 980, 982 (6th Cir. 2001)(use of a "clone" or duplicate pager to simultaneously receive the same message as a target pager is an "interception"); *Brown v. Waddell*, 50 F.3d 285, 294 (4th Cir. 1995)(same).

[11] Post-cut-through dialed digits' are any numbers dialed from a telephone after the call is initially setup or 'cut-through.' Sometimes these digits are other telephone numbers, as when a party places a credit card call by first dialing the long distance carrier access number and then the phone number of the intended party. Sometimes these digits transmit real information, such as bank account numbers, Social Security numbers, prescription numbers, and the like. In the latter case, the digits represent communications content; in the former, they are non-content call processing numbers," *In re United States*, 441 F.Supp.2d 816, 818 (S.D. Tex. 2006).

[12] *In re United States for Orders (1) Authorizing Use of Pen Registers and Trap and Trace Devices*, 515 F.Supp.2d 325, 328-38 (E.D.N.Y. 2007); *In re United States*, 441 F.Supp.2d 816, 818-27 (S.D. Tex. 2006).

[13] *United States v. Jones*, 451 F.Supp.2d 71, 75 (D.D.C. 2006)(government's acquisition from the phone company of text messages was not an interception because it did not involve contemporaneous access and because no electronic, mechanical, or other devices were used).

[14] '[E]lectronic, mechanical, or other device' means any device or apparatus which can be used to intercept a wire, oral, or electronic communication other than – (a) any telephone or telegraph instrument, equipment or facility, or any component thereof, (I) furnished to the subscriber or user by a provider of wire or electronic communication service in the ordinary course of its business and being used by the subscriber or user in the ordinary course of its business or furnished by such subscriber or user for connection to the facilities of such service and used in the ordinary course of its business; or (ii) being used by a provider of wire or electronic communication service in the ordinary course of its business, or by an investigative or law enforcement officer in the ordinary course of his duties; (b) a hearing aid or similar device being used to correct subnormal hearing to not better than normal," 18 U.S.C. 2510(5).

[15] *See* the cases cited and commentary in Barnett & Makar, *"In the Ordinary Course of Business": The Legal Limits of Workplace Wiretapping*, 10 HASTINGS JOURNAL OF COMMUNICATIONS AND ENTERTAINMENT LAW 715 (1988); *Application to Extension Telephones of Title III of the Omnibus Crime Control and Safe Streets Act of 1968 (18U.S.C. §§2510 et seq.), Pertaining to Interceptions of Wire Communications*, 58 ALR Fed. 594; *Eavesdropping on Extension Telephone as Invasion of Privacy*, 49 ALR 4th 430.

[16] *See e.g., Deal v. Spears*, 780 F.Supp. 618, 623 (W.D.Ark. 1991), *aff'd*, 980 F.2d 1153 (8th Cir. 1992)(employer regularly taped employee calls by means of a device attached to an extension phone; most of the calls were personal and recording and disclosing them served no business purpose).

[17] *Adams v. Battle Creek*, 250 F.3d 980, 983 (6th Cir. 2001); *Arias v. Mutual Central Alarm Service*, 202 F.3d 553, 558 (2d Cir. 2000); *Berry v. Funk*, 146 F.3d 1003, 1008 (D.C.Cir. 1998); *Sanders v. Robert Bosch Corp.*, 38 F.3d 736, 741 (4th Cir. 1994). *See also, Hall v. Earthlink Network Inc.*, 396 F.3d 500, 503-04 (2d Cir. 2005)

(Internet service provider's receipt and storage of former customer's e-mail after termination of the customer's account was done in ordinary course of business and consequently did not constitute an interception).
Some courts include surreptitious, extension phone interceptions conducted within the family home as part of the "business extension" exception, *Anonymous v. Anonymous*, 558 F.2d 677, 678-79 (2d Cir. 1977); *Scheib v. Grant*, 22 F.3d 149, 154 (7th Cir. 1994); *Newcomb v. Ingle*, 944 F.2d 1534, 1536 (10th Cir. 1991); *contra, United States v. Murdock*, 63 F.3d 1391, 1400 (6th Cir. 1995).

18 *See e.g.,United States v. Lewis*, 406 F.3d 11, 18 (1st Cir. 2005); *United States v. Hammond*, 286 F.3d 189, 192 (4th Cir. 2002); *Smith v. U.S.Dept. of Justice*, 251 F.3d 1047, 1049-50 (D.C.Cir. 2001); *United States v. Poyck*, 77 F.3d 285, 292 (9th Cir. 1996); *United States v. Daniels*, 902 F.2d 1238, 1245 (7th Cir. 1990); *United States v. Paul*, 614 F.2d 115, 117 (6th Cir. 1980).

19 *Amati v. Woodstock*, 176 F.3d 952, 955 (7th Cir. 1999)("Investigation is within the ordinary course of law enforcement, so if 'ordinary' were read literally warrants would rarely if ever be required for electronic eavesdropping, which was surely not Congress's intent. Since the purpose of the statute was primarily to regulate the use of wiretapping and other electronic surveillance for investigatory purposes, 'ordinary' should not be read so broadly; it is more reasonably interpreted to refer to routine noninvestigative recording of telephone conversations"). *Accord United States v. Lewis*, 406 F.3d at 19 (1st Cir. 2005); *Colandrea v. Orangetown*, 490 F.Supp.2d 342, 347-48 (S.D.N.Y. 2007).

20 The exception, however, does not permit a county to record all calls in and out of the offices of county judges merely because a detention center and the judges share a common facility, *Abraham v. Greenville*, 237 F.3d 386, 390 (4th Cir. 2001), nor does it permit jailhouse telephone monitoring of an inmate's confession to a clergyman, *Mockaitis v. Harcleroad*, 104 F.3d 1522, 1530 (9th Cir. 1997). The courts are divided over whether private corrections officials are covered by the law enforcement exception. *Compare United States v. Faulkner*, 323 F. Supp. 2d 1111, 1113-17 (D. Kan. 2004), aff'd on other grounds, 439 F.3d 1221 (10th Cir. 2006) (not covered) *with United States v. Rivera*, 292 F. Supp. 2d 838, 842-43 (E.D. Va. 2003) (covered).

21 [O]ral communication' means any oral communication uttered by a person exhibiting an expectation that such communication is not subject to interception under circumstances justifying such expectation, but such term does not include any electronic communication," 2510(2). *Pattee v. Georgia Ports Authority*, 512 F.Supp.2d 1372, 1376-377 (S.D.Ga. 2007)("the section contains two slightly different requirements: (1) that the circumstances justify an expectation that the communication is not being intercepted; and (2) that the speaker exhibits that expectation"). Note that unlike the definitions of wire and electronic communications, *infra*, there is no reference to interstate or foreign commerce here.

22 [W]ire communication' means any aural transfer made in whole or in part through the use of facilities for the transmission of communications by the aid of wire, cable, or other like connection between the point of origin and the point of reception (including the use of such connection in a switching station) furnished or operated by any person engaged in providing or operating such facilities for the transmission of interstate or foreign communications or communications affecting interstate or foreign commerce," 18 U.S.C. 2510(1).

23 [E]lectronic communication' means any transfer of signs, signals, writing, images, sounds, data, or intelligence of any nature transmitted in whole or in part by a wire, radio, electromagnetic, photoelectronic or photooptical system that affects interstate or foreign commerce, but does not include – (A) the radio portion of a cordless telephone communication that is transmitted between the cordless handset and the base unit; (B) any wire or oral communication; (C) any communication made through a tone-only paging device; or (D) any communication from a tracking device (as defined in section 3117 of this title)," 18 U.S.C. 2510(12).

24 *On Lee v. United States*, 343 U.S. 747 (1952); *Lopez v. United States*, 373 U.S. 427 (1963); *United States v. White*, 401 U.S. 745 (1971).

25 *United States v. White*, 401 U.S. at 751 (1971)("Concededly a police agent who conceals his police connections may write down for official use his conversations with a defendant and testify concerning them, without a warrant authorizing his encounters with the defendant and without otherwise violating the latter's Fourth Amendment rights . . . . For constitutional purposes, no different result is required if the agent instead of immediately reporting and transcribing his conversations with defendant, either (1) simultaneously records them with electronic equipment which he is carrying on his person, *Lopez v. United States, supra*; (2) or carries radio equipment which simultaneously transmits the conversations either to recording equipment located elsewhere or to other agents monitoring the transmitting frequency. *On Lee v. United States, supra.* If the conduct and revelations of an agent operating without electronic equipment do not invade the defendant's constitutionally justifiable expectations of privacy, neither does a simultaneous recording of the same conversations made by the agent or by others from transmissions received from the agent to whom the defendant is talking and whose trustworthiness the defendant necessarily risks"); *Lopez v. United States* 373 U.S. 427, 439 (1963)("Stripped to its essentials, petitioner's argument amounts to saying that he has a constitutional right to rely on possible flaws in the agent's memory, or to challenge the agent's credibility without being beset by corroborating evidence that is not susceptible of impeachment. For no other argument can justify excluding an accurate version of a conversation that the agent could testify to from memory. We think the risk that petitioner took in offering a bribe to Davis fairly includedthe risk that the offer would be accurately reproduced in court, whether by faultless memory or mechanical recording").

[26] (c) It shall not be unlawful under this chapter for a person acting under color of law to intercept a wire, oral, or electronic communication, where such person is a party to the communication or one of the parties to the communication has given prior consent to such interception.
"(d) It shall not be unlawful under this chapter for a person not acting under color of law to intercept a wire, oral, or electronic communication where such person is a party to the communication or where one of the parties to the communication has given prior consent to such interception unless such communication is intercepted for the purpose of committing any criminal or tortious act in violation of the Constitution or laws of the United States or of any State," 18 U.S.C. 2511(2)(c), (d).

[27] For citations to state law, see Appendix II.

[28] *United States v. Friedman*, 300 F.3d 111, 122-23 (2d Cir. 2002)(inmate use of prison phone);*United States v. Faulkner*, 439 F.3d 1221, 1224 (10th Cir. 2006)(same); *United States v. Hammond*, 286 F.3d 189, 192 (4th Cir. 2002) (same); *United States v. Footman*, 215 F.3d 145, 154-55 (1st Cir. 2000) (same); *Griggs-Ryan v. Smith*, 904 F.2d 112, 116-17 (1st Cir. 1990) (use of landlady's phone); *United States v. Rivera*, 292 F. Supp. 2d 838, 843-45 (E.D. Va. 2003)(inmate use of prison phone monitored by private contractors); see also, *United States v. Conley*, 531 F.3d 56, 58-9(1st Cir. 2008)(explicit consent as a condition for phone privileges).

[29] *Anthony v. United States*, 667 F.2d 870, 876 (10th Cir. 1981).

[30] *United States v. Antoon*, 933 F.2d 200, 203-204 (3d Cir. 1991). *But see O'Ferrell v. United States*, 968 F.Supp. 1519, 1541 (M.D. Ala. 1997) (an individual who spoke to his wife on the telephone after being told by FBI agents who were then executing a search warrant at his place of business that he could only speak to her with the agents listening in consented to the interception, even if FBI's initial search was unconstitutional).

[31] 18 U.S.C. 2511(2)(d); *United States v. Lam*, 271 F.Supp.2d 1182, 1183-184 (N.D.Cal. 2003).

[32] S.Rept. 99-541, at 17-8 (1986); H.Rept. 99-647, at 39-40 (1986).

[33] (g) It shall not be unlawful under this chapter or chapter 121 of this title for any person – (I) to intercept or access an electronic communication made through an electronic communication system that is configured so that such electronic communication is readily accessible to the general public;
"(ii) to intercept any radio communication which is transmitted – (I) by any station for the use of the general public, or that relates to ships, aircraft, vehicles, or persons in distress; (II) by any governmental, law enforcement, civil defense, private land mobile, or public safety communications system, including police and fire, readily accessible to the general public; (III) by a station operating on an authorized frequency within the bands allocated to the amateur, citizens band, or general mobile radio services; or (IV) by any marine or aeronautical communications system;
"(iii) to engage in any conduct which – (I) is prohibited by section 633 of the Communications Act of 1934; or (II) is excepted from the application of section 705(a) of the Communications Act of 1934 by section 705(b) of that Act;
"(iv) to intercept any wire or electronic communication the transmission of which is causing harmful interference to any lawfully operating station or consumer electronic equipment, to the extent necessary to identify the source of such interference; or
"(v) for other users of the same frequency to intercept any radio communication made through a system that utilizes frequencies monitored by individuals engaged in the provision or the use of such system, if such communication is not scrambled or encrypted," 18 U.S.C. 2511(2)(g).

[34] *Except as otherwise specifically provided in this chapter* any person who (a) intentionally intercepts . . . ." 18 U.S.C. 2511(1)(emphasis added).

[35] Notwithstanding any other provision of this chapter, any investigative or law enforcement officer, specially designated by the Attorney General, the Deputy Attorney General, the Associate Attorney General, or by the principal prosecuting attorney of any State or subdivision thereof acting pursuant to a statute of that State, who reasonably determines that – (a) an emergency situation exists that involves – (I) immediate danger of death or serious physical injury to any person, (ii) conspiratorial activities threatening the national security interest, or (iii) conspiratorial activities characteristic of organized crime, [–] that requires a wire, oral, or electronic communication to be intercepted before an order authorizing such interception can, with due diligence, be obtained, and (b) there are grounds upon which an order could be entered under this chapter to authorize such interception, may intercept such wire, oral, or electronic communication if an application for an order approving the interception is made in accordance with this section within forty-eight hours after the interception has occurred, or begins to occur. In the absence of an order, such interception shall immediately terminate when the communication sought is obtained or when the application for the order is denied, whichever is earlier. In the event such application for approval is denied, or in any other case where the interception is terminated without an order having been issued, the contents of any wire, oral, or electronic communication intercepted shall be treated as having been obtained in violation of this chapter, and an inventory shall be served as provided for in subsection (d) of this section on the person named in the application," 18 U.S.C. 2518(7).

[36] (I) It shall not be unlawful under this chapter for a person acting under color of law to intercept the wire or electronic communications of a computer trespasser transmitted to, through, or from the protected computer, if — (I) the owner or operator of the protected computer authorizes the interception of the computer trespasser's

communications on the protected computer; (II) the person acting under color of law is lawfully engaged in an investigation; (III) the person acting under color of law has reasonable grounds to believe that the contents of the computer trespasser's communications will be relevant to the investigation; and (IV) such interception does not acquire communications other than those transmitted to or from the computer trespasser," 18 U.S.C. 2511(2)(I).

[37] (e) Notwithstanding any other provision of this title or section 705 or 706 of the Communications Act of 1934, it shall not be unlawful for an officer, employee, or agent of the United States in the normal course of his official duty to conduct electronic surveillance, as defined in section 101 of the Foreign Intelligence Surveillance Act of 1978, as authorized by that Act," 18 U.S.C. 2511(2)(e).

[38] (h) It shall not be unlawful under this chapter – (I) to use a pen register or a trap and trace device (as those terms are defined for the purpose of chapter 206). . . ." 18 U.S.C. 2511(2)(h). Neither the stored communications sections in chapter 121 nor the pen register and trap and trace device in chapter 206 authorize the contemporaneous interception of the contents of a communication. For the citations to state statutes permitting judicial authorization of law enforcement interception of wire, oral or electronic communications, for access to stored electronic communications, and for the use of pen registers and trap and trace devices, see Appendix V.

[39] (a)(I) It shall not be unlawful under this chapter for an operator of a switchboard, or an officer, employee, or agent of a provider of wire or electronic communication service, whose facilities are used in the transmission of a wire or electronic communication, to intercept, disclose, or use that communication in the normal course of his employment while engaged in any activity which is a necessary incident to the rendition of his service or to the protection of the rights or property of the provider of that service, except that a provider of wire communication service to the public shall not utilize service observing or random monitoring except for mechanical or service quality control checks . . .

"(h) It shall not be unlawful under this chapter . . .

"(ii) for a provider of electronic communication service to record the fact that a wire or electronic communication was initiated or completed in order to protect such provider, another provider furnishing service toward the completion of the wire or electronic communication, or a user of that service, from fraudulent, unlawful or abusive use of such service," 18 U.S.C. 2511(2)(a)(I), (h).

[40] (ii) Notwithstanding any other law, providers of wire or electronic communication service, their officers, employees, and agents, landlords, custodians, or other persons, are authorized to provide information, facilities, or technical assistance to persons authorized by law to intercept wire, oral, or electronic communications or to conduct electronic surveillance, as defined in section 101 of the Foreign Intelligence Surveillance Act of 1978, if such provider, its officers, employees, or agents, landlord, custodian, or other specified person, has been provided with –

(A) a court order directing such assistance signed by the authorizing judge, or

(B) a certification in writing by a person specified in section 2518(7) of this title or the Attorney General of the United States that no warrant or court order is required by law, that all statutory requirements have been met, and that the specified assistance is required,

setting forth the period of time during which the provision of the information, facilities, or technical assistance is authorized and specifying the information, facilities, or technical assistance required. No provider of wire or electronic communication service, officer, employee, or agent thereof, or landlord, custodian, or other specified person shall disclose the existence of any interception or surveillance or the device used to accomplish the interception or surveillance with respect to which the person has been furnished a court order or certification under this chapter, except as may otherwise be required by legal process and then only after prior notification to the Attorney General or to the principal prosecuting attorney of a State or any political subdivision of a State, as may be appropriate. Any such disclosure, shall render such person liable for the civil damages provided for in section 2520. No cause of action shall lie in any court against any provider of wire or electronic communication service, its officers, employees, or agents, landlord, custodian, or other specified person for providing information, facilities, or assistance in accordance with the terms of a court order, statutory authorization, or certification under this chapter," 18 U.S.C. 2511(2)(a)(ii).

[41] (b) It shall not be unlawful under this chapter for an officer, employee, or agent of the Federal Communications Commission, in the normal course of his employment and in discharge of the monitoring responsibilities exercised by the Commission in the enforcement of chapter 5 of title 47 of the United States Code, to intercept a wire or electronic communication, or oral communication transmitted by radio, or to disclose or use the information thereby obtained," 18 U.S.C. 2511(2)(b).

[42] *Pollock v. Pollock*, 154 F.3d 601, 611 (8th Cir. 1998); *Wagner v. Wagner*, 64 F.Supp. 2d 895, 889-901 (D.Minn. 1999); *Campbell v. Price*, 2 F.Supp. 2d 1186, 1191-192 (E.D.Ark. 1998); *Thompson v. Dulaney*, 838 F.Supp. 1535, 1544-45 (D.Utah 1993).

[43] *Glazner v. Glazner*, 347 F.3d 1212, 1215-16 (11th Cir. 2003); *Heggy v. Heggy*, 944 F.2d 1537, 1539 (10th Cir. 1991); *Kempf v. Kempf*, 868 F.2d 970, 972 (8th Cir. 1989); *Pritchard v. Pritchard*, 732 F.2d 372, 374 (4th Cir. 1984); *United States v. Jones*, 542 F.2d 661, 667 (6th Cir. 1976); *Kratz v. Kratz*, 477 F.Supp. 463, 467-70 (E.D.Pa. 1979); *Heyman v.Heyman*, 548 F.Supp. 1041, 1045-47 (N.D.Ill.1982); *Lombardo v. Lombardo*, 192 F.Supp. 2d 885, 809 (N.D.Ill. 2002).

[44] *Simpson v. Simpson*, 490 F.2d 803, 809 (5th Cir. 1974); *Perfit v. Perfit*, 693 F.Supp. 851, 854-56 (C.D.Cal. 1988); see generally, *Applicability, in Civil Action, of Provisions of Omnibus Crime Control and Safe Streets Act of 1968 Prohibiting Interception of Communications (18 USCS §2511(1)), to Interception by Spouse, or Spouse's Agent, of Conversations of Other Spouse*, 139 ALR FED. 517, and the cases discussed therein.

[45] *Anonymous v. Anonymous*, 558 F.2d 677, 678-79 (2d Cir. 1977); *Scheib v. Grant*, 22 F.3d 149, 154 (7th Cir. 1994); *Newcomb v. Ingle*, 944 F.2d 1534, 1536 (10th Cir. 1991); *contra, United States v. Murdock*, 63 F.3d 1391, 1400 (6th Cir. 1995).

[46] Except as provided in (b) of this subsection or in subsection (5), whoever violates subsection (1) of this section shall be fined under this title* or imprisoned not more than five years, or both." 18 U.S.C. 2511(4)(a).
* Section 3559 of title 18 classifies as a felony any offense with a maximum penalty of imprisonment of more than one year; and as a Class A misdemeanor any offense with a maximum penalty of imprisonment set at between six months and one year. Unless Congress clearly rejects the general fine ceilings it provides, section 3571 of title 18 sets the fines for felonies at not more than $250,000 for individuals and not more than $500,000 for organizations, and for class A misdemeanors at not more than $100,000 for individuals and not more than $200,000 for organizations. If there is monetary loss or gain associated with the offense, the offender may alternatively be fined not more than twice the amount of the loss or gain, 18 U.S.C. 3571.

[47] (b) Conduct otherwise an offense under this subsection that consists of or relates to the interception of a satellite transmission that is not encrypted or scrambled and that is transmitted — (I) to a broadcasting station for purposes of retransmission to the general public; or (ii) as an audio subcarrier intended for redistribution to facilities open to the public, but not including data transmissions or telephone calls, is not an offense under this subsection unless the conduct is for the purpose of direct or indirect commercial advantage or private financial gain," 18 U.S.C. 2511(4)(b).

[48] (5)(a)(I) If the communication is — (A) a private satellite video communication that is not scrambled or encrypted and the conduct in violation of this chapter is the private viewing of that communication and is not for a tortious or illegal purpose or for purposes of direct or indirect commercial advantage or private commercial gain; or (B) a radio communication that is transmitted on frequencies allocated under subpart D of part 74 of the rules of the Federal Communications Commission that is not scrambled or encrypted and the conduct in violation of this chapter is not for tortious or illegal purpose or for purposes of direct or indirect commercial advantage or private commercial gain, then the person who engages in such conduct shall be subject to suit by the Federal Government in a court of competent jurisdiction. (ii) In an action under this subsection — (A) if the violation of this chapter is a first offense for the person under paragraph (a) of subsection (4) and such person has not been found liable in a civil action under section 2520 of this title, the Federal Government shall be entitled to appropriate injunctive relief; and (B) if the violation of this chapter is a second or subsequent offense under paragraph (a) of subsection (4) or such person has been found liable in any prior civil action under section 2520, the person shall be subject to a mandatory $500 civil fine.
"(b) The court may use any means within its authority to enforce an injunction issued under paragraph (ii)(A), and shall impose a civil fine of not less than $500 for each violation of such an injunction." 18 U.S.C. 2511(5).
Under 18 U.S.C. 2520, victims may recover the greater of actual damages or statutory damages of not less than $50 and not more than $500 for the first offense; those amounts are increased to $100 and $1000 for subsequent offenses.

[49] 18 U.S.C. 2513 ("Any electronic, mechanical, or other device used, sent, carried, manufactured, assembled, possessed, sold, or advertised in violation of section 2511 or section 2512 of this chapter may be seized and forfeited to the United States. . ."); 18 U.S.C. 983(a)(3)(C)("In lieu of, or in addition to, filing a civil forfeiture complaint, the Government may include a forfeiture allegation in a criminal indictment. . .").

[50] A good faith reliance on – (1) a court warrant or order, a grand jury subpoena, a legislative authorization, or a statutory authorization; (2) a request of an investigative or law enforcement officer under section 2518(7) of this title; or (3) a good faith determination that section 2511(3) [electronic communications provider authority to disclose content of an electronic communication "(i) as otherwise authorized in section 2511(2)(a) or 2517 of this title; (ii) with the lawful consent of the originator or any addressee or intended recipient of such communication; (iii) to a person employed or authorized, or whose facilities are used, to forward such communication to its destination; or (iv) which were inadvertently obtained by the service provider and which appear to pertain to the commission of a crime, if such divulgence is made to a law enforcement agency] or 2511(2)(I) [interception of communications of a trespasser in a computer system] of this title permitted the conduct complained of; is a complete defense against any civil or criminal action brought under this chapter or any other law," 18 U.S.C. 2520(d).

[51] The $10,000 lump sum for liquidated damages is limited to a single award per victim rather than permitting $10,000 multiples based on the number of violations or the number of types of violations, as long as the violations are "interrelated and time compacted," *Smoot v. United Transportation Union*, 246 F.3d 633, 642-645 (6th Cir. 2001); *Desilets v. Wal-Mart Stores, Inc.*, 171 F.3d 711, 713 (1st Cir. 1999).

[52] The text of 18 U.S.C. 2520 is appended.

[53] *Compare*, e.g., *DIRECTV, Inc. v. Brown*, 371 F.3d 814, 818 (11th Cir. 2004); *Dorris v. Absher*, 179 F.3d, 420, 429-30 (6th Cir. 1999); *Nalley v. Nalley*, 53 F.3d 649, 651-53 (4th Cir. 1995), *Reynolds v. Spears*, 93 F.3d 428,

433 (8th Cir. 1996); *DIRECTV, Inc. v. Neznak*, 371 F.Supp.2d 130, 133-34 (D.Conn. 2005) (each concluding that courts have discretion), *with, Rodgers v. Wood*, 910 F.2d 444, 447-49 (7th Cir. 1990) and *Menda Biton v. Menda*, 812 F.Supp. 283, 284 (D. Puerto Rico 1993) (courts have no such discretion) (note that after *Menda*, the First Circuit in *Desilets v. Wal-Mart Stores, Inc.*, 171 F.3d at 716-17 treated as a matter for the trial court's discretion the question of whether the award of plaintiff's attorneys' fees should be reduced when punitive damages have been denied).

[54] *Adams v. Battle Creek*, 250 F.3d 980, 984 (6th Cir. 2001); *Organizacion JD Ltda. v. United States Department of Justice*, 18 F.3d 91, 94-5 (2d Cir. 1994); *Connor v. Tate*, 130 F.Supp. 2d 1370, 1374 (N.D.Ga. 2001); *Dorris v. Absher*, 959 F.Supp. 813, 820 (M.D.Tenn. 1997), *aff'd/rev'd in part on other grounds*, 179 F.3d 420 (6th Cir. 1999); *PBA Local No. 38 v. Woodbridge Police Department*, 832 F.Supp. 808, 822-23 (D.N.J. 1993) (each concluding that governmental entities may be held liable); *contra, Abbott v. Winthrop Harbor*, 205 F.3d 976, 980 (7th Cir. 2000); *Amati v. Woodstock*, 176 F.3d 952, 956 (7th Cir. 1999).

[55] *Compare, Berry v. Funk*, 146 F.3d 1003, 1013 (D.C.Cir. 1998)(no immunity), *with, Tapley v. Collins*, 211 F.3d 1210, 1216 (11th Cir. 2000)(immunity); *Blake v. Wright*, 179 F.3d 1003, 1011-13(6th Cir. 1999)(same); see generally, *Qualified Immunity as Defense in Suit Under Federal Wiretap Act (18 U.S.C.A. §§2510 et seq.)*, 178 ALR FED. 1.

[56] *Williams v. Poulos*, 11 F.3d 271, 285 (1st Cir. 1993); *United States v. Wuliger*, 981 F.2d 1497, 1507 (6th Cir. 1992).

[57] The text of 18 U.S.C. 2712 is appended.

[58] If a court or appropriate department or agency determines that the United States or any of its departments or agencies has violated any provision of this chapter, and the court or appropriate department or agency finds that the circumstances surrounding the violation raise serious questions about whether or not an officer or employee of the United States acted willfully or intentionally with respect to the violation, the department or agency shall, upon receipt of a true and correct copy of the decision and findings of the court or appropriate department or agency promptly initiate a proceeding to determine whether disciplinary action against the officer or employee is warranted. If the head of the department or agency involved determines that disciplinary action is not warranted, he or she shall notify the Inspector General with jurisdiction over the department or agency concerned and shall provide the Inspector General with the reasons for such determination," 18 U.S.C. 2520(f).

[59] *Ala. Opinion 84-22* (1984); *People v. Smith*, 778 P.2d 685, 686, 687 (Colo. 1989); *Haw. Formal Opinion No. 30* (1988); *Ind.State Bar Ass'n Op.No.1* (2000); *Iowa State Bar Ass'n v. Mollman*, 488 N.W.2d 168, 169-70, 171-72 (Iowa 1992); *Mo.Advisory Comm. Op. Misc. 30* (1978); *Tex.Stat.Bar Op. 514* (1996); *Va. LEO #1635* (1995), *Va. LEO #1324*; *Gunte v. Virginia State Bar*, 238 Va. 617, 621-22, 385 S.E.2d 597, 600 (1989).
The federal courts seem to have been in accord, *Parrott v. Wilson*, 707 F.2d 1262 (11th Cir. 1983); *Moody v. IRS*, 654 F.2d 795 (D.C. Cir. 1981); *Ward v. Maritz, Inc.*, 156 F.R.D. 592 (D.N.J. 1994); *Wilson v. Lamb*, 125 F.R.D. 142 (E.D.Ky. 1989); *Haigh V. Matsushita Electric Corp.*, 676 F.Supp. 1332 (E.D.Va. 1987).

[60] *Ariz. Opinion No. 95-03* (1995); *Alaska Bar Ass'n Eth.Comm. Ethics Opinions No. 95-5 (1995) and No. 91-4* (1991); *Idaho Formal Opinion 130* (1989); *Kan.Bar.Ass'n Opinion 969* (1997); *Ky.Opinion E-279* (1984); *Minn.Law.Prof. Resp.Bd. Opinion No. 18* (1996); *Ohio Bd.Com.Griev.Disp. Opinion No. 97-3* (1997); *S.C. Ethics Advisory Opinion 92-17* (1992); *Tenn.Bd.Prof.Resp. Formal Ethics Opinion No. 86-F-14(a)* (1986).

[61] *D.C. Opinion No. 229* (1992) (recording was not unethical because it occurred under circumstances in which the uninformed party should have anticipated that the conversation would be recorded or otherwise memorialized); *Mississippi Bar v. Attorney ST.*, 621 So.2d 229 (Miss. 1993)(context of the circumstances test); *Conn.Bar Ass''n Op. 98-9* (1998)(same); *Mich.State Bar Op. RI-309* (1998)(same); *Me.State Bar Op.No. 168* (1999)(same); *N.M.Opinion 1996-2* (1996)(members of the bar are advised that there are no clear guidelines and that the prudent attorney avoids surreptitious recording); *N.C. RPC 171* (1994)(lawyers are encouraged to disclose to the other lawyer that a conversation is being tape recorded); *Okla.Bar Ass'n Opinion* 307 (1994)(a lawyer may secretly recording his or her conversations without the knowledge or consent of other parties to the conversation unless the recording is unlawful or in violation of some ethical standard involving more than simply recording); *Ore.State Bar Ass'n Formal Opinion No. 1991-74* (1991) (an attorney with one party consent he or she may record a telephone conversation "in absence of conduct which would reasonably lead an individual to believe that no recording would be made"); *Utah State Bar Ethics Advisory Opinion No. 96-04* (1996) ("recording conversations to which an attorney is a party without prior disclosure to the other parties is not unethical when the act, considered within the context of the circumstances, does not involve dishonesty, fraud, deceit or misrepresentation"); *Wis.Opinion E-94-5* ("whether the secret recording of a telephone conversation by a lawyer involves dishonesty, fraud, deceit or misrepresentation' under SCR 20:8.4(c) depends upon all the circumstances operating at the time"). In New York, the question of whether an attorney's surreptitiously recording conversations is ethically suspect is determined by locality, compare, *Ass'n of the Bar of City of N.Y. Formal Opinion No. 1995-10* (1995)(secret recording is per se unethical), with, *N.Y.County Lawyer's Ass'n Opinion No. 696* (1993)(secret recording is not per se unethical).

[62] *Cf., Nissan Motor Co., Ltd. v. Nissan Computer Corp.*, 180 F.Supp.2d 1089, 1095-97 (C.D.Cal. 2002).

[63] *See, e.g., State v. Murtagh*, 169 P.3d 602, 617-18 (Alaska 2007)("undisclosed recording is not unethical"); *In re Crossen*, 450 Mass. 533, 558, 880 N.E.2d 352, 372 (2008) (undisclosed was unethical where it was part of scheme to coerce or manufacture testimony against the judge presiding over pending litigation); *Midwest Motor Sports v. Arctic Cat Sales, Inc.*, 347 F.3d 693, 699 (8th Cir. 2003) (citing *ABA Comm. on Ethics and Prof'l Responsibility*, Formal Op. 01-422, which states that recording without consent should be prohibited when circumstances make it unethical); *United States v. Smallwood*, 365 F. Supp. 2d 689, 697-98 (E.D. Va. 2005) (holding that a lawyer cannot ethically record a conversation without the consent of all parties, even though doing so is not illegal under Virginia law). Declaring the new ABA opinion to be an "overcorrection," one bar association explained that secret taping should not be routine practice, but that it should be permitted if it advances a "societal good." *Ass'n of the Bar of the City of New York Formal Opinion No. 2003-02* (2003), *available at* [http://www.abcny.org]. For a New York state bar opinion employing a similar line of reasoning, see *Mena v. Key Food Stores Cooperative, Inc.*, 758 N.Y.S.2d 246, 247-50 (N.Y. Sup. Ct. 2003) (conduct of attorney who obtained a private investigator's services for a client and instructed the client on the use of recording equipment held *not* to warrant severe sanctions, because there was a compelling public interest in exposing the racial discrimination that was the subject of the secret recordings).

[64] "Whenever any *wire or oral communication* has been intercepted, no part of the contents of such communication and no evidence derived therefrom may be received in evidence in any trial, hearing, or other proceeding in or before any court, grand jury, department, officer, agency, regulatory body, legislative committee, or other authority of the United States, a State, or a political subdivision thereof if the disclosure of that information would be in violation of this chapter," 18 U.S.C. 2515 (emphasis added); *United States v. Lam*, 271 F.Supp.2d 1182, 1183-184 (N.D.Cal. 2003). Note that suppression does not extend to unlawfully intercepted *electronic* communications, *United States v. Steiger*, 318 F.3d 1039, 1050-52 (11th Cir. 2003); *United States v. Jones*, 364 F. Supp. 2d 1303, 1308-09 (D. Utah 2005); nor does it extend to evidence secured in violation the pen register/trap and trace provisions, *United States v. German*, 486 F.3d 849, 852-53 (5th Cir. 2007).

[65] 18 U.S.C. 2510(11)("'aggrieved person' means a person who was a party to any an intercepted wire, oral, or electronic communication or a person against whom the interception was directed"); *United States v. Gonzales*, 412 F.3d 1102, 1115-117 (9th Cir. 2005).

[66] The text of 18 U.S.C. 2518(10)(a) is appended.

[67] *United States v. Williams*, 124 F.3d 411, 426 (3d Cir. 1997)("The Supreme Court has explained the relationship between these two provisions. In *United States v. Giordano*, 416 U.S. 505 (1974), the Court wrote that 'what disclosures are forbidden under 2515 and we subject to motions to suppress is . . . governed by 2518(10)(a).' Thus, evidence may be suppressed only if one of the grounds set out in 2518(10)(a) is met. Moreover not every failure to comply fully with any requirement provided in Title III would render the interception of wire or oral communications unlawful under 2518(10)(a)(I). *United States v. Donovan*, 429 U.S. 413, 433 (1977), quoting *United States v. Chavez*, 416 U.S. 562 (1974). Rather suppression is mandated only for a failure to satisfy any of those statutory requirements that directly and substantially implement the congressional intention to limit the use of intercept procedures to those situations clearly calling for the employment of this extraordinary investigative device, *Donovan*, 429 U.S. at 433-34, quoting *Girodano*, 416 U.S. at 527"); *United States v. Lopez*, 300 F.3d 46, 55-6 (1st Cir. 2002); *United States v. Staffeldt*, 451 F.3d 578, 582-85 (9th Cir. 2006); *United States v. Gray*, 521 F.3d 514, 522 (6th Cir. 2008). This is the case even where the court is clearly troubled by the government's failure to comply with the requirements of Title III, *United States v. Callum*, 410 F.3d 571, 579 (9th Cir. 2005)("Under the force of precedent, we uphold the challenged wiretap applications and orders. Still, we note that the Department of Justice and its officers did not cover themselves with glory in obtaining the wiretap orders at issue in this case. Title III is an exacting statute obviously meant to be followed punctiliously, yet the officers repeatedly ignored its clear requirements").

[68] *United States v. Moore*, 41 F.3d 370, 376 (8th Cir. 1994); *United States v. Ambrosio*, 898 F.Supp. 177, 187 (S.D.N.Y. 1995); *United States v. Malelzadeh*, 855 F.2d 1492, 1497 (11th Cir. 1988); *United States v. Mullen*, 451 F.Supp.2d 509, 530-31 (W.D.N.Y. 2006); *contra*, *United States v. Rice*, 478 F.3d 704, 711-14 (6th Cir. 2007).

Gelbard held that a grand jury witness might claim the protection of section 2515 through a refusal to answer questions based upon an unlawful wiretap notwithstanding the fact that the Fourth Amendment exclusionary rule does not apply in grand jury proceedings. *Gelbard*, 408 U.S. at 51-52. The good faith exception to the Fourth Amendment exclusionary rule permits the admission of evidence secured in violation of the Fourth Amendment, if the officers responsible for the breach were acting in good faith reliance upon the apparent authority of a search warrant or some like condition negating the remedial force of the rule, *United States v. Leon*, 468 U.S. 897, 909 (1984).

[69] *Culbertson v. Culbertson*, 143 F.3d 825, 827-28 (4th Cir. 1998); *United States v. Echavarria-Olarte*, 904 F.2d 1391 (9th Cir. 1990); *United States v. Vest*, 813 F.2d 477, 484 (1st Cir. 1987).

[70] *United States v. Thompson,* 130 F.3d 676, 683 (5th th Cir. 1997); *United States v. Panaro*, 241 F.3d 1104, 1111 (9th Cir. 2001); *United States v. Smith*, 242 F.3d 737, 741 (7th Cir. 2001).

[71] *United States v. Webster*, 84 F.3d 1056, 1064 (8th Cir. 1996); *United States v. Green*, 175 F.3d 822, 830 n.3 (10th Cir. 1999); *United States v. Green*, 324 F.3d 375, 379 (5th Cir. 2003)(citing 4 of the 7 factors); *cf., United*

States v. Calderin-Rodriguez, 244 F.3d 977, 98687 (8th Cir. 2001). These seven factors have been fairly widely cited since they were first announced in *United States v. McKeever*, 169 F.Supp. 426, 430 (S.D.N.Y. 1958), *rev'd on other grounds*, 271 F.2d 669 (2d Cir. 1959). They are a bit formalistic for some courts who endorse a more ad hoc approach to the assessment of whether the admission of what purports to be a taped conversation will introduce fraud or confusion into the court, *see e.g.*, *Stringel v. Methodist Hosp. of Indiana, Inc.*, 89 F.3d 415, 420 (7th Cir. 1996)(*McKeever* "sets out a rather formal, seven step checklist for the authentication of tape recordings, and we have looked to some of the features [in the past]"); *United States v. White*, 116 F.3d 903, 921 (D.C.Cir. 1997)("tapes may be authenticated by testimony describing the process or system that created the tape or by testimony from parties to the conversation affirming that the tapes contained an accurate record of what was said"); *United States v. Tropeano*, 252 F.3d 653, 661 (2d Cir. 2001)("[T]his Circuit has never expressly adopted a rigid standard for determining the admissibility of tape recordings"); *United States v. Westmoreland*, 312 F.3d 302, 310-11 (7th Cir. 2002); *United States v. Dawson*, 425 F.3d 389, 393 (7th Cir. 2005)("But there are no rigid rules, such as chain of custody, for authentication; all that is required is adequate evidence of genuineness. (There are such rules for electronic surveillance governed by Title III, but Title III is inapplicable to conversations that, as here, are recorded with the consent of one of the participants")).

In: Privacy: An Overview of Federal Law…
Editor: Alderic Jimenez
ISBN: 978-1-60741-654-8

Chapter 5

ILLEGAL DISCLOSURE OF INFORMATION OBTAINED BY WIRETAPPING OR ELECTRONIC EAVESDROPPING

Although often overlooked, it is also a federal crime to disclose information obtained from illicit wiretapping or electronic eavesdropping, 18 U.S.C. 2511(1)(c):

- any person [who]
- intentionally
- discloses or endeavors to disclose to another person
  - the contents of any wire, oral, or electronic communication
  - having reason to know
  - that the information was obtained through the interception of a wire, oral, or electronic communication
  - in violation of 18 U.S.C. 2511(1)
  - is subject to the same sanctions and remedies as the wiretapper or electronic eavesdropper.

This is true of the wiretapper or electronic eavesdropper and of all those who disclose information, that in fact can be traced to a disclosure by the original wiretapper or eavesdropper, with reason to know of the information's illicit origins, except to the extent the First Amendment bans application.[1] The legislative history speaks of a common knowledge limitation on the statute's coverage, but it is not clear whether it refers to common knowledge at the time of interception or at the time disclosure, S.Rept. 90-1097, at 93 (1967).[2] By definition a violation of paragraph 2511(1)(c) requires an earlier unlawful interception under subsection 2511(1). If there is no predicate unlawful interception there can be no violation of paragraph 2511(1)(c).

The results of electronic eavesdropping authorized under Title III/ECPA may be disclosed and used for law enforcement purposes [3] and for testimonial purposes.[4]

It is also a federal crime to disclose, with an intent to obstruct criminal justice, any information derived from lawful police wiretapping or electronic eavesdropping, *i.e.*:

- any person [who]
- intentionally discloses, or endeavors to disclose, to any other person

- the contents of any wire, oral, or electronic communication
- intercepted by means authorized by sections:
  2511(2)(a)(ii) (communication service providers, landlords, etc. who assist police setting up wiretaps or electronic eavesdropping devices
  2511(2)(b) (FCC regulatory activity)
  2511(2)(c) (police one party consent)
  2511(2)(e) (Foreign Intelligence Surveillance Act)
  2516 (court-ordered, police wiretapping or electronic surveillance)
  2518 (emergency wiretaps or electronic surveillance)
- knowing or having reason to know that:
  - the information was obtained through the interception of such a communication
  - in connection with a criminal investigation
  - having obtained or received the information in connection with a criminal investigation
  - with intent to improperly obstruct, impede, or interfere with a duly authorized criminal investigation,
  - is subject to the same sanctions and remedies as one who illegally wiretaps, 18 U.S.C. 2511(1)(e).[5]

The proscriptions in 2511(1)(e) would appear to apply to efforts to obstruct justice by information gleaned from either federal or state police wiretaps. Use of the word "authorized" in conjunction with a list of federal statutes might suggest that the paragraph was only intended to protect wiretap information gathered by federal rather than by federal or state authorities. But most of the cited sections do not "authorize" anything; they simply confine the reach of the statutory prohibitions. And several are as likely to involve state interceptions as federal, e.g., the one-party-consent-undercolor-of-law interceptions.

Essentially, the same consequences flow from an unlawful disclosure under paragraphs 2511(1)(c) or 2511(1)(e) as follow unlawful interception under paragraphs 2511(1)(a) or 2511(1)(b):

- maximum five year prison terms and fines of not more than $250,000 or $500,000, depending upon whether the offender is an individual or organization;[6]
- exposure to civil liability including equitable relief and actual or statutory damages.[7]

End Notes

[1] *Bartnicki v. Vopper*, 532 U.S. 514, 533-34 (2001), pointed out that the First Amendment right to free speech bars the application of section 2511(1)(c) to the disclosure of illegally intercepted, but lawfully acquired, communications dealing with a matter of unusual public concern. Bartnicki was a union negotiator whose telephone conversations with the union's president were surreptitiously intercepted and recorded a discussion negotiation of a teachers' contract. During the conversation, the possibility of using violence against school board members was mentioned. After the teachers' contract was signed, the unknown wiretapper secretly supplied Yocum, a critic of the union's position, with a copy of the tape. Yocum in turn played it for members of the school board and turned it over to Vopper, a radio talk show host, who played it on his show. Other

stations and media outlets published the contents as well. Bartnicki sued Vopper and Yocum for use and disclosure in violation of sections 2511(1)(c) and 2511(1)(d). Vopper and Yocum offered a free speech defense, which the Supreme Court accepted. *But see*, *Quigley v. Rosenthal*, 327 F.3d 1044, 1067-68 (10th Cir. 2003) (denying First Amendment protection for those knowingly involved with interceptors of private matters (not public concerns)); *Boehner v. McDermott*, 484 F.3d 573, 577-81 (D.C. Cir. 2007)(Members of Congress do not have a First Amendment right to disclose unlawful wiretap information in violation of House rules). For a more extensive examination of *Bartnicki, see*, CRS Report RS20974, *The Right to Publish Lawfully Obtained But Illegally Intercepted Material of Public Concern: Bartnicki v. Vopper*.

[2] "Subparagraphs (c) and (d) prohibit, in turn, the disclosure or use of the contents of any intercepted communication by any person knowing or having reason to know the information was obtained through an interception in violation of this subsection. The disclosure of the contents of an intercepted communication that had already become 'public information' or 'common knowledge' would not be prohibited. The scope of this knowledge required to violate either subparagraph reflects existing law (*Pereira v. United States*, 347 U.S. 1 (1954))." The remark may also have been influenced by the high level of intent (willfully rather than intentionally) included in the disclosure provision as reported out.

[3] "Any investigative or law enforcement officer who, by any means authorized by this chapter, has obtained knowledge of the contents of any wire, oral, or electronic communication, or evidence derived therefrom, may disclose such contents to another investigative or law enforcement officer to the extent that such disclosure is appropriate to the proper performance of the official duties of the officer making or receiving the disclosure," 18 U.S.C. 2517(1).

[4] "Any person who has received, by any means authorized by this chapter, any information concerning a wire, oral, or electronic communication, or evidence derived therefrom intercepted in accordance with the provisions of this chapter may disclose the contents of that communication or such derivative evidence while giving testimony under oath or affirmation in any proceeding held under the authority of the United States or of any State or political subdivision thereof," 18 U.S.C. 2517(3). This does not entitle private litigants to disclosure in the view of at least one court, *In re Motion to Unseal Electronic Surveillance Evidence*, 990 F.2d 1015 (8th Cir. 1993).

When court-ordered interception results in evidence of a crime other than the crime with respect to which the order was issued, the evidence is admissible only upon a judicial finding that it was otherwise secured in compliance with Title III/ECPA requirements, 18 U.S.C. 2517(5).

[5] When acting with a similar intent, disclosure of the *fact* of authorized federal wiretap or foreign intelligence gathering is proscribed elsewhere in title 18. "Whoever, having knowledge that a Federal investigative or law enforcement officer has been authorized or has applied for authorization under chapter 119 to intercept a wire, oral, or electronic communication, in order to obstruct, impede, or prevent such interception, gives notice or attempts to give notice of the possible interception to any person shall be fined under this title or imprisoned not more than five years, or both."

"Whoever, having knowledge that a Federal officer has been authorized or has applied for authorization to conduct electronic surveillance under the Foreign Intelligence Surveillance Act of 1978 (50 U.S.C. 1801, et seq.), in order to obstruct, impede, or prevent such activity, gives notice or attempts to give notice of the possible activity to any person shall be fined under this title or imprisoned not more than five years, or both," 18 U.S.C. 2232(d),(e).

[6] "[W]hoever violates subsection (1) of this section shall be fined under this title or imprisoned not more than five years, or both," 18 U.S.C. 2511(4)(a).

[7] "(a) . . . any person whose wire, oral, or electronic communication is . . . disclosed . . . used in violation of this chapter may in a civil action recover from the person or entity, other than the United States, which engaged in that violation such relief as may be appropriate. . . .(g) Any willful disclosure . . . by an investigative or law enforcement officer or governmental entity of information beyond the extent permitted by section 2517 is a violation of this chapter for purposes of section 2520(a)," 18 U.S.C. 2520(a),(g).

In: Privacy: An Overview of Federal Law…
Editor: Alderic Jimenez
ISBN: 978-1-60741-654-8

Chapter 6

ILLEGAL USE OF INFORMATION OBTAINED BY UNLAWFUL WIRETAPPING OR ELECTRONIC EAVESDROPPING

The prohibition on the use of information secured from illegal wiretapping or electronic eavesdropping mirrors the disclosure provision, 18 U.S.C. 2511(1)(d):

- any person [who]
- intentionally
  - uses or endeavors to use to another person
  - the contents of any wire, oral, or electronic communication
  - having reason to know
  - that the information was obtained through the interception of a wire, oral, or electronic communication
  - in violation of 18 U.S.C. 2511(1)
  - is subject to the same sanctions and remedies as the wiretapper or electronic eavesdropper.

The available case law under the use prohibition of section 2511(1)(d) is scant, and the section has rarely been invoked except in conjunction with the disclosure prohibition of section 2511(1)(c). The wording of the two is clearly parallel, the legislative history describes them in the same breath,[1] and they are treated alike for law enforcement purposes.[2] Bartnicki seems destined to change all of that, because it appears to parse the constitutionally suspect ban on disclosure from the constitutionally permissible ban on use.[3] In doing so, it may also resolve a conflict among the lower federal appellate courts over the so-called "clean hands" exception. A few courts had recognized an exception to the disclosure-use bans of section 2511(1) where law enforcement officials might disclose or use the results of an illegal interception in which they had played no role.[4] *Bartnicki* appears to dim the prospects of a clean hands exception because, to illustrate situations to which the section 2511(1)(d) use might be constitutionally outlawed, it points to one of the cases which rejected to the exception.[5]

The consequences of unlawful use of intercepted communications in violation of paragraph 2511(d) are similar to those for unlawful disclosure in violation of paragraphs

2511(1)(c) or 2511(1)(e), or for unlawful interception under paragraphs 2511(1)(a) or 2511(1)(b):

- maximum five year prison terms and fines of not more than $250,000 or $500,000, depending upon whether the offender is an individual or organization, 18 U.S.C. 2511(4)(a);
- exposure to civil liability including equitable relief and actual or statutory damages, 18 U.S.C. 2520(a), (g).

End Notes

1 “Subparagraphs (c) and (d) prohibit, in turn, the disclosure or use of the contents of any intercepted communication by any person knowing or having reason to know the information was obtained through an interception in violation of this subsection,” S.Rept. 90-1097, at 93 (1967).

2 *Compare*, 18 U.S.C. 2517(1)(“Any investigative or law enforcement officer who, by any means authorized by this chapter, has obtained knowledge of the contents of any wire, oral, or electronic communication, or evidence derived therefrom, may disclose such contents to another investigative or law enforcement officer to the extent that such disclosure is appropriate to the proper performance of the official duties of the officer making or receiving the disclosure”), *with* 18 U.S.C. 2517(2)(“Any investigative or law enforcement officer who, by any means authorized by this chapter, has obtained knowledge of the contents of any wire, oral, or electronic communication or evidence derived therefrom may use such contents to the extent such use is appropriate to the proper performance of his official duties”).

3 “[T]he naked prohibition against disclosures is fairly characterized as a regulation of pure speech. Unlike the prohibition against the <use’ of the contents of an illegal interception in §2511(1)(d), subsection (c) is not a regulation of conduct,” 532 U.S. at 526-27.

4 *Forsyth v. Barr*, 19 F.3d 1527, 1541-545 (5th Cir. 1994); *United States v. Murdock*, 63 F.3d 1391, 1400-403 (6th Cir. 1995); *contra*, *Berry v. Funk*, 146 F.3d 1003, 1011-13 (D.C.Cir. 1998); *Chandler v. United States Army*, 125 F.3d 1296, 1300-302 (9th Cir. 1997); *In re Grand Jury*, 111 F.3d 1066, 1077 (3d Cir. 1997); *United States v. Vest*, 813 F.2d 477, 481 (1st Cir. 1987); *United States v. Lam*, 271 F.Supp.2d 1182, 1184-187 (N.D.Cal. 2003); see also, *United States v. Gray*, 521 F.3d 514, 530 (6th Cir. 2008)(noting that doctrine is only available in cases of government use).

5 “Unlike the prohibition against the ‘use’ of the contents of an illegal interception in §2511(1)(d),* subsection (c) is not a regulation of conduct.
*”The Solicitor General has catalogued some of the cases that fall under subsection (d): . . . . The statute has also been held to bar the use of illegally intercepted communications for important and socially valuable purposes, see, *In re Grand Jury* , 111 F.3d 1066, 1077-79 (3d Cir. 1997),” 532 U.S. at 527 (footnote 10 of the Court’s opinion quoted after the *).

In: Privacy: An Overview of Federal Law…
Editor: Alderic Jimenez
ISBN: 978-1-60741-654-8

Chapter 7

SHIPPING, MANUFACTURING, DISTRIBUTING, POSSESSING OR ADVERTISING WIRE, ORAL, OR ELECTRONIC COMMUNICATION INTERCEPTION DEVICES

The proscriptions for possession and trafficking in wiretapping and eavesdropping devices are even more demanding than those that apply to the predicate offense itself. There are exemptions for service providers,[1] government officials and those under contract with the government,[2] but there is no exemption for equipment designed to be used by private individuals, lawfully but surreptitiously.[3]

The three prohibitions in section 2512 present generally common features, declaring that:

- any person who
- intentionally
- either

(a)

sends through the mail or sends or carries in interstate or foreign commerce
any electronic, mechanical, or other device
knowing or having reason to know
that the design of such device renders it primarily useful
for the purpose of the surreptitious interception of wire, oral, or electronic communications; or

(b)

manufactures, assembles, possesses, or sells
any electronic, mechanical, or other device
knowing or having reason to know
that the design of such device renders it primarily useful
for the purpose of the surreptitious interception of wire, oral, or electronic communications, and
that such device or any component thereof has been or will be sent through the mail or transported in interstate or foreign commerce; or

(c)

places in any newspaper, magazine, handbill, or other publication or disseminates electronically
any advertisement of —
any electronic, mechanical, or other device
knowing or having reason to know
that the design of such device renders it primarily useful
for the purpose of the surreptitious interception of wire, oral, or electronic communications; or
any other electronic, mechanical, or other device
where such advertisement promotes the use of such device
for the purpose of the surreptitious interception of wire, oral, or electronic communications
knowing the content of the advertisement and knowing or having reason to know
that such advertisement will be sent through the mail or transported in interstate or foreign commerce
shall be imprisoned for not more than five years and/or fined not more than $250,000 (not more than $500,000 for organizations), 18 U.S.C. 2512.

The legislative history lists among the items Congress considered "primarily useful for the purpose of the surreptitious interception of communications: the martini olive transmitter, the spike mike, the infinity transmitter, and the microphone disguised as a wristwatch, picture frame, cuff link, tie clip, fountain pen, stapler, or cigarette pack," S.Rept. 90-1097, at 95 (1968).

Questions once raised over whether section 2512 covers equipment designed to permit unauthorized reception of scrambled satellite television signals have been resolved.[4] Each of the circuits to consider the question has now concluded that 2512 outlaws such devices,[5] but simple possession does not give rise to a private cause of action.[6] Their use is also proscribed by 47 U.S.C. 605.[7]

End Notes

[1] "It shall not be unlawful under this section for – (a) a provider of wire or electronic communication service or an officer, agent, or employee of, or a person under contract with, such a provider, in the normal course of the business of providing that wire or electronic communication service . . . to send through the mail, send or carry in interstate or foreign commerce, or manufacture, assemble, possess, or sell any electronic, mechanical, or other device knowing or having reason to know that the design of such device renders it primarily useful for the purpose of the surreptitious interception of wire, oral, or electronic communications," 18 U.S.C. 2512(2)(a).

[2] "(2) It shall not be unlawful under this section for . . . (b) an officer, agent, or employee of, or a person under contract with, the United States, a State, or a political subdivision thereof, in the normal course of the activities of the United States, a State, or a political subdivision thereof, to send through the mail, send or carry in interstate or foreign commerce, or manufacture, assemble, possess, or sell any electronic, mechanical, or other device knowing or having reason to know that the design of such device renders it primarily useful for the purpose of the surreptitious interception of wire, oral, or electronic communications.

"(3) It shall not be unlawful under this section to advertise for sale a device described in subsection (1) of this section if the advertisement is mailed, sent, or carried in interstate or foreign commerce solely to a domestic provider of wire or electronic communication service or to an agency of the United States, a State, or a political subdivision thereof which is duly authorized to use such device," 18 U.S.C. 2512(2)(b),(3).

[3] *United States v. Spy Factory, Inc.*, 951 F.Supp. 450, 473-75 (S.D.N.Y. 1997); *United States v. Bast*, 495 F.2d 138, 141 (D.C.Cir. 1974).

[4] The two appellate panel decisions that found the devices beyond the bounds of section 2512, *United States v. Herring*, 933 F.2d 932 (11th Cir. 1991) and *United States v. Hux*, 940 F.2d 314 (8th Cir. 1991) were overturned en banc, *United States v. Herring*, 993 F.2d 784, 786 (11th Cir. 1993); *United States v. Davis*, 978 F.2d 415, 416 (8th Cir. 1992).

[5] *United States v. Harrell*, 983 F.2d 36, 37-39 (5th Cir. 1993); *United States v. One Macom Video Cipher II*, 985 F.2d 258, 259-61 (6th Cir. 1993); *United States v. Shriver*, 989 F.2d. 898, 901-06 (7th Cir. 1992); *United States v. Davis*, 978 F.2d 415, 417-20 (8th Cir. 1992); *United States v. Lande*, 968 F.2d 907, 910-11 (9th Cir. 1992); *United States v. McNutt*, 908 F.2d 561, 564-65 (10th Cir. 1990); *United States v. Herring*, 993 F.2d 784, 786-89 (11th Cir. 1991).

[6] *DIRECTV, Inc. v. Treworgy*, 373 F.3d 1124, 1129 (11th Cir. 2004); *DIRECTV, Inc. v. Robson*, 420 F.3d 532, 538-39 (5th Cir. 2005)(citing several district court cases that have reached the same conclusion). Proof that the possessor used the device to intercept satellite transmission evidences a violation of section 2511 and exposure to civil liability under section 2520, *DIRECTV, Inc. v. Nicholas*, 403 F.3d 223, 227-28 (4th Cir. 2005); *DIRECTV, Inc. v. Pepe*, 431 F.3d 162, 169 (3d Cir. 2005).

[7] The text of the section is appended.

In: Privacy: An Overview of Federal Law…
Editor: Alderic Jimenez
ISBN: 978-1-60741-654-8

Chapter 8

STORED ELECTRONIC COMMUNICATIONS

In its original form Title III was ill-suited to ensure the privacy of those varieties of modern communications which are equally vulnerable to intrusion when they are at rest as when they are in transmission. Surreptitious "access" is as least as great a threat as surreptitious "interception" to the patrons of electronic mail (e-mail), electronic bulletin boards, voice mail, pagers, and remote computer storage.

Accordingly, Title III/ECPA also bans surreptitious access to communications at rest, although it does so beyond the confines of that apply to interception, 18 U.S.C. 2701 - 2711. These separate provisions afford protection for e-mail, voice mail, and other electronic communications somewhat akin to that available for telephone and face to face conversations under 18 U.S.C. 2510-2522. Thus, subject to certain exceptions, it is a federal crime to:

- intentionally
- either
- access without authorization or
- exceed an authorization to access
    - a facility through which an electronic communication service is provided
    - and thereby obtain, alter, or prevent authorized access to a wire or electronic communication while it is in electronic storage in such system, 18 U.S.C. 2701(a).

The exceptions cover electronic storage facility operators, their customers, and – under procedural counterparts to court ordered wiretapping – governmental entities.[1]

Violations committed for malicious, mercenary, tortious or criminal purposes are punishable by imprisonment for not more than five years and/or a fine of not more than $250,000 (not more than 10 years for a subsequent conviction); lesser transgressions, by imprisonment for not more than one year (not more than five years for a subsequent conviction) and/or a fine of not more than $100,000.[2] Those who provide the storage service and other victims of unlawful access have a cause of action for equitable relief, reasonable attorneys' fees and costs, damages equal the loss and gain associated with the offense but not less than $1000.[3] Both criminal and civil liability are subject to good faith defenses.[4]

Service providers, nevertheless, may incur civil liability for unlawful disclosures,[5] unless they can take advantage of one of a fairly extensive list of exceptions and defenses.[6]

Violations by the United States may give rise to a cause of action and may result in disciplinary action against offending officials or employees under the same provisions that apply to U.S. violations of Title III,[7] but unlike Title III there is no statutory rule for the exclusion of evidence as a consequence of a violation.[8] A Sixth Circuit panel has held, in a decision since vacated en banc, that the Fourth Amendment precludes government access to the content of stored communications (e-mail) held by service providers in the absence of a warrant, subscriber consent, or other indication that the subscriber has waived his or her expectation of privacy.[9] Where the government instead secures access through a subpoena or court order as section 2703 permits, the evidence may be subject to both the Fourth Amendment exclusionary rule and the exceptions to the rule.[10]

Unlawful access to electronic communications may involve violations of several other federal and state laws, including for instance the federal computer fraud and abuse statute, 18 U.S.C. 1030, and state computer abuse statutes.[11]

End Notes

[1] "Subsection (a) of this section does not apply with respect to conduct authorized – (1) by the person or entity providing a wire or electronic communications service; (2) by a user of that service with respect to a communication of or intended for that user; or (3) in section 2703 [requirements for government access], 2704 [backup preservation] or 2518 [court ordered wiretapping or electronic eavesdropping] of this title," 18 U.S.C. 2701(c).

Section 2709 creates an exception for counterintelligence access to telephone records.

[2] "The punishment for an offense under subsection (a) of this section is – (1) if the offense is committed for purposes of commercial advantage, malicious destruction or damage, or private commercial gain, or in furtherance of any criminal or tortious act in violation of the constitution and laws of the United States or any state – (A) a fine under this title or imprisonment for not more than 5 years, or both, in the case of a first offense under this subparagraph; and (B) a fine under this title or imprisonment for not more than 10 years, or both, for any subsequent offense under this subparagraph; and (2)(A) a fine under this title or imprisonment for not more than 1 year or both, in the case of a first offense under this paragraph; and (B) a fine under this title or imprisonment for not more than 5 years, or both, in the case of an offense under this subparagraph that occurs after a conviction of another offense under this section,"18 U.S.C. 2701(b).

[3] "(a) Cause of action – Except as provided in section 2703(e)[relating to immunity for compliance with judicial process], any provider of electronic communication service, subscriber, or customer aggrieved by any violation of this chapter in which the conduct constituting the violation is engaged in with a knowing or intentional state of mind may, in a civil action, recover from the person or entity other than the United States which engaged in that violation such relief as may be appropriate.

"(b) Relief – In a civil action under this section, appropriate relief includes – (1) such preliminary and other equitable or declaratory relief as may be appropriate; (2) damages under subsection(c); and (3) a reasonable attorney's fee and other litigation costs reasonably incurred;

"(c) Damages – The court may assess as damages in a civil action under this section the sum of the actual damages suffered by the plaintiff and any profits made by the violator as a result of the violation, but in no case shall a person entitled to recover receive less than the sum of $1,000. . . ." 18 U.S.C. 2707.

[4] "A good faith reliance on – (1) a court warrant or order, a grand jury subpoena, a legislative authorization, or a statutory authorization (including a request of a governmental entity under section 2703(f) of this title) [relating to an official request to for a service provider preserve evidence]; (2) a request of an investigative or law enforcement officer under section 2518(7) of this title [relating to emergency wiretapping and electronic eavesdropping]; or (3) a good faith determination that section 2511(3) of this title [relating to the circumstances under which an electronic communications provider may divulge the contents of communication] permitted the conduct complained of – is a complete defense to any civil or criminal action brought under this chapter or any other law," 18 U.S.C. 2707(e).

[5] "Except as in subsection (b) or (c) – (1) a person or entity providing an electronic communication service to the public shall not knowingly divulge to any person or entity the contents of a communication while in electronic storage by that service; (2) a person or entity providing remote computing service to the public shall not knowingly divulge to any person or entity the contents of any communication which is carried or maintained on that service – (A) on behalf of, and received by means of electronic transmission from (or created by means

of computer processing of communications received by means of electronic transmission from), a subscriber or customer of such service; and (B) solely for the purpose of providing storage or computer processing services to such subscriber or customer, if the provider is not authorized to access the contents of any such communications for purposes of providing any services other than storage or computer processing; and (3) a provider of remote computing service or electronic communication service to the public shall not knowingly divulge a record or other information pertaining to a subscriber to or customer of such service (not including the contents of communications covered by paragraph (1) or (2)) to any government entity," 18 U.S.C. 2702(a).

Section 2702 makes no mention of any consequences that follow a breach of its commands, but 2707 establishes a civil cause of action for the victims of any violation of chapter 121 (18 U.S.C. 2701 - 2711).

[6] "A provider described in subsection (a) may divulge the contents of a communication – (1) to an addressee or intended recipient of such communication or an agent of such addressee or intended recipient; (2) as otherwise authorized in section 2517, 2511(2)(a), or 2703 of this title; (3) with the lawful consent of the originator or an addressee or intended recipient of such communication, *or the subscriber in the case of remote computing service;* (4) to a person employed or authorized or whose facilities are used to forward such communication to its destination; (5) as may be necessarily incident to the rendition of the service or to the protection of the rights or property of the provider of that service; (6) to the National Center for Missing and Exploited Children, in connection with a report submitted thereto under section 227 of the Victims of Child Abuse Act of 1990; (7) to a law enforcement agency – (A) if the contents – (I) were inadvertently obtained by the service provider; and (ii) appear to pertain to the commission of a crime; (8) to a Federal, State, or local government entity, if the provider, in good faith, believes that an emergency involving danger of death or serious physical injury to any person requires disclosure without delay of communications relating to the emergency," 18 U.S.C. 2702(b).

The Ninth Circuit recently noted that a remote computer service provider may disclose to a subscriber (as noted in italics above), but that an electronic service provider, such as one who provides text messaging services, may not, even when the material disclosed resides in storage, *Quon v. Arch Wireless Operating Co., Inc.*, 529 F.3d 892, 900-901(9th Cir. 2008).

[7] "Any person who is aggrieved by any willful violation this chapter or of chapter 119 of this title [18 U.S.C. 2510-2520] . . . may commence an action in United States District Court . . . .If . . . any of the departments or agencies has violated any provision of this chapter . . . the department or agency shall . . . promptly initiate a proceeding to determine whether disciplinary action . . . is warranted. . . ."18 U.S.C. 2712(a),(c).

[8] *United States v. Steiger*, 318 F.3d 1039, 1049 (11th Cir. 2003); *United States v. Perrine*, 518 F.3d 1196, 1202 (10th Cir. 2008).

[9] *Warshak v. United States*, 490 F.3d 455, 468-82 (6th Cir. 2007), vac'd en banc, 532 F.3d 521 (6th Cir. 2008)(vacated on grounds that the issue was not ripe for decision).

[10] *United States v. Ferguson*, 508 F.Supp.2d 7, 8-10 (D.D.C. 2007)(even if a Fourth Amendment violation occurred, officers could rely in good faith on the magistrate's order issued before any court had raised the specter of constitutional suspicion which surfaced later in *Warshak*).

[11] See generally, CRS Report 97-1025, *Cybercrime: An Overview of the Federal Computer Fraud and Abuse Statute and Related Federal Criminal Laws*. Citations to the various state computer abuse statutes are appended.

In: Privacy: An Overview of Federal Law… ISBN: 978-1-60741-654-8
Editor: Alderic Jimenez

Chapter 9

PEN REGISTERS AND TRAP AND TRACE DEVICES

A trap and trace device identifies the source of incoming calls, and a pen register indicates the numbers called from a particular phone.[1] Since neither allows the eavesdropper to overhear the "contents" of the phone conversation, they were not considered interceptions within the reach of Title III prior to the enactment of ECPA, *United States v. New York Telephone Co.*, 434 U.S. 159 (1977). Although Congress elected to expand the definition of interception, it chose to continue to regulate these devices beyond the boundaries of Title III for most purposes, 18 U.S.C. 3121 - 3127.

As noted earlier, however, the Title III wiretap provisions apply when due to the nature of advances in telecommunications technology pen registers and trap and trace devices are able to capture wire communication "content."[2]

The USA PATRIOT Act enlarged the coverage of sections 3121-3127 to include sender/addressee information relating to e-mail and other forms of electronic communications, 115 Stat. 288-91 (2001).

The use or installation of pen registers or trap and trace devices by anyone other than the telephone company, service provider, or those acting under judicial authority is a federal crime, punishable by imprisonment for not more than a year and/or a fine of not more than $100,000 ($200,000 for an organization).[3] There is no accompanying exclusionary rule, however, and consequently a violation of section 3121 will not serve as a basis to suppress any resulting evidence.[4]

Unlike other violations of Title III/ECPA, there is no separate federal private cause of action for victims of a pen register or trap and trace device violation. Some of the states have established a separate criminal offense for unlawful use of a pen register or trap and trace device, yet most of these do seem to follow the federal lead and decline to establish a separate private cause of action, *See* Appendix III.

End Notes

[1] "(3) the term 'pen register' means a device which records or decodes electronic or other impulses which identify the numbers dialed or otherwise transmitted on the telephone line to which such device is attached, but such term does not include any device used by a provider or customer of a wire or electronic communication service for billing, or recording as an incident to billing, for communications services provided by such provider or any device used by a provider or customer of a wire communication service for cost accounting or

other like purposes in the ordinary course of its business; (4) the term 'trap and trace device' means a device which captures the incoming electronic or other impulses which identify the originating number of an instrument or device from which a wire or electronic communication was transmitted," 18 U.S.C. 3127(3),(4)). Although clone pagers are not considered pen registers, *Brown v. Waddell*, 50 F.3d 285, 290-91 (4th Cir. 1995), "caller id" services have been found to constitute trap and trace devices, *United States v. Fregoso*, 60 F.3d 1314, 1320 (8th Cir. 1995).

[2] "'Post-cut-through dialed digits' are any numbers dialed from a telephone after the call is initially setup or 'cut-through.' Sometimes these digits are other telephone numbers, as when a party places a credit card call by first dialing the long distance carrier access number and then the phone number of the intended party. Sometimes these digits transmit real information, such as bank account numbers, Social Security numbers, prescription numbers, and the like. In the latter case, the digits represent communications content; in the former, they are non-content call processing numbers," *In re United States*, 441 F.Supp.2d 816, 818 (S.D. Tex. 2006); *In re United States for Orders (1) Authorizing Use of Pen Registers and Trap and Trace Devices*, 515 F.Supp.2d 325, 328-38 (E.D.N.Y. 2007).

[3] "(a) *In general* – Except as provided in this section, no person may install or use a pen register or a trap and trace device without first obtaining a court order under section 3123 of this title or under the Foreign Intelligence Surveillance Act of 1978 (50 U.S.C. 1801 et seq.). (b) *Exception* – The prohibition of subsection (a) does not apply with respect to the use of a pen register or a trap and trace device by a provider of electronic or wire communication service – (1) relating to the operation, maintenance, and testing of a wire or electronic communication service or to the protection of the rights or property of such provider, or to the protection of users of that service from abuse of service or unlawful use of service; or (2) to record the fact that a wire or electronic communication was initiated or completed in order to protect such provider, another provider furnishing service toward the completion of the wire communication, or a user of that service, from fraudulent, unlawful or abusive use of service; or (3) where the consent of the user of that service has been obtained. (c) *Limitation* – A government agency authorized to install and use a pen register or trap and trace device under this chapter or under State law shall use technology reasonably available to it that restricts the recording or decoding of electronic or other impulses to the dialing, routing, addressing, and signaling information utilized in identifying the origination or destination of wire or electronic communications. (d) *Penalty*. – Whoever knowingly violates subsection (a) shall be fined under this title or imprisoned not more than one year, or both," 18 U.S.C. 3121.

[4] *United States v. German*, 486 F.3d 849, 852-53 (5th Cir. 2007); *United States v. Fregoso*, 60 F.3d 1314, 1320 (8th Cir. 1995); *United States v. Thompson*, 936 F.2d 1249, 1249-250 (11th Cir. 1991). To the extent that the unlawful use captures content, the Fourth Amendment exclusionary rule may apply, *cf.*, *In re United States for Orders (1) Authorizing Use of Pen Registers and Trap and Trace Devices*, 515 F.Supp.2d 325, 328-38 (E.D.N.Y. 2007); *United States v. Ferguson*, 508 F.Supp.2d 7 (D.D.C. 2007).

In: Privacy: An Overview of Federal Law…
Editor: Alderic Jimenez
ISBN: 978-1-60741-654-8

Chapter 10

FOREIGN INTELLIGENCE SURVEILLANCE ACT

The Foreign Intelligence Surveillance Act (FISA) authorizes special court orders for four purposes: electronic surveillance, physical searches, installation and use pen registers/trap and trace devices, and orders to disclose tangible items, 50 U.S.C. 1801-1861. The electronic surveillance portion of FISA, 50 U.S.C. 1801-1811, creates a procedure for judicially supervised "electronic surveillance" (wiretapping) conducted for foreign intelligence gathering purposes. The Act classifies four kinds of wiretapping as "electronic surveillance." The four classes of *electronic surveillance* involve wiretapping that could otherwise only be conducted under court order:

> "(1) the acquisition by an electronic, mechanical, or other surveillance device of the contents of any wire or radio communication sent by or intended to be received by a particular, known United States person who is in the United States, if the contents are acquired by intentionally targeting that United States person, under circumstances in which a person has a reasonable expectation of privacy and a warrant would be required for law enforcement purposes;
>
> "(2) the acquisition by an electronic, mechanical, or other surveillance device of the contents of any wire communication to or from a person in the United States, without the consent of any party thereto, if such acquisition occurs in the United States, does not include the acquisition of those communications of computer trespassers that would be permissible under section 2511(2)(I) of title 18, United States Code;
>
> "(3) the intentional acquisition by an electronic, mechanical, or other surveillance device of the contents of any radio communication, under circumstances in which a person has a reasonable expectation of privacy and a warrant would be required for law enforcement purposes, and if both the sender and all intended recipients are located within the United States; or
>
> "(4) the installation or use of an electronic, mechanical, or other surveillance device in the United States for monitoring to acquire information, other than from a wire or radio communication, under circumstances in which a person has a reasonable expectation of privacy and a warrant would be required for law enforcement purposes," 50 U.S.C. 1801(f).

Section 1809 proscribes:

- intentionally
- either

  engaging in *electronic surveillance*
  under color of law
  except as authorized by statute, or
  disclosing or using
  information obtained under color of law
  by *electronic surveillance*,
  knowing or having reason to know
  that the information was obtained by electronic surveillance not authorized by statute, 50 U.S.C. 1809.

The prohibitions of section 1809 apply only to federal officers and employees,[1] but do not apply to a law enforcement officer operating under a warrant or court.[2] Violations are punishable by imprisonment for not more than five years and/or a fine of not more than $250,000, *id.* and expose the offender to civil liability.[3] By virtue of USA PATRIOT Act amendments, victims of any improper use of information secured under a FISA surveillance order may also be entitled to actual or statutory damages.[4]

FISA also has its own exclusionary rule for electronic surveillance and physical searches.[5] However, Congress anticipated,[6] and the courts have acknowledged, that surveillance conducted under FISA for foreign intelligence purposes may result in admissible evidence of a crime.[7]

The physical search portion of FISA authorizes the issuance of physical search orders for foreign intelligence gathering purposes, 50 U.S.C. 1821-1829. Its accompanying criminal proscriptions and civil liability provisions, and are identical to those used in the electronic surveillance portion of FISA.[8]

End Notes

[1] "There is Federal jurisdiction over an offense under this section if the person committing the offense was an officer or employee of the United States at the time the offense was committed," 50 U.S.C. 1809(d). The criminal proscriptions and exemptions of Title III/ECPA (18 U.S.C. 2510-2518) may apply as well.

[2] "It is a defense to a prosecution under subsection (a) of this section that the defendant was a law enforcement or investigative officer engaged in the course of his official duties and the electronic surveillance was authorized by and conducted pursuant to a search warrant or court order of a court of competent jurisdiction," 50 U.S.C. 1809(b).

[3] "An aggrieved person, other than a foreign power or an agent of a foreign power, as defined in section 1801(a) or (b)(1)(A) of this title, respectively, who has been subjected to an electronic surveillance or about whom information obtained by electronic surveillance of such person has been disclosed or used in violation of section 1809 of this title shall have a cause of action against any person who committed such violation and shall be entitled to recover – (a) actual damages, but not less than liquidated damages of $1,000 or $100 per day for each day of violation, whichever is greater; (b) punitive damages; and (c) reasonable attorney's fees and other investigation and litigation costs reasonably incurred," 50 U.S.C. 1810. Victims are not entitled to injunctive relief, *ACLU Foundation of Southern California v. Barr*, 952 F.2d 457, 469-70 (D.C.Cir. 1992). The court did not address the question of whether conduct in violation of both FISA and Title III/EPCA might be enjoined under 18 U.S.C. 2520(b)(1). The Sixth Circuit, however, has held that the proscriptions of Title III/ECPA do not apply to interception in this country for foreign intelligence gathering purposes of

communications between parties in the United States and those in other nations, *ACLU v. National Security Agency*, 493 F.3d 644, 680 (6th Cir. 2007), citing, 18 U.S.C. 2511(2)(f).

[4] "Any person who is aggrieved by any willful violation of . . . section[] 106(a) . . . of the Foreign Intelligence Surveillance Act [relating to the use of information acquired from electronic surveillance under the Act] may commence an action in United States District Court against the United States to recover money damages. In any such action, if a person who is aggrieved successfully establishes a violation of . . . the above special provisions of title 50, the Court may assess as damages – (1) actual damages, but not less than $10,000, whichever amount is greater; and (2) litigation costs, reasonably incurred," 18 U.S.C. 2712(a).

[5] "If the United States district court pursuant to subsection (f) of this section determines that the surveillance was not lawfully authorized or conducted, it shall, in accordance with the requirements of law, suppress the evidence which was unlawfully obtained or derived from electronic surveillance of the aggrieved person or otherwise grant the motion of the aggrieved person. If the court determines that the surveillance was lawfully authorized and conducted, it shall deny the motion of the aggrieved person except to the extent that due process requires discovery or disclosure," 50 U.S.C. 1806(g); 1825(f); *United States v. Campa*, 529 F.3d 980, 993 (11th Cir. 2008). The text of 50 U.S.C. 1825 and 1806(f) are appended.

[6] S.Rept. 95-701, at 61 (1978); 50 U.S.C. 1806(b)(". . . such information . . . may only be used in a criminal proceeding with the advance authorization of the Attorney General").

[7] When FISA required certification that the acquisition of foreign intelligence was "the" purpose for seeking the a FISA surveillance order, there was some debate among the courts over how prominent the foreign intelligence purpose had to be in order to permit the evidence it unearthed under as FISA order to be used in a criminal prosecution, *United States v. Johnson*, 952 F.2d 565, 572 (1st Cir. 1992); *United States v. Duggan*, 743 F.2d 59, 77 (2d Cir. 1984); *United States v. Sarkissian*, 841 F.2d 959, 964 (9th Cir. 1988); *United States v. Badia*, 827 F.2d 1458, 1463 (11th Cir. 1987). The USA PATRIOT Act changed "the purpose" to "a significant purpose," a change which the FISA review court concluded demands only that the government have a "measurable" foreign intelligence purpose when it seeks a FISA surveillance order, *In re Sealed Case*, 310 F.3d 717, 734-35 (F.I.S.Ct.Rev. 2002); see also, Seamon & Gardner, *The Patriot Act and the Wall Between Foreign Intelligence and Law Enforcement*, 28 HARVARD JOURNAL OF LAW AND PUBLIC POLICY 319 (2005).

[8] 50 U.S.C. 1827 ("A person is guilty of an offense if he intentionally – (1) under color of law for the purpose of obtaining foreign intelligence information, executes a physical search within the United States except as authorized by statute . . . ."); 50 U.S.C. 1828 ("An aggrieved person, other than a foreign power or an agent of a foreign power, as defined in section 1801(a) or (b)(1)(A), respectively, of this title, whose premises, property, information, or material has been subjected to a physical search within the United States or about whom information obtained by such a physical search has been disclosed or used in violation of section 1827 of this title shall have a cause of action against any person who committed such violation . . . ."); 18 U.S.C. 2712(a)("Any person who is aggrieved by any willful violation of . . . section[] 305(a) . . . of the Foreign Intelligence Surveillance Act [relating to the use of information acquired from a physical search under the Act] may commence an action in United States District Court against the United States to recover money damages. . . . ").

In: Privacy: An Overview of Federal Law…
Editor: Alderic Jimenez
ISBN: 978-1-60741-654-8

Chapter 11

PROCEDURE

Each of the prohibitions mentioned above recognizes a procedure for government use notwithstanding the general ban, usually under judicial supervision. Although Fourth Amendment concerns supply a common theme, the procedures are individually distinctive.

In: Privacy: An Overview of Federal Law... ISBN: 978-1-60741-654-8
Editor: Alderic Jimenez

Chapter 12

LAW ENFORCEMENT WIRETAPPING AND ELECTRONIC EAVESDROPPING

Title III/ECPA authorizes both federal and state law enforcement wiretapping and electronic eavesdropping, under court order, without the prior consent or knowledge of any of the participants, 18 U.S.C. 2516 - 2518. At the federal level, a senior Justice Department official must approve the application for the court order.[1] The procedure is only available where there is probable cause to believe that the wiretap or electronic eavesdropping will produce evidence of one of a long, but not exhaustive, list of federal crimes,[2] or of the whereabouts of a "fugitive from justice" fleeing from prosecution of one of the offenses on the predicate offense list, 18 U.S.C. 2516(1)(*l*). Any federal prosecutor may approve an application for a court order under section 2518 authorizing the interception of e-mail or other electronic communications during transmission.[3]

At the state level, the principal prosecuting attorney of a state or any of its political subdivisions may approve an application for an order authorizing wiretapping or electronic eavesdropping based upon probable cause to believe that it will produce evidence of a felony under the state laws covering murder, kidnaping, gambling, robbery, bribery, extortion, drug trafficking, or any other crime dangerous to life, limb or property. State applications, court orders and other procedures must at a minimum be as demanding as federal requirements.[4]

Applications for a court order authorizing wiretapping and electronic surveillance include:

- the identity of the applicant and the official who authorized the application;
- a full and complete statement of the facts including
  details of the crime,
  a particular description of nature, location and place where the interception is to occur,[5]
  a particular description of the communications to be intercepted, and
  the identities (if known) of the person committing the offense and of the persons whose communications are to be intercepted;
- a full and complete statement of the alternative investigative techniques used or an explanation of why they would be futile or dangerous;

- a statement of period of time for which the interception is to be maintained and if it will not terminate upon seizure of the communications sought, a probable cause demonstration that further similar communications are likely to occur;
- a full and complete history of previous interception applications or efforts involving the same parties or places;
- in the case of an extension, the results to date or explanation for the want of results; and
- any additional information the judge may require, 18 U.S.C. 2518(1), (2).

Before issuing an order authorizing interception, the court must find:

- probable cause to believe that an individual is, has or is about to commit one or more of the predicate offenses;
- probable cause to believe that the particular communications concerning the crime will be seized as a result of the interception requested;
- that normal investigative procedures have been or are likely to be futile or too dangerous; and
- probable cause to believe that "the facilities from which, or the place where, the wire, oral, or electronic communications are to be intercepted are being used, or are about to be used, in connection with the commission of such offense, or are leased to, listed in the name of, or commonly used by such person," 18 U.S.C. 2518(3).

Subsections 2518(4) and (5) demand that any interception order include:

- the identity (if known) of the persons whose conversations are to be intercepted;
- the nature and location of facilities and place covered by the order;
- a particular description of the type of communication to be intercepted and an indication of the crime to which it relates;
- individual approving the application and the agency executing the order;
- the period of time during which the interception may be conducted and an indication of whether it may continue after the communication sought has been seized;
- an instruction that the order shall be executed
  as soon as practicable, and
- so as to minimize the extent of innocent communication seized; and
- upon request, a direction for the cooperation of communications providers and others necessary or useful for the execution of the order, 18 U.S.C. 2518(4).

Compliance with these procedures may be postponed briefly until after the interception effort has begun, upon the approval of senior Justice Department officials in emergency cases involving organized crime or national security threatening conspiracies or involving the risk of death or serious injury, 18 U.S.C. 2518(7).[6]

The court orders remain in effect only as long as required but not more than 30 days. After 30 days, the court may grant 30 day extensions subject to the procedures required for issuance of the original order, 18 U.S.C. 2518(5). During that time the court may require progress reports at such intervals as it considers appropriate, 18 U.S.C. 2518(6).

Intercepted communications are to be recorded and the evidence secured and placed under seal (with the possibility of copies for authorized law enforcement disclosure and use) along with the application and the court's order, 18 U.S.C. 2518(8)(a),(b).

Within 90 days of the expiration of the order those whose communications have been intercepted are entitled to notice, and evidence secured through the intercept may be introduced into evidence with 10 days' advance notice to the parties, 18 U.S.C. 2518(8)(d), (9).

Title III also circumscribes the conditions under which information derived from a court ordered interception may be disclosed or otherwise used. Nevertheless, it may be disclosed to and used for official purposes by:

- other law enforcement officials including foreign officials, 18 U.S.C. 2517(1), (2), (5), (7);
- federal intelligence officers to the extent that it involves foreign intelligence information, 18 U.S.C. 2517(6);[7]
- other American or foreign government officials to the extent that it involves the threat of hostile acts by foreign powers, their agents, or international terrorists, 18 U.S.C. 2517(8).[8]

It may also be disclosed by witnesses testifying in federal or state proceedings, 18 U.S.C. 2517(3), (5),[9] provided the intercepted conversation or other communication is not privileged, 18 U.S.C. 2517(4).

End Notes

[1] "The Attorney General, Deputy Attorney General, Associate Attorney General, or any Assistant Attorney General, any acting Assistant Attorney General, or any Deputy Assistant Attorney General or acting Deputy Assistant Attorney General in the Criminal Division specially designated by the Attorney General, may authorize an application to a Federal judge of competent jurisdiction for, and such judge may grant in conformity with section 2518 of this chapter an order authorizing or approving the interception of wire or oral communications by the Federal Bureau of Investigation, or a Federal agency having responsibility for the investigation of the offense as to which the application is made, when such interception may provide or has provided evidence of [the predicate offenses]. . ." 18 U.S.C. 2516(1).

[2] The list appears in 18 U.S.C. 2516(1) the text of which is appended.

[3] "Any attorney for the Government (as such term is defined for the purposes of the Federal Rules of Criminal Procedure) may authorize an application to a Federal judge of competent jurisdiction for, and such judge may grant, in conformity with section 2518 of this title, an order authorizing or approving the interception of electronic communications by an investigative or law enforcement officer having responsibility for the investigation of the offense as to which the application is made, when such interception may provide or has provided evidence of any Federal felony," 18 U.S.C. 2516(3). The less demanding procedures of 18 U.S.C. 2701-2711 may be used with respect to e-mail or other electronic communications that are in storage; recourse to subsection 2516(3) is only necessary when wire, oral or electronic communications are to be "intercepted."

[4] 18 U.S.C. 2516(2). The text of subsection 2516(2) is appended.

[5] Identification of the place where, or facilities over, which the targeted communications are to occur may be excused where the court finds that the suspect has or will take steps to thwart interception, 18 U.S.C. 2518(11), (12)(text is appended).

[6] The text of section 2518(7) is appended.

[7] "'[F]oreign intelligence information', for purposes of section 2517(6) of this title, means – (A) information, whether or not concerning a United States person, that relates to the ability of the United States to protect

against – (I) actual or potential attack or other grave hostile acts of a foreign power or an agent of a foreign power; (ii) sabotage or intentional terrorism by a foreign power or an agent of a foreign power; or (iii) clandestine intelligence activities by and intelligence service or network of a foreign power or by an agent of a foreign power; or (B) information, whether or not concerning a United States person, with respect to a foreign power or foreign territory that relates to – (I) the national defense or the security of the United States; or (ii) the conduct of the foreign affairs of the United States," 18 U.S.C. 2510(19).

[8] The text of 18 U.S.C. 2578(1), (2), (5), (6), (7), and (8)is appended.

[9] The text of 18 U.S.C. 2517(3) and (4) is appended.

In: Privacy: An Overview of Federal Law… ISBN: 978-1-60741-654-8
Editor: Alderic Jimenez

Chapter 13

STORED ELECTRONIC OR WIRE COMMUNICATIONS

The procedural requirements for law enforcement access to stored wire or electronic communications and transactional records are less demanding but equally complicated, 18 U.S.C. 2701-2712. They deal with two kinds of information – often in the custody of the telephone company or some other service provider rather than of any of the parties to the communication – communications records and th content of electronic or wire communications. Law enforcement officials are entitled to access:

- with the consent of the one of the parties;[1]
- on the basis of a court order or similar process under the procedures established in Title III/ECPA;[2]
- in certain emergency situations;[3] or
- under one of the other statutory exceptions to the ban on service provider disclosure.[4]

Section 2703, which affords law enforcement access to the content of stored wire and electronic communications, distinguishes between recent communications and those that have been in electronic storage for more than six months. Government officials may gain access to wire or electronic communications in electronic storage for less than six months under a search warrant issued upon probable cause to believe a crime has been committed and the search will produce evidence of the offense.[5]

The government must used the same warrant procedure to acquire older communications or those stored in remote computer storage if access is to be afforded without notice to the subscriber or customer.[6] If government officials are willing to afford the subscriber or customer notice or at least delayed notice, access may be granted under a court order showing that the information sought is relevant and material to a criminal investigation or under an administrative subpoena, a grand jury subpoena, a trial subpoena, or court order.[7]

Under the court order procedure, the court may authorize delayed notification in 90 day increments when contemporaneous notice might have an adverse impact.[8] Government supervisor officials may certify the need for delayed notification in the case of a subpoena.[9] Traditional exigent circumstances and a final general inconvenience justification form the grounds for delayed notification in either case:

- endangering the life or physical safety of an individual;
- flight from prosecution;
- destruction of or tampering with evidence;
- intimidation of potential witnesses; or
- otherwise seriously jeopardizing an investigation or unduly delaying a trial, 18 U.S.C. 2705(a)(2), (b).[10]

Comparable, if less demanding, procedures apply when the government seeks other customer information from a service provider (other than the content of a customer's communications). The information can be secured:

- with a warrant;
- with a court order;
- with customer consent;
- with a written request in telemarketing fraud cases; or
- with a subpoena in some instances.[11]

Most customer identification, use, and billing information can be secured simply with a subpoena and without customer notification.[12]

End Notes

[1] "(b) A provider described in subsection (a) may divulge the contents of a communication . . . (3) with the lawful consent of the originator or an addressee or intended recipient of such communication, or the subscriber in the case of remote computing service. . . . (c) . . . A provider described in subsection (a) may divulge a record or other information pertaining to a subscriber to or customer of such service, (not including the contents of communications covered by subsection (a)(1) or (a)(2)) . . . (2) with the lawful consent of the customer or subscriber. " 18 U.S.C. 2702(b)(3),(c)(2).

[2] "A provider described in subsection (a) may divulge the contents of a communication . . . (2) as otherwise authorized in section 2517, 2511(2)(a), or 2703 . . . .(c) . . . A provider described in subsection (a) may divulge a record or other information pertaining to a subscriber to or customer of such service, (not including the contents of communications covered by subsection (a)(1) or (a)(2)) (1) as otherwise authorized in section 2703, " 18 U.S.C. 2702(b)(2), (c)(1).

[3] "(b) A provider described in subsection (a) may divulge the contents of a communication . . . (8) to a governmental entity, if the provider, in good faith, believes that an emergency involving danger of death or serious physical injury to any person requires disclosure without delay of communications relating to the emergency. (c) . . . A provider described in subsection (a) may divulge a record or other information pertaining to a subscriber to or customer of such service, (not including the contents of communications covered by subsection (a)(1) or (a)(2)) . . .(4) to a government entity, if the provider, in good faith, believes that an emergency involving danger of death or serious physical injury to any person requires disclosure without delay of the information relating to the emergency," 18 U.S.C. 2702(b)(8),(c)(4).

[4] "(b) A provider described in subsection (a) may divulge the contents of a communication — (1) to an addressee or intended recipient of such communication or an agent of such addressee or intended recipient; . . . (4) to a person employed or authorized or whose facilities are used to forward such communication to its destination; (5) as may be necessarily incident to the rendition of the service or to the protection of the rights or property of the provider of that service; (6) to the National Center for Missing and Exploited Children, in connection with a report submitted thereto under section 227 of the Victims of Child Abuse Act of 1990; (7) to a law enforcement agency – (A) if the contents – (I) were inadvertently obtained by the service provider; and (ii) appear to pertain to the commission of a crime . . . (c) . . . A provider described in subsection (a) may divulge a record or other information pertaining to a subscriber to or customer of such service, (not including the contents of communications covered by subsection (a)(1) or (a)(2)) . . . (3) as may be necessarily incident to

the rendition of the service or to the protection of the rights or property of the provider of that service," 18 U.S.C. 2702(b)(1),(4),(5),(6),(7); (c)(3).

[5] 18 U.S.C. 2703(a)(text is appended). The 21st Century Department of Justice Appropriations Authorization Act, 116 Stat. 1822 (2002), amended section 2703 to permit execution of the warrant by service providers and others without requiring the presence of a federal officer, 18 U.S.C. 2703(g)("Notwithstanding section 3105 of this title, the presence of an officer shall not be required for service or execution of a search warrant issued in accordance with this chapter requiring disclosure by a provider of electronic communications service or remote computing service of the contents of communications or records or other information pertaining to a subscriber to or customer of such service"), see *United States v. Bach*, 310 F.3d 1063 (8th Cir. 2002)(the Fourth Amendment does not require the presence of a federal officer when technicians execute a search warrant on a service provider's server).

[6] 18 U.S.C. 2703(a), (b)(1)(A), (b)(2) (text is appended).

[7] 18 U.S.C. 2703(b)(1)(B), (d) (text is appended).

[8] 18 U.S.C. 2705(a)(1)(A), (4) (text is appended).

[9] 18 U.S.C. 2705(a)(1)(B), (4) (text is appended).

[10] A Sixth Circuit panel, in a decision later vacated en banc on grounds of ripeness, held that the Fourth Amendment precluded the seizure of stored e-mail from a service provider under a section 2703 court order which featured a delayed notice authorization under section 2705, *Warshak v. United States*, 490 F.3d 455, 468-82 (6th Cir. 2007), vac'd en banc, 532 F.3d 521 (6th Cir. 2008). The panel did not address whether exigent circumstances would permit seizure with delayed notice, perhaps because the government apparently did not raise the question, 490 F.3d at 464-65.

[11] "(1) A government entity may require a provider of electronic communication service or remote computing service to disclose a record or other information pertaining to a subscriber to or customer of such service (not including the contents of communications) – (A) obtains a warrant issued using the procedures described in the Federal Rules of Criminal Procedure by a court with jurisdiction over the offense under investigation or equivalent State warrant; (B) obtains a court order for such disclosure under subsection (d) of this section; (C) has the consent of the subscriber or customer to such disclosure; or (D) submits a formal written request relevant to a law enforcement investigation concerning telemarketing fraud for the name, address, and place of business of a subscriber or customer of such provider, which subscriber or customer is engaged in telemarketing (as such term is defined in section 2325 of this title); or (E) seeks information under paragraph (2) . . . (3) A governmental entity receiving records or information under this subsection is not required to provide notice to a subscriber or customer," 18 U.S.C. 2703(c)(1),(3).

[12] "(2) A provider of electronic communication service or remote computing service shall disclose to a governmental entity the (A) name; (B) address; (C) local and long distance telephone connection records, or records of session times and durations; (D) length of service (including start date) and types of service utilized; (E) telephone or instrument number or other subscriber number or identity, including any temporarily assigned network address; and (F) means and source of payment (including any credit car or bank account number), of a subscriber to or customer of such service, when the governmental entity uses an administrative subpoena authorized by a Federal or State statute or a Federal or State grand jury or trial subpoena or any means available under paragraph (1). (3) A governmental entity receiving records or information under this subsection is not required to provide notice to a subscriber or customer," 18 U.S.C. 2703(c)(2),(3).

In: Privacy: An Overview of Federal Law...
Editor: Alderic Jimenez
ISBN: 978-1-60741-654-8

Chapter 14

PEN REGISTERS AND TRAP AND TRACE DEVICES

Pen registers and trap and trace devices identify the source of calls placed to or from a particular telephone. Federal government attorneys and state and local police officers may apply for a court order authorizing the installation and use of a pen register and/or a trap and trace device upon certification that the information that will provide is relevant to a pending criminal investigation.[1]

An order authorizing installation and use of a pen register or trap and trace device must:

- specify
    - the person (if known) upon whose telephone line the device is to be installed,
    - the person (if known) who is the subject of the criminal investigation,
    - the telephone number, (if known) the location of the line to which the device is to be attached, and geographical range of the device,
    - a description of the crime to which the investigation relates;
- upon request, direct carrier assistance pursuant to section 3124;
- terminate within 60 days, unless extended;
- involve a report of particulars of the order's execution in Internet cases; and
- impose necessary nondisclosure requirements.[2]

Senior Justice Department or state prosecutors may approve the installation and use of a pen register or trap and trace device prior to the issuance of court authorization in emergency cases that involving either an organized crime conspiracy, an immediate danger of death or serious injury, an threat to national security, or a serious attack on a "protected computer."[3]

Federal authorities have applied for court orders, under the Stored Communications Act (18 U.S.C. 2701-2712) and the trap and trace authority of 18 U.S.C. 3121-3127, seeking to direct communications providers to supply them with the information necessary to track cell phone users in conjunction with an ongoing criminal investigation. Thus far, their efforts have met with mixed success.[4]

End Notes

[1] 18 U.S.C. 3122 (text is appended).
[2] 18 U.S.C. 3123 (text is appended).
[3] 18 U.S.C. 3125 (text is appended).
[4] E.g., *In re Application of the United States*, 497 F.Supp.2d 301 (D. P.R. 2007); *In re United States*, 441 F.3d 816 (S.D. Tex. 2006); *In re Application of the Untied States,* 416 F.Supp. 390 (D.Md. 2006); *In re Application of the United States*, 415 F.Supp.2d 211 (W.D.N.Y. 2006); *In re Application of the United States*, 412 F.Supp.2d 947 (E.D.Wis. 2006); *In re Application of the United States*, 407 F.Supp.2d 134 (D.D.C. 2006) (each denying the application); but see, *In re Application of the United States*, 509 F.Supp.2d 76 (D.Mass. 2007); *In re Application of the United States*, 460 F.Supp.2d 448 (S.D.N.Y. 2006); *In re Application of the United States*, 433 F.Supp.2d 804 (S.D. Tex. 2006); *In re Application of the United States*, 411 F.Supp.2d 678 (W.D.La. 2006).

In: Privacy: An Overview of Federal Law… ISBN: 978-1-60741-654-8
Editor: Alderic Jimenez

Chapter 15

FOREIGN INTELLIGENCE SURVEILLANCE ACT

The procedure for securing wiretapping court orders under the Foreign Intelligence Surveillance Act (FISA), 50 U.S.C. 1801-1811, is the most distinctive of the wiretap-related procedures.[1] First, its focus is different. It was designed to secure foreign intelligence information – not evidence of a crime.[2] Second, it operates in a highly secretive manner. But its most individualistic feature is that the procedure is conducted entirely before members of an independent court convened for no other purpose. The Act operates in the field of foreign intelligence gathering, primarily through a Foreign Intelligence Surveillance Court whose judges grant or reject petitions for wiretap and electronic surveillance orders, orders authorizing physical searches and seizures, pen register and trap and trace orders, and orders relating to the surrender of tangible items.

The Foreign Intelligence Surveillance Court is comprised of eleven federal court judges designated by the Chief Justice to sit on the Court for a single seven year term.[3] In the area of wiretaps and physical searches,[4] the judges of the Court individually receive and approve or reject requests,[5] authorized by the Attorney General, to conduct the four specific types of electronic surveillance noted earlier[6] of the communications and activities of foreign powers.[7]

The contents of FISA application include:

- the identity of the individual submitting the application;
- the identity or a description of the person whose communications are to be intercepted;
- an indication of
    - why the person is believed to be a foreign power or the agent of a foreign power, and
    - why foreign powers or their agents are believed to use the targeted facilities or places;
- a summary of the minimization procedures[8] to be followed;
- a description of the communications to be intercepted and the information sought;[9]
- certification by a senior national security or senior defense official designed by the President that

- the information sought is foreign intelligence information,
- a significant purpose of interception is to secure foreign intelligence information,
- the information cannot reasonably be obtained using alternative means,[10]
- a summary statement of the means of accomplishing the interception (including whether a physical entry will be required);11
- a history of past interception applications involving the same persons, places or facilities;
- the period of time during which the interception is to occur, whether it will terminate immediately upon obtaining the information sought, and if not, the reasons why interception thereafter is likely to be productive intercepted.[12]

FISA court judges issue orders approving electronic surveillance or physical searches upon a finding that the application requirements have been met and that there is probable cause to believe that the target is a foreign power or the agent of a foreign power and that the targeted places or facilities are used by foreign powers of their agents.[13]

Orders approving electronic surveillance must:

- specify
  - the identity or a description of the person whose communications are to be intercepted,
  - the nature and location of the targeted facilities or places, if known,
  - type of communications or activities targeted and the kind of information sought,
  - the means by which interception is to be accomplished and whether physical entry is authorized,
  - the tenure of the authorization, and
  - whether more than one device are to be used and if so their respective ranges and associated minimization procedures;

- require
  - that minimization procedures be adhered to,
  - upon request, that carriers and others provide assistance,[14]
  - that those providing assistance observe certain security precautions, and be compensated;[15]
  - direct the applicant to advise the court of the particulars relating to surveillance directed at additional facilities and places when the order permits surveillance although the nature and location of targeted facilities and places were unknown at the time of issuance;
  - expire when its purpose is accomplished but not later than after 90 days generally (after 120 days in the case of certain foreign agents and after a year in the case of foreign governments or their entities or factions of foreign nations) unless extended (extensions may not exceed one year).[16]

As in the case of law enforcement wiretapping and electronic eavesdropping, there is authority for interception and physical searches prior to approval in emergency situations,[17] but there is also statutory authority for foreign intelligence surveillance interceptions and physical searches without the requirement of a court order when the targets are limited to communications among or between foreign powers or involve nonverbal communications from places under the open and exclusive control of a foreign power.[18] The second of these is replete with reporting requirements to Congress and the FISA court.[19] These and the twin war time exceptions[20] may be subject to constitutional limitations, particularly when Americans are the surveillance targets.[21]

FISA has detailed provisions governing the use of the information acquired through the use of its surveillance or physical search authority that include:

- confidentiality requirements, 50 U.S.C. 1806(a), 1825(a);
- notice of required Attorney General approval for disclosure, 50 U.S.C. 1806(b), 1825(b);
- notice to the "aggrieved" of the government's intention to use the results as evidence, 50 U.S.C. 1806(c),(d), 1825(c),(d);
- suppression procedures, 50 U.S.C. 1806(e), (f), (g), (h), 1825(e), (f), (g), (h);[22]
- inadvertently captured information, 50 U.S.C. 1806(I), 1825(b);
- notification of emergency surveillance or search for which no FISA order was subsequently secured, 50 U.S.C. 1806(j), 1825(j); and
- clarification that those who execute FISA surveillance or physical search orders may consult with federal and state law enforcement officers, 50 U.S.C. 1806(k), 1825(k).

Both the surveillance and the physical search authorities are subject to Congressional oversight in the form of semiannual reports on the extent and circumstances of their use, 50 U.S.C. 1808, 1826.

PEN REGISTERS AND TRAP AND TRACE DEVICES

FISA pen register and trap and trace procedures, 50 U.S.C. 1841-1846, are similar to those of their law enforcement counterparts, but with many of the attributes of other FISA provisions. The orders may be issued either by a member of the FISA court or by a FISA magistrate upon the certification of a federal officer that the information sought is likely to be relevant to an investigation of international terrorism or clandestine intelligence activities, 50 U.S.C. 1842. The order may direct service providers to supply customer information related to order, 50 U.S.C. 1842.(d)(2)(C). The statute allows the Attorney General to authorize emergency installation and use as long as an application is filed within 48 hours, 50 U.S.C. 1843, and restricts the use of any resulting evidence if an order is not subsequently granted, 50 U.S.C. 1843(c)(2). The provisions for use of the information acquired run parallel to those that apply to FISA surveillance and physical search orders, 50 U.S.C. 1845. The USA PATRIOT Improvement and Reauthorization Act increased the level of Congressional oversight by requiring that the semiannual report on the government's recourse to FISA pen register/trap and trace authority including statistical information on the extent its use, 50 U.S.C. 1846.

TANGIBLE ITEMS

FISA's tangible item orders, 50 U.S.C. 1861, are perhaps its most interesting feature. Prior to the USA PATRIOT Act, senior FBI officials could approve an application to a FISA judge or magistrate for an order authorizing common carriers, or public accommodation, storage facility, or vehicle rental establishments to release their business records based upon certification of a reason to believe that the records pertained to a foreign power or the agent of a foreign power, 50 U.S.C. 1862 (2000 ed.). The USA PATRIOT Act and later the USA PATRIOT Improvement and Reauthorization Act temporarily rewrote the procedure. In its temporary form, it requires rather than authorizes access; it is predicated upon relevancy rather than probable cause; it applies to all tangible property (not merely records); and it applies to the tangible property of both individuals or organizations, commercial and otherwise.[23] It is limited, however, to investigations conducted to secure foreign intelligence information or to protect against international terrorism or clandestine intelligence activities, 50 U.S.C. 1861(a).

Recipients are prohibited from disclosing the existence of the order, but are expressly authorized to consult an attorney with respect to their rights and obligations under the order, 50 U.S.C. 1861(d). They enjoy immunity from civil liability for good faith compliance, 50 U.S.C. 1861(e). They may challenge the legality of the order and/or ask that its disclosure restrictions be lifted or modified, 50 U.S.C. 1861(f). The grounds for lifting the secrecy requirements are closely defined, but petitions for reconsideration may be filed annually, 50 U.S.C. 1861(f)(2)(C)(iii). The decision to set aside, modify or let stand either the disclosure restrictions of an order or the underlying order itself are subject to appellate review, 50 U.S.C. 1861(f)(3),(4),(5).

As addition safeguards, Congress has:

- insisted upon the promulgation of minimization standards, 50 U.S.C. 1861(g);
- established use restrictions, 50 U.S.C. 1861(h),
- required the approval of senior officials in order to seek orders covering the records of libraries and certain other types of records, 50 U.S.C. 1861(a)(3);
- confirmed and reenforced reporting requirements, 50 U.S.C. 1862; and
- directed the Justice Department's Inspector General to conduct an audit of the use of the FISA tangible item authority, P.L. 109-177, §106A, 120 Stat. 200-202 (2006).

PROTECT AMERICA ACT (EXPIRED)

The Protect America Act (Protect Act) granted the Attorney General and the Director of National Intelligence the power, under limited conditions, to authorize gathering foreign intelligence information,[24] including by electronic surveillance, (for up to a year) relating to persons believed to be overseas.[25] In order to exercise that power, the Attorney General and the Director of National Intelligence were required to certify under oath that the collection effort involved:

- procedures reasonably calculated to assure that the information sought concerned a person outside the United States;
- communications to which service providers or others had access;
- a desire, at least in significant part, to gather foreign intelligence information;
- accompanying minimization procedures; and
- no electronic surveillance other than that directed at a person reasonably believed to be abroad, 50 U.S.C. 1805b(a)(expired).[26]

That having been done or in emergency situations with their oral approval,[27] the Attorney General and Director of National Intelligence might direct the communications providers, or others with access, to immediately assist in the gathering of the foreign intelligence information in a manner least disruptive of service to the target and under confidentiality restrictions imposed by the Attorney General and the Director of National Intelligence, 50 U.S.C. 1805b(e)(expired). The directive came with the promise of compensation at prevailing rates as well as immunity from civil liability and was enforceable through the contempt power of the FISA court, 50 U.S.C. 1805b(f), (g), (*l*)(expired). Recipients were entitled to seek judicial modification of a directive, issued contrary to the statute or otherwise unlawfully, in the FISA court under expedited procedures, 50 U.S.C. 1805b(h), (I), (j), (k) (expired).

The FISA court was also tasked with the responsibility of reviewing the procedures crafted to ensure that the authority was only invoked with respect to persons reasonably believed to be found overseas, 50 U.S.C. 1805c(expired). Should the court have determined that the procedures were clearly erroneous, the government was free to amend them or to appeal the determination initially to the Foreign Intelligence Surveillance Court of Review and then to the Supreme Court, *id.*

Foreign Intelligence Surveillance Act of 1978 Amendments Act of 2008 (P.L. 110-261)

P.L. 110-261 (H.R. 6304), signed July 10, 2008, addresses four FISA-related matters.[28] First, in a manner reminiscent of the Protect Act, it provides temporary authorityto gatherforeign intelligence information from overseas targets.[29] Second, it reasserts the exclusivity of FISA and Title III/ECPA as a basis for governmental electronic surveillance.[30] Third, it instructs the Inspectors General in various agencies to conduct a review and report to Congress on the Terrorist Surveillance Program.[31] Fourth, it seeks to protect those who assist government surveillance activities from civil liability.[32]

Overseas Targets

P.L. 110-261 repeals the Protect Act.[33] Yet like the Protect Act, it establishes a temporary set of three procedures to authorize the acquisition of foreign intelligence information by targeting an individual or entity thought to be overseas.[187] One, 50 U.S.C. 1881a, applies to the targeting of an overseas person or entity that is not a U.S. person.[35] Another, 50 U.S.C. 1881b, covers situations when the American target is overseas but the gathering involves electronic communications or stored electronic communications or data acquired in this country.[36] The third, 50 U.S.C. 1881c, applies to situations when the American target is overseas, but section 1881b is not available, either because acquisition occurs outside of the United States or because it involves something other than electronic surveillance or the acquisition of stored communications or data, e.g., a physical search.[37]

In the case of targets who are not U.S. persons, section 1881a(a) declares "upon the issuance of an order in accordance with subsection (i)(3) or a determination under subsection (c)(2), the Attorney General and the Director of National Intelligence may authorize jointly, for a period of up to 1 year from the effective date of the authorization, the targeting of persons reasonably believed to be located outside the United States to acquire foreign intelligence information." It makes no mention of authorizing acquisition. It merely speaks of targeting with an eye to acquisition. Moreover, it gives no indication of whether the anticipated methods of acquisition include the capture of a target's communications, of communications relating to a target, of communications of a person or entity related to the target, or information concerning one of the three. The remainder of the section, however, seems to dispel some of the questions. Section 1881a is intended to empower the Attorney General and the Director of National Intelligence to authorize the acquisition of foreign intelligence information and the methods that may be used to the capture of communications and related information.

The procedure begins either with a certification presented to the FISA court for approval or with a determination by the two officials that exigent circumstances warrant timely authorization prior court approval.[38] In the certification process, they must assert in writing and under oath that:

- a significant purpose for the effort is the acquisition of foreign intelligence information
- the effort will involve the assistance of an electronic communication service provider
- the court has approved, or is being asked to approve, procedures designed to ensure that acquisition is limited to targeted persons found outside the U.S. and to prevent the capture of communications in which all the parties are within the U.S.
- minimization procedures, which the court has approved or is being asked to approve and which satisfy the requirements for such procedures in the case of FISA electronic surveillance and physical searches, will be honored
- guidelines to ensure compliance with limitations imposed in the section have been adopted and the limitations will be observed
- these procedures and guidelines are consistent with Fourth Amendment standards.[39]

The certification is be accompanied by a copy of the targeting and minimization procedures, any supporting affidavits from senior national security officials, an indication of the effective date of the authorization, and a notification of whether pre-approval emergency authorization has been given.[40] The certification, however, need not describe the facilities or places at which acquisition efforts will be directed.[41]

The limitations preclude intentionally targeting a person in the U.S., "reverse targeting" (intentionally targeting a person overseas purpose of targeting a person within the U.S.), intentionally targeting a U.S. person outside the U.S., intentionally acquiring a communication in which all of the parties are in the U.S., or conducting the acquisition in a manner contrary to the demands of the Fourth Amendment.[42]

The Attorney General, in consultation with the Director of National Intelligence, is obligated to promulgate targeting and minimization procedures and guidelines to ensure that the section's limitations are observed.[43] The minimization procedures must satisfy the standards required for similar procedures required for FISA electronic surveillance and physical searches.[44] The targeting procedures must be calculated to avoid acquiring communications in which all of the parties are in the U.S. and to confine targeting to persons located outside the U.S.[45] Both are subject to review by the FISA court for sufficiency when it receives the request to approve the certification.[46] Copies of the guidelines, which also provide directions concerning the application for FISA court approval under the section, must be supplied to court and to the congressional intelligence and judiciary committees.[47]

The Attorney General and Director of National Intelligence may instruct an electronic communications service provider to assist in the acquisition. Cooperative providers are entitled to compensation and are immune from suit for their assistance.[48] They may also petition the FISA court to set aside or modify the direction for assistance, if directive is unlawful.[49] The Attorney General may petition the court to enforce a directive against an uncooperative provider.[50] The court's decisions concerning certification approval, modification of directions for assistance, and enforcement of the directives are each appealable to the Foreign Intelligence Court of Review and on certiorari to the Supreme Court.[51]

Except with respect to disclosure following a failure to court approval of an emergency authorization, section 1806, discussed earlier, governs the use of information obtained under the authority of section 1881a.[52]

When the overseas target is an American individual or entity and acquisition is to occur in this country, the FISA court may authorize acquisition by electronic surveillance or by capturing stored electronic communications or data under section 1881b. The Attorney General must approve the application which must be made under oath and indicate:

- the identity of the applicant
- the identity, if known, or description of the American target
- the facts establishing that reason to believe that the person is overseas and a foreign power or its agent, officer, or employee
- the applicable minimization procedures
- a description of the information sought and the type of communications or activities targeted
- certification by the Attorney General or a senior national security or defense official that
    - foreign intelligence information is to be sought
    - a significant purpose of the effort is to obtain such information
    - the information cannot otherwise reasonable be obtained (and the facts upon which this conclusion is based)
    - the nature of the information (e.g., relating to terrorism, sabotage, the conduct of U.S. foreign affairs, etc.)(and the facts upon which this conclusion is based)

- the means of acquisition and whether physical entry will be necessary
- the identity of the service providing assisting (targeted facilities and premises need not be identified)
- a statement of previous applications relating to the same American and actions taken
- the proposed tenure of the order (not to exceed 90 days), and
- any additional information the FISA court may require.[53]

The court must issue an acquisition order upon a finding that the application satisfies statutory requirements, the minimization procedures are adequate, and there is probable cause to believe that the American target is located overseas and is a foreign power or its agent, officer or employee.[54] The court must explain in writing any finding that the application's assertion of probable cause, minimization procedures, or certified facts is insufficient.[55] Such findings are appealable to the Foreign Intelligence Surveillance Court of Review and under certiorari to the Supreme Court.[56]

The court's order approving acquisition is to include the identity or description of the American target, the type of activities targeted, the nature of the information sought, the means of acquisition, and duration of the order.[57] The order will also call for compliance with the minimization procedures, and when appropriate, for confidential, minimally disruptive provider assistance, compensated at a prevailing rate.[58] Providers are immune from civil liability for any assistance they are directed to provide.[59]

As in other instances, in emergency cases the Attorney General may authorize acquisition pending approval of the FISA court.[60] The court must be notified of the Attorney General's decision and the related application must be filed within 7 days.[61] If emergency acquisition is not judicially approved subsequently, no resulting evidence may be introduce any judicial, legislative or regulatory proceedings unless the target is determined not to be an American, nor may resulting information be shared with other federal officials without the consent of the target, unless the Attorney General determines that the information concerns a threat of serious bodily injury.[62] Except with respect to disclosure following a failure to court approval of an emergency authorization, section 1806, discussed earlier, governs the use of information obtained under the authority of section 1881a.[63]

The second provision for targeting an American overseas in order to acquire foreign intelligence information, section 1881c, is somewhat unique. Both FISA and Title III/ECPA have been understood to apply only to interceptions within the United States. Neither has been thought to apply overseas. Section 1881c, however, may be used for acquisitions outside the United States. Moreover, it may be used for acquisitions inside the United States as long as the requirements that would ordinarily attend such acquisition are honored.[64]

Otherwise, section 1881c features many of the same application, approval, and appeal provisions as section 1881b. Authorization is available under a FISA court order or in emergency circumstances under the order of the Attorney General.[65] Acquisition activities must be discontinued during any period when the target is thought to be in the United States.[66] Unlike 1881b, however, it is not limited to electronic surveillance or the acquisition of stored electronic information. Moreover, it declares that in the case of acquisition abroad recourse to a FISA court order need only be had when the target American, found overseas, has a reasonable expectation of privacy and a warrant would be required if the acquisition efforts had taken place in the United States and for law enforcement purposes.[67]

Exclusivity

Title III/ECPA has long declared that it should not be construed to confine governmental activities authorized under FISA, but that the two – Title III/ECPA and FISA – are the exclusive authority under which governmental electronic surveillance may be conducted in this country.[68] The Justice Department suggested, however, that in addition to the President's constitutional authority the Authorization for the Use of Military Force Resolution,[69] enacted in response to the events of September 11, established an implicit exception to the exclusivity requirement.[70] Section 102 of P.L. 110-261 seeks to overcome the suggestion by establishing a second exclusivity section which declares that it exceptions may only be created by explicit statutory language.[71]

Inspector General Reviews

Section 301 of P.L. 110-261 instructs the Inspectors General of the Justice and Defense Departments, of the Office of the Director of National Intelligence, of the National Security Agency, and of any pertinent intelligence agency to conduct a comprehensive review of their agency's activities relating to presidentially authorized intelligence activities involving communications, including the Terrorist Surveillance Program.[72] It further directs them to provide the Judiciary and Intelligence Committees with interim reports within 60 days of enactment and final reports within 1 year.[73]

Immunity for Assistanc

P.L. 110-261 bars the initiation or continuation of civil suits in either state or federal court based on charges that the defendant assisted any of the U.S. intelligence agencies.[74] Dismissal is required upon the certification of the Attorney General that the person either:

- did not provide the assistance charged;
- provided the assistance under order of the FISA court;
- provided the assistance pursuant to a national security letter issued under 18 U.S.C. 2709;
- provided the assistance pursuant to 18 U.S.C. 2511(2)(a)(ii)(B) and 2518(7) under assurances from the Attorney General or a senior Justice Department official, empowered to approve emergency law enforcement wiretaps, that no court approval was required;
- provided the assistance in response to a directive from the President through the Attorney General relating to communications between or among foreign powers pursuant to 50 U.S.C. 1802(a)(4);
- provided the assistance in response to a directive from the Attorney General and the Director of National Intelligence relating to the acquisition of foreign intelligence information concerning persons believed to be overseas pursuant to 50 U.S.C. 1805b (Protect Act);
- provided the assistance in response to a directive from the Attorney General and the Director of National Intelligence relating to the acquisition of foreign

intelligence information targeting non-U.S. persons thought to be overseas pursuant to 50 U.S.C. 1881a(h); or

- provided the assistance in connection with intelligence activities authorized by the President between September 11, 2001 and January 17, 2007 relating to terrorist attacks against the United States.[75]

Only telecommunications carriers, electronic service providers, and other communication service providers may claim the protection afforded those who assisted activities authorized between 9/11 and January 17, 2007.[76] The group which may claim protection for assistance supplied under other grounds is larger. It includes not only communication service providers but also any "landlord, custodian or other person" ordered or directed to provide assistance.[77]

The Attorney General's certification is binding if supported by substantial evidence, and the court is to consider challenges and supporting evidence ex parte and in camera where the Attorney General asserts that disclosure would harm national security.[78] Cases filed in state court may be removed to federal court.[79]

P.L. 11-261 also preempts state regulatory authority over communication service providers with respect to assistance provide intelligence agencies.[80] Moreover, it directs the Attorney General to report to the Judiciary and Intelligence Committees on implementation of the protective provisions.[81]

End Notes

[1] See generally, CRS Report RL30465, *The Foreign Intelligence Surveillance Act: An Overview of the Statutory Framework*, by Elizabeth B. Bazan.

[2] In its original form, gathering foreign intelligence was "the" purpose for which FISA surveillance orders were sought, 50 U.S.C. 1804(a)(7)(B) (1982 ed.). Although amended by the USA PATRIOT Act, gathering foreign intelligence must still provide a "significant" reason for seeking a FISA surveillance order, 50 U.S.C. 1804(a)(7)(B); In re Sealed Case, 310 F.3d 717, (F.I.S.Ct.Rev. 2002); *United States v. Ning Wen*, 477 F.3d 896, 897 (7th Cir. 2007).

[3] 50 U.S.C. 1803(a),(b),(d) (text is appended).

[4] The FISA procedures relating to wiretapping and electronic surveillance orders, 50 U.S.C. 1801-1811, and those relating to physical searches, 50 U.S.C. 1821-1829, are virtually identical and consequently are treated together here.

[5] P.L. 110-261 explicitly granted the FISA court judges the authority to sit as a group on their own initiative or on the petition of the government when a majority of court concludes that a particular matter is exceptional significance or in order uniformity of interpretation among the members of the court, 50 U.S.C. 1803(a)(2).

[6] 50 U.S.C. 1801(f)(text is appended). The courts have noted that, unlike surveillance under Title III/EPCA, silent video surveillance falls within the purview of FISA by virtue of subsection 1801(f)(4), *United States v. Koyomejian*, 970 F.2d 536, 540 (9th Cir. 1992); *United States v. Mesa-Rincon*, 911 F.2d 1433, 1438 (10th Cir. 1990); *United States v. Biasucci*, 786 F.2d 504, 508 (2d Cir. 1986).

[7] "'Foreign power' means – (1) a foreign government or any component thereof, whether or not recognized by the United States; (2) a faction of a foreign nation or nations, not substantially composed of United States persons; (3) an entity that is openly acknowledged by a foreign government or governments to be directed and controlled by such foreign government or governments; (4) a group engaged in international terrorism or activities in preparation therefor; (5) a foreign-based political organization, not substantially composed of United States persons; (6) an entity that is directed and controlled by a foreign government or governments; or *an entity not substantially composed of United States persons that is engaged in the international proliferation of weapons of mass destruction*," 50 U.S.C. 1801(a)(language in italics added in P.L. 110-261). Note that the definition of foreign power includes international terrorists groups regardless of whether any nexus to a foreign power can be shown, 50 U.S.C. 1801(a)(4) and includes agents of foreign powers that no longer exist, *United States v. Squillacote*, 221 F.3d 542, 554 (4th Cir. 2000) (agents of East Germany intercepted under an order granted after unification). Moreover, at least until it expires on December 31, 2009, the definition of "agent of foreign power" (50 U.S.C.1801(b)(1)(c)) includes international terrorists with no necessary to

connection to a foreign power or group. The FISA physical search provisions adopt by cross reference the definitions of "foreign power" and "agent of a foreign power," 50 U.S.C. 1821(1).

[8] "Minimization procedures" are defined in 50 U.S.C. 1801(h). They are essentially those procedures designed to minimize the unnecessary acquisition, retention, and dissemination of information relating to U.S. persons (American citizens, permanent resident aliens, U.S. corporations, and organizations a substantial number of whose members are Americans). Like the procedures in Title III, they are crafted to minimize the amount of "innocent" communications captured with the communications which are the target of the order and require a good faith effort on the part of the government to avoid the capture and retention of irrelevant material, *United States v. Hammoud*, 381 F.3d 316, 334 (4th Cir. 2004), vac'd on other grounds, 543 U.S. 1097 (2004), reinstated in pertinent part after remand, 405 F.3d 1034 (4th Cir. 2005); *United States v. Rosen*, 447 F.Supp.2d 538, 550-51 (E.D.Va. 2006).

[9] Section 104(a)(1)(c) of P.L. 110-261 eliminated the requirement of a "detailed" description.

[10] Section 104(a)(1)(D) of P.L. 110-261 authorized the President to designate the Deputy Director of the Federal Bureau of Investigation as a certifying official as well.

[11] Section 104(a)(1)(E) of P.L. 11-261 added that the statement need only be "summary."

[12] 50 U.S.C. 1804 (text is appended). 50 U.S.C. 1823 relating to applications for a FISA physical search order is essentially the same. Section 104(a)(1)(A) of P.L. 110-261 eliminated the requirement that the application indicate that the Attorney General approved the application and that the President had authorized him to do so. It also eliminated the requirement that the application indicate whether more than one interception device was to be used and if so their range and the minimization procedures associated with each. Section 104(a)(2) of P.L. 110-261, however, repealed the language once found in 50 U.S.C. 1804(b) which, when the target of the surveillance was a foreign power, excused the inclusion of multiple device information, of a statement of the means of execution, of a statement relating to the basis for the "last resort" and foreign intelligence information certifications, and of a description of the information sought and the type of communications targeted.

[13] 50 U.S.C. 1805(a) (text is appended); 50 U.S.C. 1824(a) is to the same effect with respect to physical search orders.

[14] "An order approving an electronic surveillance under this section shall . . . (2) direct – (B) that, upon the request of the applicant, a specified communication or other common carrier, landlord, custodian, or other specified person , *or in circumstances where the Court finds that the actions of the target of the application may have the effect of thwarting the identification of a specified person, such other persons,* furnish the applicant forthwith all information, facilities, or technical assistance necessary to accomplish the electronic surveillance in such a manner as will protect its secrecy and produce a minimum of interference with the services that such carrier, landlord, custodian, or other person is providing that target of electronic surveillance," 50 U.S.C. 1805(c)(2)(B). By virtue of section 102(b) of the USA PATRIOT Improvement and Reauthorization Act, the language in italics expires on December 31, 2009, unless statutorily extended or made permanent, P.L. 109-177, §102(b) 120 Stat. 195 (2006).

[15] 50 U.S.C. 1805(c)(2)(C),(D); 50 U.S.C. 1824(c)(2)(C),(D)(text is appended). FISA physical search orders must also direct "the federal officer conducting the physical search promptly report to the court the circumstances and results of the physical search," 50 U.S.C. 1824(c)(2)(E).

The USA PATRIOT Act's amendments make it clear that those who provide such assistance are immune from civil suit, 18 U.S.C. 1805(i) ("No cause of action shall lie in any court against any provider of a wire or electronic communication service, landlord, custodian, or other persons (including any officer, employee, agent, or other specified person thereof) that furnishes any information, facilities, or technical assistance in accordance with a court order or request for emergency assistance under this Act for electronic surveillance or physical search"). As discussed at greater length later, P.L. 110261 affords service providers retroactive protection for foreign intelligence assistance provided outside the confines of FISA.

[16] 50 U.S.C. 1805(c); 1824(c) (text is appended).

[17] 50 U.S.C. 1805(f); 1824(e) (text is appended). P.L. 110-261 extends the permissible length of emergency authorizations absent court approval from 72 hours to 7 days. It also removes earlier language which called for review of a FISA court denial of an application to approve an emergency authorization. Finally, it states that the Attorney General is to assess compliance with the statutory provisions which permit use of the information secured under an authorization which fails to secure judicial approval.

[18] 50 U.S.C. 1802(a)(1),(4); 1822(a)(1), (4) (text is appended).

[19] 50 U.S.C. 1802(a)(2),(3); 1822(a)(2), (3) (text is appended).

[20] "Notwithstanding any other law, the President, through the Attorney General, may authorize electronic surveillance without a court order under this subchapter to acquire foreign intelligence information for a period not to exceed fifteen calendar days following a declaration of war by the Congress, " 50 U.S.C. 1811.

"Notwithstanding any other provision of law, the President, through the Attorney General, may authorize physical searches without a court order under this subchapter to acquire foreign intelligence information for a period not to exceed 15 calendar days following a declaration of war by the Congress," 50 U.S.C. 1829.

[21] Over the years, however, the vast majority of courts have rejected the suggestion that FISA is vulnerable to constitutional attack on Fourth Amendment grounds or any other, *In re Sealed Case*, 310 F.3d 717, 737-46 (F.I.S.Ct.Rev. 2002); *United States v. Damrah*, 412 F.3d 618, 624-25 (6th Cir. 2005); *United States v. Mubayyid*, 521 F.Supp.2d 125, 135-36 (D. Mass. 2007); *United States v. Benkahla*, 437 F.Supp.2d 541, 554-55 (E.D.Va. 2006); *contra, Mayfield v. United States*, 504 F.Supp.2d 1023, 1036-43 (D. Ore. 2007).

[22] Consideration of a motion to suppress occurs ex parte and in camera when the government files a notice that national security would otherwise be compromised, 50 U.S.C. 1806(f); *In re Grand Jury Proceedings*, 347 F.3d 197, 203 (7th Cir. 2003); *United States v. Damrah*, 412 F.3d 618, 623-24 (6th Cir. 2005); review is the same as that afforded by the FISA court, statutory compliance; there is no authority to "second guess the executive branches certification," *In re Grand Jury Proceedings*, 347 F.3d 197, 204-205 (7th Cir. 2003); *United States v. Campa*, 529 F.3d 980, 993 (11th Cir. 2008); *United States v. Amawi*, 531 F.Supp.2d 832, 837 (N.D. Ohio 2008); *United States v. Abu-Jihaad*, 531 F.Supp.2d 299, 312 (D.Conn. 2008).

[23] Unless legislative extended, the authority reverts to its pre-USA PATRIOT Act form on December 31, 2009, 50 U.S.C. 1861 note; P.L. 109-177, §102(b), 120 Stat. 195 (2006).

[24] "'Foreign intelligence information' means – (1) information that relates to, and if concerning a United States person is necessary to, the ability of the United States to protect against – (A) actual or potential attack or other grave hostile acts of a foreign power or an agent of a foreign power; (B) sabotage, international terrorism, *or the international proliferation of weapons of mass destruction* by a foreign power or an agent of a foreign power; or (C) clandestine intelligence activities by an intelligence service or network of a foreign power or by an agent of a foreign power; or (2) information with respect to a foreign power or foreign territory that relates to, and if concerning a United States person is necessary to – (A) the national defense or the security of the United States; or (B) the conduct of the foreign affairs of the United States," 50 U.S.C. 1801(e)(language in italics added by P.L. 110-261 did not apply when the Protect Act was in effect).

[25] P.L. 110-55, §§2, 3, 121 Stat. 552 (2007), 50 U.S.C. 1805a -1805c. By operation of section 6(c) of the Public Law, sections 2, 3, 4, and 5 expired 180 days after enactment; the deadline was extended to 195 days on January 31, 2008, by P.L. 110-182, 122 Stat. 605 (2008); and the sections expired when the deadline ran out in mid-February. Section 6(b) of the Act provides that orders issued and extended under the authority of the Act remain in effect until they expire under the terms of the order, the Act, and the FISA provisions in effect when they were issued. See generally, CRS Report RL34143, *P.L.110-55, the Protect America Act of 2007: Modifications to the Foreign Intelligence Surveillance Act*, by Elizabeth B. Bazan.

[26] Section 1805b(a)(2) simply called for a determination that "the acquisition does not constitute electronic surveillance," but section 1805a had declared that "nothing in the definition of electronic surveillance under section 101(f)[which provides the definition of terms used in the subchapter in which section 1805b is found] shall be construed to encompass surveillance directed at a person reasonably believed to be located outside the United States."

[27] In emergency situations, information gathering could begin prior certification under oral instructions as long as minimization procedures were followed and certification was provided within 72 hours, 50 U.S.C. 1805b(a), (d)(expired).

[28] For a general discussion of the debate leading up to enactment see CRS Report RL34279, *The Foreign Intelligence Surveillance Act: An Overview of Selected Issues*, by Elizabeth B. Bazan.

[29] 50 U.S.C. 1881-1881g.

[30] 50 U.S.C. 1812 ("(a) Except as provided in subsection (b), the procedures of chapters 119, 121, and 206 of title 18, United States Code, and this Act shall be the exclusive means by which electronic surveillance and the interception of domestic wire, oral, or electronic communications may be conducted. (b) Only an express statutory authorization for electronic surveillance or the interception of domestic wire, oral, or electronic communications, other than as an amendment to this Act or chapters 119, 121, or 206 of title 18, United States Code, shall constitute an additional exclusive means for the purpose of subsection (a)").

[31] P.L. 110-261, tit. III, 122 Stat. 2471 (2008).

[32] P.L. 110-261, tit. II, 122 Stat. 2467 (2008); 50 U.S.C. 1885-1885c (text is appended). For a general discussion of the immunity provisions see CRS Report RL34600, *Retroactive Immunity Provided by the FISA Amendments Act of 2008*, by Edward C. Liu.

[33] P.L. 110-261, §403(a)(1)(A), 122 Stat. 2473 (2008)(repealing 50 U.S.C. 1805a, 1985b, and 1805c).

[34] Sections 1881a-1881g are repealed effective December 31, 2012, P.L. 110-261, §403(b)(1), 122 Stat. 2474 (2008).

[35] "United States person" includes United States citizens, permanent resident aliens of the United States, corporations incorporated in the United States, and unincorporated associates made up of a substantial number of U.S. citizens, 50 U.S.C. 1881(a), 1801(j).

[36] 50 U.S.C. 1881b.

[37] 50 U.S.C. 1881c.

[38] 50 U.S.C. 1881a(a), (i)(3), (c)(2).

[39] 50 U.S.C. 1881a(g)(2).

[40] *Id.*

[41] 50 U.S.C. 1881a(g)(4).
[42] 50 U.S.C. 1881a(b).
[43] 50 U.S.C. 1881a(d), (e), (f).
[44] 50 U.S.C. 1881a(e).
[45] 50 U.S.C. 1881a(d).
[46] 50 U.S.C. 1881a(d), (e), (i).
[47] 50 U.S.C. 1881a(f).
[48] 50 U.S.C. 1881(h)(1)-(3).
[49] 50 U.S.C. 1881(h)(4).
[50] 50 U.S.C. 1881(h)(5).
[51] 50 U.S.C. 1881a(h)(6), (i).
[52] 50 U.S.C. 1881e(a).
[53] 50 U.S.C. 1881b(b).
[54] 50 U.S.C. 1881b(c)(1). An American may not be considered a foreign power or its agent, officer or employee based solely on activities protected by the First Amendment, 50 U.S.C. 1881b(c)(2).
[55] 50 U.S.C. 1881b(c)(3).
[56] 50 U.S.C. 1881b(f).
[57] 50 U.S.C. 1881b(c)(4).
[58] 50 U.S.C. 1881b(c)(5).
[59] 50 U.S.C. 1881b(e).
[60] 50 U.S.C. 1881b(d)(1).
[61] *Id.*
[62] 50 U.S.C. 1881b(d)(4).
[63] 50 U.S.C. 1881e(a).
[64] 50 U.S.C. 1881c(a)(3)(B)("If an acquisition for foreign intelligence purposes is to be conducted inside the United States and could be authorized under section 703 [1881b], the acquisition may only be conducted if authorized under section 703 or in accordance with another provision of this Act other than this section").
50 U.S.C. 1881d("(a) *Joint applications and orders*.– If an acquisition targeting a United States person under section 703 or 704 is proposed to be conducted both inside and outside the United States, a judge having jurisdiction under section 703(a)(1) or 704(a)(1) may issue simultaneously, upon the request of the Government in a joint application complying with the requirements of sections 703(b) and 704(b), orders under sections 703(c) and 704(c), as appropriate. (b) *Concurrent authorization*– If an order authorizing electronic surveillance or physical search has been obtained under section 105 or 304, the Attorney General may authorize, for the effective period of that order, without an order under section 703 or 704, the targeting of that United States person for the purpose of acquiring foreign intelligence information while such person is reasonably believed to be located outside the United States").
[65] 50 U.S.C. 1881c(a).
[66] 50 U.S.C. 1881c(a)(3).
[67] 50 U.S.C. 1881c(a)(2).
[68] 18 U.S.C. 2511(2)(f).
[69] Section 2(a), P.L. 107-40, 115 Stat. 224 (2001), 50 U.S.C. 1541 note ("That the President is authorized to use all necessary and appropriate force against those nations, organizations, or persons he determines planned, authorized, committed, or aided the terrorist attacks that occurred on September 11, 2001, or harbored such organizations or persons, in order to prevent any future acts of international terrorism against the United States by such nations, organizations or persons").
[70] H.Rept. 110-373, at 9-10 (2007), citing a letter from Assistant Attorney General William E. Moschella.
[71] 50 U.S.C. 1812 ("(a) Except as provided in subsection (b), the procedures of chapters 119, 121, and 206 of title 18, United States Code, and this Act shall be the exclusive means by which electronic surveillance and the interception of domestic wire, oral, or electronic communications may be conducted. (b) Only an express statutory authorization for electronic surveillance or the interception of domestic wire, oral, or electronic communications, other than as an amendment to this Act or chapters 119, 121, or 206 of title 18, United States Code, shall constitute an additional exclusive means for the purpose of subsection (a)").
[72] P.L. 110-261, §301(b), (a)(3), 122 Stat. 2471(2008).
[73] P.L. 110-261, §301(c), 122 Stat. 2471(2008).
[74] 50 U.S.C. 1885a(a)("Notwithstanding any other provision of law, a civil action may not lie or be maintained in a Federal or State court against any person for providing assistance to an element of the intelligence community, and shall be promptly dismissed. . .").
[75] 50 U.S.C. 1885a(a). On January 17,2007, the Attorney General notified Congress that any subsequent electronic surveillance conducted as part of the Terrorist Surveillance Program would conducted pursuant to FISA court approval, S. Rept. 110-209, at 4 (2007).
[76] 50 U.S.C. 1885a(a)(4); 1885(6)("(A) a telecommunications carrier, as that term is defined in section 3 of the Communications Act of 1934 (47 U.S.C. 153); (B) a provider of electronic communication service, as that

term is defined in section 2510 of title 18, United States Code; (C) a provider of a remote computing service, as that term is defined in section 2711 of title 18, United States Code; (D) any other communication service provider who has access to wire or electronic communications either as such communications are transmitted or as such communications are stored; (E) a parent, subsidiary, affiliate, successor, or assignee of an entity described in subparagraph (A), (B), (C), or (D); or (F) an officer, employee, or agent of an entity described in subparagraph (A), (B), (C), (D), or (E)").

[77] 50 U.S.C. 1885a(a)(1)-(3), (5); 1885(7).

[78] 50 U.S.C. 1885a(b), (c).

[79] 50 U.S.C. 1885a(g).

[80] 50 U.S.C. 1885b.

[81] 50 U.S.C. 1885c.

In: Privacy: An Overview of Federal Law… ISBN: 978-1-60741-654-8
Editor: Alderic Jimenez

Chapter 16

APPENDIX A

STATE STATUTES OUTLAWING THE INTERCEPTION OF WIRE(W), ORAL(O) AND ELECTRONIC COMMUNICATIONS(E)

Alabama: Ala.Code §§13A-11-30 to 13A-11-37(w/o); **Alaska**: Alaska Stat. §§42.20.300 to 42.20.390 (w/o/e); **Arizona**: Ariz.Rev.Stat.Ann. §§13-3001 to 133009 (w/o/e); **Arkansas**: Ark.Code §§5-60-120, 23-17-107(w/o/e); **California**: Cal.Penal Code §§631(w), 632(o), 632.7(e); **Colorado**: Colo.Rev.Stat. §§18-9-301 to 18-9-305(w/o/e);	**New Jersey**: N.J.Stat.Ann. §§ 2A:156A-2, 2A:156A-3(w/o/e); **New Mexico**: N.M.Stat.Ann. §30-12-(w); **New York**: N.Y.Penal Law §§ 250.00, 250.05(w/o/e); **North Carolina**: N.C.Gen.Stat. §§ 15A-286, 15A-287(w/o/e); **New Hampshire**: N.H.Rev.Stat.Ann. §§ 570-A:1, 570-A:2 (w/o);
Connecticut: Conn.Gen.Stat.Ann. §§53a-187 to 53a-189, 54-41t (w/o); **Delaware**: Del.Code tit.11 §§ 2401, 2402(w/o/e); **Florida**: Fla.Stat.Ann. §§ 934.02, 934.03(w/o/e); **Georgia**: Ga.Code §16-11-62 (w/o/e); **Hawaii**: Hawaii Rev.Stat. §§ 711-1111, 803-41, 803-42(w/o/e); **Idaho**: Idaho Code §§ 18-6701, 18-6702(w/o/e);	**New Jersey**: N.J.Stat.Ann. §§ 2A:156A-2, 2A:156A-3(w/o/e); **New Mexico**: N.M.Stat.Ann. §30-12-1(w); **New York**: N.Y.Penal Law §§ 250.00, 250.05(w/o/e); **North Carolina**: N.C.Gen.Stat. §§ 15A-286, 15A-287(w/o/e); **North Dakota**: N.D.Cent.Code §§12.1-15-02, 12.1-15-04 (w/o);
Indiana: Ind.Code Ann. §§ 35-33.5-1-5, 35-33.55-5(w/e);	**Ohio**: Ohio Rev.Code §§ 2933.51, 2933.52 (w/o/e);

(Continued)

Iowa: Iowa Code Ann. §§272.8, 808B.2(w/o/e); **Kansas**: Kan.Stat.Ann. §21-4001(w/o); 21-4002(w); **Kentucky**: Ky.Rev.Stat. §§526.010, 526.020(w/o); **Louisiana**: La.Rev.Stat.Ann. §§ 15:1302, 15:1303 (w/o/e); **Maine**: Me.Rev.Stat.Ann. tit. 15 §§ 709, 710(w/o);	**Oklahoma**: Okla.Stat.Ann. tit.13 §§ 176.2, 176.3 (w/o/e); **Oregon**: Ore.Rev.Stat. §§165.535 to 165.545 (w/o/e); **Pennsylvania**: Pa.Stat.Ann. tit.18 §§ 5702, 5703 (w/o/e); **Rhode Island**: R.I.Gen.Laws §§11-35-21(w/o/e); **South Carolina**: S.C. Code Ann. §§16-17-470, 17-30-10 to 17-30-20 (w/o/e);
Maryland: Md.Cts. & Jud.Pro.Code Ann. §§ 10-401, 10-402(w/o/e); **Massachusetts**: Mass.Gen.Laws Ann. ch.272 §99 (w/o); **Michigan**: Mich.Comp.Laws Ann. §§750.539a, 750.539c(o); 750.540(w); **Minnesota**: Minn.Stat.Ann. §§ 626A.01, 626A.02 (w/o/e);	**South Dakota**: S.D.Cod.Laws §§ 23A-35A-1, 23A-35A-20 (w/o); **Tennessee**: Tenn.Code Ann. §39-13-601(w/o/e); **Texas**: Tex.Penal Code. § 16.02; Tex. Crim. Pro. Code art. 18.20 (w/o/e); **Utah**: Utah Code Ann. §§ 76-9-405, 77-23a-3, 7723a-4 (w/o/e);
Mississippi: Miss.Code §41-29-533(w/o/e) **Missouri**: Mo.Ann.Stat. §§ 542.400 to 542.402 (w/o); **Montana**: Mont.Code Ann. §45-8-213(w/o/e); **Nebraska**: Neb.Rev.Stat. §§ 86-701 to 86-712 (w/o/e); **Nevada**: Nev.Rev.Stat. §§ 200.610, 200.620(w), 200.650(o); **New Hampshire**: N.H.Rev.Stat.Ann. §§ 570-A:1, 570-A:2 (w/o);	**Virginia**: Va.Code §§ 19.2-61, 19.2-62(w/o/e); **Washington**: Wash.Rev.Code Ann.§9.73.030 (w/o); **West Virginia**: W.Va.Code §§ 62-1D-2, 62-1D3(w/o/e); **Wisconsin**: Wis.Stat.Ann. §§ 968.27, 968.31(w/o/e); **Wyoming**: Wyo.Stat. §§ 7-3-701, 7-3-702(w/o/e); **District of Columbia**: D.C.Code §§ 23-541, 23542(w/o).

ISBN: 978-1-60741-654-8

Chapter 17

APPENDIX B

CONSENT INTERCEPTIONS UNDER STATE LAW

Alabama: Ala.Code §13A-11-30 (one party consent); **Alaska**: Alaska Stat. §§42.20.310, 42.20.330 (one party consent); **Arizona**: Ariz.Rev.Stat.Ann. §13-3005 (one party consent); **Arkansas**: Ark.Code §5-60-120 (one party consent); **California**: Cal. Penal Code §§ 631, 632 (one party consent for police; all party consent otherwise), 632.7 (all party consent);	**Montana**: Mont.Code Ann. §§45-8-213 (all party consent with an exception for the performance of official duties); **Nebraska**: Neb.Rev.Stat. § 86-702 (one party consent); **Nevada**: Nev.Rev.Stat. §§200.620, 200.650 (one party consent); **New Hampshire**: N.H.Rev.Stat.Ann. §570-A:2 (all party consent); **New Jersey**: N.J.Stat.Ann. §§2A:156A-4 (one party consent);
Colorado: Colo.Rev.Stat. §§18-9-303, 18-9-304 (one party consent); **Connecticut**: Conn.Gen.Stat.Ann. §§53a-187, 53a188 (criminal proscription: one party consent); §52570d (civil liability: all party consent except for police); **Delaware**: Del.Code tit.11 §2402 (one party consent); **Florida**: Fla.Stat.Ann. §934.03 (one party consent for the police; all party consent for others);	**New Mexico**: N.M.Stat.Ann. §§30-12-1 (one party consent); **New York**: N.Y.Penal Law §250.00 (one party consent); **North Carolina**: N.C.Gen.Stat. §15A-287 (one party consent); **North Dakota**: N.D.Cent.Code §§12.1-15-02 (one party consent); **Ohio**: Ohio Rev.Code §2933.52 (one party consent);
Georgia: Ga.Code §16-11-66 (one party consent); **Hawaii**: Hawaii Rev.Stat. §§ 711-1111, 803-42 (one party consent);	**Oklahoma**: Okla.Stat.Ann. tit.13 §176.4 (one party consent); **Oregon**: Ore.Rev.Stat. §165.540 (one party consent for wiretapping and all

(Continued)

Idaho: Idaho Code §18-6702 (one party consent); **Illinois**: Ill.Comp.Stat.Ann. ch.720 §§5/14-2, 5/14-3 (all party consent with law enforcement exceptions); **Indiana**: Ind.Code Ann. §35-33.5-1-5 (one party consent); **Iowa**: Iowa Code Ann. §808B.2 (one party consent);	parties must consent for other forms of electronic eavesdropping); **Pennsylvania**: Pa.Stat.Ann. tit.18 §5704 (one party consent for the police; all parties consent otherwise); **Rhode Island**: R.I.Gen.Laws §§11-35-21 (one party consent);
Kansas: Kan.Stat.Ann. §§21-4001, 21-4002 (one party consent); **Kentucky**: Ky.Rev.Stat. §526.010 (one party consent); **Louisiana**: La.Rev.Stat.Ann. §15:1303 (one party consent); **Maine**: Me.Rev.Stat.Ann. tit. 15 §709 (one party consent); **Maryland**: Md.Cts. & Jud.Pro.Code Ann. §10-402 (all party consent); **Massachusetts**: Mass.Gen.Laws Ann. ch.272 §99 (all parties must consent, except in some law enforcement cases);	**South Carolina**: S.C. Code Ann. § 17-30-30 (one party consent); **South Dakota**: S.D.Comp.Laws §§23A-35A-20 (one party consent); **Tennessee**: Tenn.Code Ann. §39-13-601 (one party consent) **Texas**: Tex.Penal Code §16.02 (one party consent); **Utah**: Utah Code Ann. §§77-23a-4 (one party consent); **Virginia**: Va.Code §19.2-62 (one party consent);
Michigan: Mich.Comp.Laws Ann. §750.539c (ban on eavesdropping on oral conversation: all party consent, except that the proscription does not apply to otherwise lawful activities of police officers); **Minnesota**: Minn.Stat.Ann. §626A.02 (one party consent); **Mississippi**: Miss.Code §41-29-531 (one party consent); **Missouri**: Mo.Ann.Stat. §542.402 (one party consent);	**Washington**: Wash.Rev.Code Ann. §9.73.030 (all parties must consent, except that one party consent is sufficient in certain law enforcement cases); **West Virginia**: W.Va.Code §62-1D-3 (one party consent); **Wisconsin**: Wis.Stat.Ann. §968.31 (one party consent); **Wyoming**: Wyo.Stat. §7-3-702 (one party consent); **District of Columbia**: D.C.Code §23-542 (one party consent).

In: Privacy: An Overview of Federal Law…
Editor: Alderic Jimenez

ISBN: 978-1-60741-654-8

Chapter 18

APPENDIX C

STATUTORY CIVIL LIABILITY FOR INTERCEPTIONS UNDER STATE LAW

Arizona: Ariz.Rev.Stat.Ann. §12-731; **California**: Cal. Penal Code §§ 637.2; **Colorado**: Colo.Rev.Stat. §18-9-309.5; **Connecticut**: Conn.Gen.Stat.Ann. §§54-41r, 52570d; **Delaware**: Del.Code tit.11 §2409;	**Nevada**: Nev.Rev.Stat. §200.690; **New Hampshire**: N.H.Rev.Stat.Ann. §570-A:11; **New Jersey**: N.J.Stat.Ann. §§2A:156A-24; **New Mexico**: N.M.Stat.Ann. §§30-12-11; **North Carolina**: N.C.Gen.Stat. §15A-296;
Florida: Fla.Stat.Ann. §§934.10, 934.27; **Hawaii**: Hawaii Rev.Stat. §803-48; **Idaho**: Idaho Code §18-6709; **Illinois**: Ill.Comp.Stat.Ann. ch.720 §5/14-6; **Indiana**: Ind.Code Ann. §35-33.5-5-4;	**Ohio**: Ohio Rev.Code §2933.65; **Oregon**: Ore.Rev.Stat. §133.739; **Pennsylvania**: Pa.Stat.Ann. tit.18 §§5725, 5747; **Rhode Island**: R.I.Gen.Laws §12-5.1-13; **South Carolina**: S.C. Code Ann. § 17-30-135;
Iowa: Iowa Code Ann. §808B.8; **Kansas**: Kan.Stat.Ann. §22-2518 **Louisiana**: La.Rev.Stat.Ann. §15:1312; **Maine**: Me.Rev.Stat.Ann. ch.15 §711; **Maryland**: Md.Cts. & Jud.Pro.Code Ann. §§10410, 10-4A-08;	**Tennessee**: Tenn.Code Ann. §39-13-603; **Texas**: Tex.Code Crim.Pro. art. 18.20; **Utah**: Utah Code Ann. §§77-23a-11; 77-23b-8; **Virginia**: Va.Code §19.2-69; **Washington**: Wash.Rev.Code Ann. §9.73.060;
Massachusetts: Mass.Gen.Laws Ann. ch.272 §99; **Michigan**: Mich.Comp.Laws Ann. §750.539h; **Mississippi**: Miss. Code § 41-29-529; **Minnesota**: Minn.Stat.Ann. §§626A.02, 626A.13; **Nebraska:** Neb.Rev.Stat. § 86-707.2;	**West Virginia**: W.Va.Code §62-1D-12; **Wisconsin**: Wis.Stat.Ann. §968.31; **Wyoming**: Wyo.Stat. §7-3-710; **District of Columbia**: D.C.Code §23-554.

In: Privacy: An Overview of Federal Law… ISBN: 978-1-60741-654-8
Editor: Alderic Jimenez

Chapter 19

APPENDIX D

COURT AUTHORIZED INTERCEPTION UNDER STATE LAW

Alaska: Alaska Stats. §§12.37.010 to 12.37.900; **Arizona**: Ariz.Rev.Stat.Ann. §§13-3010 to 13-3019 **California**: Cal.Penal Code §629.50 to 629.98; **Colorado**: Colo.Rev.Stat. §§16-15-101 to 16-15-104; **Connecticut**: Conn.Gen.Stat.Ann. §§54-41a to 54-41u;	**North Carolina**: N.C.Gen.Stat. §§15A-286 to 15A-298; **North Dakota**: N.D.Cent.Code §§29-29.2-01 to 29-29.2-05; **Ohio**: Ohio Rev.Code §§2933.51 to 2933.66; **Oklahoma**: Okla.Stat.Ann. tit.13 §§176.1 to 176.14 **Oregon**: Ore.Rev.Stat. §§133.721 to 133.739;
Delaware: Del.Code tit.11 §§2401 to 2412; **Florida**: Fla.Stat.Ann. §§934.02 to 934.43; **Georgia**: Ga.Code §16-11-64 to 16-11-69; **Hawaii**: Hawaii Rev.Stat. §§803-41 to 803-49; **Idaho**: Idaho Code §§18-6701 to 18-6709; 6719 to 6725;	**Pennsylvania**: Pa.Stat.Ann. tit.18 §§5701 to 5728 **Rhode Island**: R.I.Gen.Laws §§12-5.1-1 to 125.1-16; **South Carolina**: S.C. Code Ann. §§ 17-30-10 to 17-30-145;
Illinois: Ill.Stat.Ann. ch.725 §§5/108A-1 to 108B-14; **Indiana**:Ind.Code §§35-33.5-1-1 to 35-33.5-5-6; **Iowa**: Iowa Code Ann. §§808B.3 to 808B.7; **Kansas**: Kan.Stat.Ann. §§ 22-2514 to 22-2519; **Louisiana**: La.Rev.Stat.Ann. §§15:1301 to 15:1316; **Maryland**: Md.Cts. & Jud.Pro.Code Ann. §§10401 to 10-410;	**South Dakota**: S.D.Cod.Laws §§23A-35A-1 to 23A-35A-34; **Tennessee**: Tenn.Code Ann. §§40-6-301 to 40-6311; **Texas**: Tex.Crim.Pro. Code. art. 18.20; **Utah**: Utah Code Ann. §§77-23a-1 to 77-23a-16; **Virginia**: Va.Code §§19.2-61 to 19.2-70.3;

(Continued)

Massachusetts: Mass.Gen.Laws Ann. ch.272 §99; **Minnesota**: Minn.Stat.Ann. §§626A.01 to 626A.41; **Mississippi**: Miss.Code §§41-29-501 to 41-29-537; **Missouri**: Mo.Ann.Stat. §§542.400 to 542.422; **Nebraska**: Neb.Rev.Stat. §§ 86-707.1 to 86-712;	**Washington**: Wash.Rev.Code Ann. §§9.73.040 to 9.73.250; **West Virginia**: W.Va.Code §§62-1D-1 to 62-1D16; **Wisconsin**: Wis.Stat.Ann. §§968.27 to 968.33; **Wyoming**: Wyo.Stat. §§7-3-701 to 7-3-712; **District of Columbia**: D.C.Code §§23-541 to 23556, 5-1537.
Nevada: Nev.Rev.Stat. §§179.410 to 179.515; **New Hampshire**: N.H.Rev.Stat.Ann. §§570-A:1 to 570-A:9; **New Jersey**: N.J.Stat.Ann. §§2A:156A-8 to 2A:156A-26; **New Mexico**: N.M.Stat.Ann. §§30-12-1 to 30-12-11; **New York**: N.Y.Crim.Pro. Law §§700.05 to 700.70;	

In: Privacy: An Overview of Federal Law…
Editor: Alderic Jimenez
ISBN: 978-1-60741-654-8

Chapter 20

APPENDIX E

STATE STATUTES REGULATING STORED ELECTRONIC COMMUNICATIONS (SE), PEN REGISTERS (PR) AND TRAP AND TRACE DEVICES (T)

Alaska: Alaska Stats. §§12.37.200 (PR&T), 12.37.300(SE); **Arizona**: Ariz.Rev.Stat.Ann. §§13-3016 (SE); 13-3005, 13-3017 (PR&T); **Arkansas**: Ark. Code Ann. § 5-60-120(g) (PR&T); **Colorado**: Colo. Rev. Stat. § 18-9-305 (PR&T); **Delaware**: Del.Code tit.11 §§ 2401; 2421 to 2427 (SE); 2430 to 2434 (PR&T);	**New Jersey**; N.J.Stat.Ann. §§2A:156A-27 to 2A:156A-34 (SE); **New York**: N.Y.Crim.Pro.Law §§705.00 to 705.35 (PR&T); **North Carolina**: N.C.Gen.Stat. §§15A-260 to 15A-264 (PR&T); **North Dakota**: N.D.Cent.Code §§29-29.3-01 to 29-29.3-05 (PR&T);
Florida: Fla.Stat.Ann. §§934.02; 934.21 to 934.28 (SE); 934.32 to 934.34(PR&T); **Georgia**: Ga.Code Ann. §§16-11-60 to 16-11-64.2 (PR &T); 2005 Ga. Laws 46 (to be codified at § 16-9-109) (SE); **Hawaii**: Hawaii Rev.Stat. §§803-41; 803-44.5, 803-44.6 (PR&T), 803-47.5 to 803.47.9 (SE); **Idaho**: Idaho Code §§18-6719 to 18-6725 (PR&T); **Iowa**: Iowa Code Ann. §§808B.1, 808B.10 to 808B.14 (PR&T);	**Ohio**: Ohio Rev.Code §2933.76 (PR&T); **Oklahoma**: Okla.Stat.Ann. tit.13 §177.1 to 177.5 (PR&T); **Oregon**: Ore.Rev.Stat. §§165.657 to 165.673 (PR&T); **Pennsylvania**: Pa.Stat.Ann. tit.18 §§5741 to 5749 (SE), 5771 to 5775 (PR&T); **Rhode Island**; R.I.Gen.Laws §§12-5.2-1 to 125.2-5 (PR&T);
Kansas: Kan.Stat.Ann. §§22-2525 to 22-2529 (PR&T);	**South Carolina**: S.C.Code §§17-29-10 to 17-2950, 17-30-45 to 17-30-50 (PR&T);

(Continued)

Louisiana: La.Rev.Stat.Ann. §§15:1302, 15:1313 to 15:1316 (PR&T); **Maryland**: Md.Cts. & Jud.Pro.Code Ann. §§104A-01 to 10-4A-08 (SE), 10-4B-01 to 10-4B-05 (PR&T); **Minnesota**: Minn.Stat.Ann. §§626A.01; 626A.26 to 626A.34; (SE), 626A.35 to 636A.391 (PR&T); **Mississippi**: Miss.Code §41-29-701(PR&T);	**South Dakota**: S.D.Cod.Laws §§23A-35A-22 to 23A-35A-34 (PR&T); **Tennessee**: Tenn.Code Ann. §40-6-311 (PR&T); **Texas**: Tex.Code Crim.Pro. art. 18.20, 18.21; Tex. Penal Code §§ 16.03, 16.04 (SE, PR&T); **Utah**: Utah Code Ann. §§77-23a-13 to 77-23a-15 (PR&T); 77-23b-1 to 77-23b-9(SE);
Missouri: Mo.Ann.Stat. §542.408 (PR); **Montana**: Mont.Code Ann. §§46-4-401 to 46-4-405 (PR&T); **Nebraska**: Neb.Rev.Stat. §§ 86-707.03 to 86707.06 (PR&T); 86-707.09 to 86-707.14 (SE); **Nevada**: Nev.Rev.Stat. §§179.530 (PR&T), 205.492 to 205.513(SE); **New Hampshire**: N.H.Rev.Stat.Ann. §§570-B:1 to 570-B:7 (PR&T);	**Virginia**: Va.Code §§19.2-70.1, 19.2-70.2 (PR&T), 19.2-70.3 (SE); **Washington**: Wash.Rev.Code Ann. §9.73.260 (PR&T); **West Virginia**: W.Va.Code §§62-1D-2, 62-1D-10 (PR&T); **Wisconsin**: Wis.Stat.Ann. §968.30 to 968.37 (PR&T); **Wyoming**: Wyo.Stat. §§7-3-801 to 7-3-806 (PR&T); **District of Columbia**: D.C. Code § 5-1537.

In: Privacy: An Overview of Federal Law…
Editor: Alderic Jimenez
ISBN: 978-1-60741-654-8

Chapter 21

APPENDIX F

STATE COMPUTER CRIME STATUTES

Alabama: Ala.Code §§13A-8-100 to 13A-8-103; **Alaska**: Alaska Stat. §11.46484; **Arizona**: Ariz.Rev.Stat.Ann. §§13-2316 to 13-2316.02; **Arkansas**: Ark.Code §§5-41-101 to 5-41-206; **California**: Cal.Penal Code §502;	**Nevada**: Nev.Rev.Stat. §§205.473 to 205.492; 205.509 to 205.513; **New Hampshire**: N.H.Rev.Stat.Ann. §638:16 to 638:19; **New Jersey**: N.J.Stat.Ann. §§2C:20-2, 2C:20-23 to 2C:20-34;
Colorado: Colo.Rev.Stat. §§18-5.5-101, 18-5.5102; **Connecticut**: Conn.Gen.Stat.Ann. §§53a-250 to 53a-261; **Delaware**: Del.Code tit.11 §§931 to 941; **Florida**: Fla.Stat.Ann. §§815.01 to 815.07; **Georgia**: Ga.Code §§16-9-92 to 16-9-94;	**New Mexico**: N.M.Stat.Ann. §§30-45-1 to 30-457; **New York**: N.Y.Penal Law §§156.00 to 156.50; **North Carolina**: N.C.Gen.Stat. §§14-453 to 14-458; **North Dakota**: N.D.Cent.Code §12.1-06.1-08; **Ohio**: Ohio Rev.Code §§2909.01, 2909.07, 2913.01 to 2913.04, 2913.421;
Hawaii: Hawaii Rev.Stat. §708-890 to 708-895.7; **Idaho**: Idaho Code §§18-2201, 18-2202; **Illinois**: Ill.Stat.Ann. ch.720 §§5/16D-1 to 5/16D7; **Indiana**: Ind.Code §§35-43-1-4 to 35-43-2-3; **Iowa**: Iowa Code Ann. §716.6B;	**Oklahoma**: Okla.Stat.Ann. tit.21 §§1951 to 1959; **Oregon**: Ore.Rev.Stat. §164.377; **Pennsylvania**: Pa.Stat.Ann. tit.18 §7611; **Rhode Island**: R.I.Gen.Laws §§11-52-1 to 11-52-8; **South Carolina**: S.C.Code §§16-16-10 to 16-1640, 26-6-210;
Kansas: Kan.Stat.Ann. §21-3755; **Kentucky**: Ky.Rev.Stat. §§434.840 to 434.860;	**South Dakota**: S.D.Cod.Laws §§43-43B-1 to 43-43B-8; **Tennessee**: Tenn.Code Ann. §§39-14-601 to 39-14-605;

(Continued)

Louisiana: La.Rev.Stat.Ann. §§14:73.1 to 14:73.7; **Maine**: Me.Rev.Stat.Ann. tit. 17-A §§431 to 433; **Maryland**: Md.Code Ann., Crim. Law. §7-302; **Massachusetts**: Mass.Gen.Laws Ann. ch.266 §120F;	**Texas**: Tex.Penal Code. §§33.01 to 33.05; **Utah**: Utah Code Ann. §§76-6-702 to 76-6-705;
Michigan: Mich.Comp.Laws Ann. §§752.791 to 752.797; **Minnesota**: Minn.Stat.Ann. §§609.87 to 609.893; **Mississippi**: Miss.Code §§97-45-1 to 97-45-29; **Missouri**: Mo.Ann.Stat. §§569.095 to 569.099; **Montana**: Mont.Code Ann. §§45-6-310, 45-6-311; **Nebraska**: Neb.Rev.Stat. §§28-1341 to 28-1348;	**Vermont**: Vt. Stat. Ann. tit. 13, §§ 4101 to 4107; **Virginia**: Va.Code §§18.2-152.1 to 18.2-152.15, 19.2-249.2; **Washington**: Wash.Rev.Code Ann. §§9A.52.110 to 9A.52.130; **West Virginia**: W.Va.Code §§61-3C-1 to 61-3C21; **Wisconsin**: Wis.Stat.Ann. §943.70; **Wyoming**: Wyo.Stat. §§6-3-501 to 6-3-505.

In: Privacy: An Overview of Federal Law…
Editor: Alderic Jimenez
ISBN: 978-1-60741-654-8

Chapter 22

APPENDIX G

SPYWARE[1]

Alaska: Alaska Stat. §§45.45.471 to 45.45.798;
Arizona: Ariz. Rev. Stat. Ann. §§ 44-7301 to 44-7304;
Arkansas: Ark. Code §§ 4-110-101 to 4-110-105;
California: Cal. Bus. & Prof. Code §§ 22947 to 22947.6;
Georgia: Ga. Code Ann. §§ 16-9-150 to 16-9-157;
Indiana: Ind. Code Ann. §§ 24-4.8-1-1 to 24-4.8-3-2;
Iowa: Iowa Code Ann. §§ 715.1 to 715.8;
Louisiana: La. Rev. Stat. Ann. §§51:2006 to 51:2014
Nevada: Nev. Rev. Stat. Ann. §205.4737;
New Hampshire: N.H. Rev. Stat. Ann. §§ 359-H:1 to 359-H:6;
Texas: Tex. Bus. & Com. Code Ann. §§ 48.001 to 48.102;
Utah: Utah Code Ann. §§ 13-40-101 to 13-40-401;
Washington: Wash. Rev. Code Ann. §§19.270.010 to19.270.900.

End Note

[1] Depending upon the definition used, spyware has been outlawed under a host of federal and state laws; this appendix is limited to those state statutes that address "spyware" as such. For a general discussion of activities at the federal level see CRS Report RL32706, *Spyware: Background and Policy Issues for Congress*.

In: Privacy: An Overview of Federal Law…
Editor: Alderic Jimenez
ISBN: 978-1-60741-654-8

Chapter 23

SELECTED BIBLIOGRAPHY

BOOKS AND ARTICLES

Bankston, *Only the DoJ Knows: The Secret Law of Electronic Surveillance*, 41 UNIVERSITY OF SAN FRANCISCO LAW REVIEW 589 (2007)

Banisar & Davies, *Global Trends in Privacy Protection: An International Survey of Privacy, Data Protection, and Surveillance Laws and Developments*, 18 JOHN MARSHALL JOURNAL OF COMPUTER AND INFORMATION LAW 1 (1999)

Barr, Post-9/11 *Electronic Surveillance Severely Undermining Freedom*, 41 VALPARAISO UNIVERSITY LAW REVIEW 1383 (2007)

Brownell, *The Public Security and Wire Tapping*, 39 CORNELL LAW QUARTERLY 154 (1954)

Caproni, *Surveillance and Transparency*, 11 LEWIS & CLARK LAW REVIEW 1087 (2007)

Carr & Bellia, THE LAW OF ELECTRONIC SURVEILLANCE (2001)

Casey, *Electronic Surveillance and the Right to Be Secure*, 41 UC DAVIS LAW REVIEW 977 (2008)

Chemerinsky, *Losing Liberties: Applying a Foreign Intelligence Model to Domestic Law Enforcement*, 51 UCLA LAW REVIEW 1619 (2004)

Chiarella & Newton, *"So Judge, How Do I Get that FISA Warrant?": The Policy and Procedure for Conducting Electronic Surveillance*, 1997 ARMY LAWYER 25 (Oct. 1997)

Cinquegrana, *The Walls (and Wires) Have Ears: The Background and First Ten Years of the Foreign Intelligence Surveillance Act of 1978*, 137 UNIVERSITY OF PENNSYLVANIA LAW REVIEW 793 (1989)

Cooper, *The Electronic Communications Privacy Act: Does the Answer to the Internet Information Privacy Problem Lie in a Fifteen-Year-Old Federal Statute? A Detailed Analysis,* 20 JOHN MARSHALL JOURNAL OF COMPUTER & INFORMATION LAW 1 (2001)

Clark, *Cell Phones as Tracking Devices*, 41 VALPARAISO UNIVERSITY LAW REVIEW 1413 (2007)

Dinger, *Should Parents Be Allowed to Record a Child's Telephone Conversations When They Believe the Child Is in Danger?: A Examination of the Federal Wiretap Statute and the Doctrine of Vicarious Consent in the Context of a Criminal Prosecution*, 28 SEATTLE UNIVERSITY LAW REVIEW 955 (2005)

Donnelly, *Comments and Caveats on the Wiretapping Controversy*, 63 YALE LAW JOURNAL 799 (1954)

Fishman, *Technologically Enhanced Visual Surveillance the Fourth Amendment: Sophistication, Availability and the Expectation of Privacy*, 26 AMERICAN CRIMINAL LAW REVIEW 315 (1989)

Fishman & McKenna, WIRETAPPING AND EAVESDROPPING (2d ed.1995) & (Mar. 2006)

Freiwald, *Online Surveillance: Remembering the Lessons of the Wiretap Act*, 56 ALABAMA LAW REVIEW 9 (2004)

Froomkin, *The Metaphor Is the Key: Cryptography, the Clipper Chip*, and the Constitution, 143 UNIVERSITY OF PENNSYLVANIA LAW REVIEW 709 (1995)

Funk, *Electronic Surveillance of Terrorism; The Intelligence/Law Enforcement /Dilemma – A History* 11 LEWIS & CLARK LAW REVIEW 1099 (2007)

Garrie, Armstrong & Harris, V*oice Over Internet Protocol and the Wiretap Act: Is Your Conversation Protected?*, 29 SEATTLE UNIVERSITY LAW REVIEW 97 (2005)

Gilbreath & Cukjati, *Tape Recording of Conversations: Ethics, Legality and Admissibility*, 59 TEXAS BAR JOURNAL 951 (1996)

Goldsmith & Balmforth, *The Electronic Surveillance of Privileged Communications: A Conflict of Doctrines*, 64 SOUTH CALIFORNIA LAW REVIEW 903 (1991)

Kash, *Prewarrant Thermal Imaging as a Fourth Amendment Violation: A Supreme Court Question in the Making*, 60 ALBANY LAW REVIEW 1295 (1997)

Kesan, *Cyber-Working or Cyber-Shirking?: A First Principles Examination of Electronic Privacy in the Workplace*, 54 FLORIDA LAW REVIEW 289 (2002)

Kastenmeier, Leavy & Beier, *Communications Privacy: A Legislative Perspective*, 1989 WISCONSIN LAW REVIEW 715

Lieb, *E-Mail and the Wiretap Laws: Why Congress Should Add Electronic Communications to Title III's Statutory Exclusionary Rule and Expressly Rejected a "Good Faith" Exception*, 34 HARVARD JOURNAL OF LEGISLATION 393 (1997)

MacArthur, *The NSA Phone Call Database: The Problematic Acquisition and Mining of call records in the United States, Canada, the United Kingdom, and Australia*, 17 DUKE JOURNAL OF COMPARATIVE AND INTERNATIONAL LAW 441 (2007)

Maclin, *The Bush Administration's Terrorist Surveillance Program and the Fourth Amendment's Warrant Requirement: Lessons from Justice Powell and the Keith Case*, 41 UC DAVIS LAW REVIEW 1259 (2008)

Maher, T*ale of the Tape: Lawyers Recording Conversations*, 15 PROFESSIONAL LAWYER 10 (2004)

McCarthy, *Don't Fear Carnivore: It Won't Devour Individual Privacy*, 66 MISSOURI LAW REVIEW 827 (2001)

Meason, *The Foreign Intelligence Surveillance Act: Time for Reappraisal*, 24 INTERNATIONAL LAWYER 1043 (1990)

National Commission for the Study of Federal and State Laws Relating to Wiretapping and Electronic Surveillance, FINAL REPORT (1976)

Rosenstein, *The Electronic Communications Privacy Act of 1986 and Satellite Descramblers: Toward Preventing Statutory Obsolescence*, 76 MINNESOTA LAW REVIEW 1451 (1992)

Seamon, *Domestic Surveillance for International Terrorists: Presidential Power and Fourth Amendment Limits*, 35 HASTINGS CONSTITUTIONAL LAW QUARTERLY 449 (2008)

Seamon & Gardner, *The Patriot Act and the Wall Between Foreign Intelligence and Law Enforcement*, 28 HARVARD JOURNAL OF LAW & PUBLIC POLICY 319 (2005)

Simons, *From Katz to Kyllo: A Blueprint for Adapting the Fourth Amendment to Twenty-First Century Technologies*, 53 HASTINGS LAW JOURNAL 1303 (2002)

Sulmasy & Yoo, *Katz and the War on Terrorism*, 41 UC DAVIS LAW REVIEW 1219 (2008)

Symposium, *The Future of Internet Surveillance Law: A Symposium to Discuss Internet Surveillance, Privacy & the USA PATRIOT Act*, 72 GEORGE WASHINGTON LAW REVIEW 1139 (2004)

- Kerr, *Foreword: The Future of Internet Surveillance Law*, 72 GEORGE WASHINGTON LAW REVIEW 1139 (2004)
- Howell, *Seven Weeks: The Making of the USA PATRIOT Act*, 72 GEORGE WASHINGTON LAW REVIEW 1145 (2004)
- Kerr, A User's Guide to the Stored Communications Act, and a Legislator's Guide to Amending It, 72 GEORGE WASHINGTON LAW REVIEW 1208 (2004)
- Schwartz, Evaluating Telecommunications Surveillance in Germany: The Lessons of the Max Plank Institute's Study, 72 GEORGE WASHINGTON LAW REVIEW 1244 (2004)
- Solove, *Reconstructing Electronic Surveillance Law*, 72 GEORGE WASHINGTON LAW REVIEW 1264 (2004)
- Swire, *The System of Foreign Intelligence Surveillance Law*, 72 GEORGE WASHINGTON LAW REVIEW 1306 (2004)
- Bellia, *Surveillance Law Through Cyberlaw's Lens*, 72 GEORGE WASHINGTON LAW REVIEW 1375 (2004)
- Dempsey & Flint, *Commercial Data and National Security*, 72 GEORGE WASHINGTON LAW REVIEW 1459 (2004)
- Fishman, Technology and the Internet: The Impending Destruction of Privacy by Betrayers, Grudgers, Snoops, Spammers, Corporations, and the Media, 72 GEORGE WASHINGTON LAW REVIEW 1503 (2004)
- Mulligan, Reasonable Expectations in Electronic Communications; A Critical Perspective on the Electronic Communications Privacy Act, 72 GEORGE WASHINGTON LAW REVIEW 1557 (2004)
- Ohm, Parallel-Effect Statutes and E-Mail "Warrants": Reframing the Internet Surveillance Debate, 72 GEORGE WASHINGTON LAW REVIEW 1559 (2004)

Symposium, *Spyware: The Latest Cyber-Regulatory Challenge*, 20 BERKELEY TECHNOLOGY LAW JOURNAL 1269 (2005)

- • Schwartz, *Privacy Inalienability and the Regulation of Spyware*, 20 BERKELEY TECHNOLOGY LAW JOURNAL 1269 (2005)
- Bellia, *Spyware and the Limits of Surveillance Law*, 20 BERKELEY TECHNOLOGY LAW JOURNAL 1283 (2005)
- Winn, *Contracting Spyware by Contract*, 20 B BERKELEY TECHNOLOGY LAW JOURNAL 1345 (2005)
- Crawford, *First Do No Harm: The Problem of Spyware*, 20 B BERKELEY TECHNOLOGY LAW JOURNAL 1433 (2005)

Symposium, *Surveillance*, 75 UNIVERSITY OF CHICAGO LAW REVIEW 47 (2008)

- Allen, Dredging Up the Past: Lifelogging, Memory, and Surveillance, 75 UNIVERSITY OF CHICAGO LAW REVIEW 47 (2008)
- Bamberger & Mulligan, *Privacy Decisionmaking in Administrative Agencies*, 75 UNIVERSITY OF CHICAGO LAW REVIEW 75 (2008)
- Beales & Muris, Choice or Consequences: Protecting Privacy in Commercial Information, 75 UNIVERSITY OF CHICAGO LAW REVIEW 109(2008)
- Bellia, *The Memory Gap in Surveillance Law*, 75 UNIVERSITY OF CHICAGO LAW REVIEW 137(2008)
- Cohen, *Privacy, Visibility, Transparency, and Exposure*, 75 UNIVERSITY OF CHICAGO LAW REVIEW 181(2008)
- Epstein &Brown, *Cybersecruity in the Payment Card Industry*, 75 UNIVERSITY OF CHICAGO LAW REVIEW 203(2008)
- Kerr, *Updating the Foreign Intelligence Surveillance Act*, 75 UNIVERSITY OF CHICAGO LAW REVIEW 225 (2008)
- Posner, *Privacy, Surveillance and Law*, 75 UNIVERSITY OF CHICAGO LAW REVIEW 245(2008)
- Rubinstein, Lee & Schwartz, Data Mining and Internet Profiling: Emerging Regulatory and Technological Approaches, 75 UNIVERSITY OF CHICAGO LAW REVIEW 261 (2008)
- Schwartz, *Reviving Telecommunications Surveillance Law*, 75 UNIVERSITY OF CHICAGO LAW REVIEW 287 (2008)
- Stobogin, *Government Data Mining and the Fourth Amendment*, 75 UNIVERSITY OF CHICAGO LAW REVIEW 317 (2008)
- Solove, *Data Mining and the Security-Liberty Debate*, 75 UNIVERSITY OF CHICAGO LAW REVIEW 343 (2008)
- Strahilevitz, *Privacy Versus Antidiscrimination*, 75 UNIVERSITY OF CHICAGO LAW REVIEW 363 (2008)

Spritzer, *Electronic Surveillance by Leave of the Magistrate: The Case in Opposition*, 118 UNIVERSITY OF PENNSYLVANIA LAW REVIEW 169 (1969)

Taylor, *Issues Raised by the Application of the Pen Register Statutes to Authorize Government Collection of Information on Packet-Switched Networks*, 6 VIRGINIA JOURNAL OF LAW & TECHNOLOGY 4 (2001)

Turkington, *Protections for Invasions of Conversational and Communications Privacy by Electronic Surveillance in Family, Marriage, and Domestic Disputes Under Federal and State Wiretap and Store Communications Acts and the Common Law Privacy Intrusion Tort*, 82 NEBRASKA LAW REVIEW 693 (2004)

Whitehead & Aden, *Forfeiting "Enduring Freedom" for "Homeland Security": A Constitutional Analysis of the USA PATRIOT Act and the Justice Department's Anti-Terrorism Initiatives*, 51 AMERICAN UNIVERSITY LAW REVIEW 1081 (2002)

NOTES AND COMMENTS

Attorney Private Eyes: Ethical Implications of a Private Attorney's Decision to Surreptitiously Record Conversations, 2003 UNIVERSITY OF ILLINOIS LAW REVIEW 1605 (2003)

The Case for Magic Lantern: September 11 Highlights the Need for Increased Surveillance, 15 HARVARD JOURNAL OF LAW & TECHNOLOGY 521 (2002)

Electronic Surveillance in the Internet Age: The Strange Case of Pen Registers, 41 AMERICAN CRIMINAL LAW REVIEW 1321 (2004)

The Fourth Amendment and the Wiretap Act Fail to Protect Against Random ISP Monitoring of E-Mails for the Purpose of Assisting Law Enforcement, 22 JOHN MARSHALL JOURNAL OF COMPUTER AND INFORMATION LAW 493 (2004)

Government Access to Transactional Information and the Lack of Subscriber Notice, 8 BOSTON UNIVERSITY JOURNAL OF SCIENCE & TECHNOLOGY 648 (2002)

Hijacking Civil Liberties: The USA PATRIOT Act of 2001, 33 LOYOLA UNIVERSITY OF CHICAGO LAW JOURNAL 933 (2002)

How the USA PATRIOT Act Will Permit Governmental Infringement Upon the Privacy of Americans in the Name of "Intelligence" Investigations, 150 UNIVERSITY OF PENNSYLVANIA LAW REVIEW 1651 (2002)

The Notice Problem, Unlawful Electronic Surveillance, and Civil Liability Under the Foreign Intelligence Surveillance Act, 61 UNIVERSITY OF MIAMI LAW REVIEW 393 (2007)

The Patriot Act's Impact on the Government's Ability to Conduct Electronic Surveillance on Ongoing Domestic Communications, 52 DUKE LAW JOURNAL 179 (2002)

Privacy Versus Protection: Exploring the Boundaries of Electronic Surveillance in the Internet Act, 29 FORDHAM URBAN LAW JOURNAL 2233 (2002)

Protect American Act of 2007, 45 HARVARD JOURNAL ON LEGISLATION 581 (2008)

Qualified Immunity as a Defense to Federal Wiretap Act Claims, 68 UNIVERSITY OF CHICAGO LAW REVIEW 1369 (2001)

The Revamped FISA: Striking a Better Balance Between the Government's Need to Protect Itself and the 4th Amendment, 58 VANDERBILT LAW REVIEW 1671 (2005)

Scowl Because You're on Candid Camera: Privacy and Video Surveillance, 31 VANDERBILT LAW REVIEW 1079 (1997)

Should "Clean Hands" Protect the Government Against §2515 Suppression Under Title III of the Omnibus Crime Control and Safe Streets Act of 1968? 53 WASHINGTON & LEE LAW REVIEW 1473 (1996)

Tapping Into Family Affairs: Examining the Federal Wiretapping Statute as It Applies to the Home, Pollock v. Pollock, 154 F.3d 601 (6th Cir. 1998), 68 UNIVERSITY OF CINCINNATI LAW REVIEW 995 (2000)

Thirty-Seventh Annual Review of Criminal Procedure: Electronic Surveillance, 37 GEORGETOWN LAW JOURNAL ANNUAL REVIEW OF CRIMINAL PROCEDURE 133 (2008)

You've Got Mail . . . And Your Boss Knows It: Rethinking the Scope of the E-Mail Monitoring Exceptions to the Electronic Communications Privacy Act, 2001 UCLA JOURNAL OF LAW & TECHNOLOGY 5

ALR NOTES

Allowable Use of Federal Pen Register and Trap and Trace Device to Trace Cell Phones and Internet Use, 15 ALR FED. 2D 537

Applicability, in Civil Action, of Provisions of Omnibus Crime Control and Safe Streets Act of 1968, Prohibiting Interception of Communications (18 USCS §2511(1)), to Interceptions by Spouse, or Spouse's Agent, of Conversations of Other Spouse, 139 ALR FED. 517

Application of Extension Telephones of Title III of the Omnibus Crime Control and Safe Streets Act of 1968 (18 USCS §§2510 et seq.) Pertaining to Interceptions of Wire Communications, 58 ALRFED. 594

Constitutionality of Secret Video Surveillance, 91 ALR 5th 585

Construction and Application of 18 USCS 2511(1)(a) and (b), Providing Criminal Penalty for Intercepting, Endeavoring to intercept, or Procuring Another to Intercept Wire, Oral or Electronic Communication, 122 ALR FED. 597

Construction and Application of Provision of Omnibus Crime and Safe Streets Act of 1968 (18 U.S.C.A. §2520) Authorizing Civil Cause of Action by Person Whose Wire, Oral, or Electronic Communication Is Intercepted, Disclosed, or Used in Violation of the Act, 164 ALR FED. 139

Construction and Application of State Statutes Authorizing Civil Cause of Action by Person Whose Wire or Oral Communications Is Intercepted, Disclosed, or Used in Violation of Statutes, 33 ALR4^{TH} 506

Eavesdropping and Wiretapping, What Constitutes "Device Which Is Primarily Useful for the Surreptitious Interception of Wire, Oral, or Electronic Communication," Under 18 USCS 2512(1)(b), Prohibiting Manufacture, Possession, Assembly, Sale of Such Device, 129 ALR FED. 549

Eavesdropping on Extension Telephone as Invasion of Privacy, 49 ALR 4th 430

Expectation of Privacy in Text Transmissions To or From Pager, Cellular Telephone, or Other Wireless Personal Communication Devices, 25 ALR 6TH 201

Interception of Telecommunications by or With Consent of Party as Exception Under 18 USCS §2511(2)(c) and (d), to Federal Proscription of Such Interceptions, 67 ALR FED. 429

Permissible Surveillance, Under State Communications Interception Statute, by Person Other than State or Local Law Enforcement Officer or One Acting in Concert with Officer, 24 ALR 4th 1208

Permissible Warrantless Surveillance, Under State Communications Interception Statute, by State or Local Law Enforcement Officer or One Acting in Concert with Officer, 27 ALR 4th 449

Propriety of Attorney's Surreptitious Sound Recording of Statements by Others Who Are or May Become Involved in Litigation, 32 ALR 5th 715

Propriety of Monitoring of Telephone Calls to or From Prison Inmates Under Title III of Omnibus Crime Control and Safe Streets Act (18 USCS §§2510 et seq.) Prohibiting Judicially Unauthorized Interception of Wire or Oral Communications, 61 ALR FED. 825

Propriety of Governmental Eavesdropping on Communications Between Accused and His Attorney, 189 ALR FED. 419

Propriety, Under 18 USCS 2517(5), of Interception or Use of Communications Relating to Federal Offenses Which Were Not Specified in Original wiretap Order, 103 ALR FED. 422

Qualified Immunity as Defense in Suit Under Federal Wiretap Act (18 U.S.C.A. §§2510 et seq.), 178 ALR FED 1

State Regulation of Radio Paging Services, 44 ALR 4th 216

Validity, Construction, and Application of Foreign Intelligence Surveillance Act of 1978 (50 USCS §§1801 et seq.) Authorizing Electronic Surveillance of Foreign Powers and Their Agents, 190 ALR FED. 385

What Constitutes Adequate Response by the Government, Pursuant to 18 U.S.C. 3504, Affirming or Denying Use of Unlawful Electronic Surveillance, 53 ALR FED. 378

What Constitutes Compliance by Government Agents With Requirement of 18 U.S.C. 2518(5) that Wire Tapping and Electronic Surveillance Be Conduct in Such Manner as to Minimize Interception of Communications Not Otherwise Subject to Interception, 181 ALR FED. 419

Who May Apply or Authorize Application for Order to Intercept Wire or Oral Communications Under Title III of the Omnibus Crime Control and Safe Streets Act of 1968 (18 U.S.C. 2510 et seq.), 169 ALR FED. 169

In: Privacy: An Overview of Federal Law...
Editor: Alderic Jimenez
ISBN: 978-1-60741-654-8

Chapter 24

TEXT OF ECPA/FISA

ELECTRONIC COMMUNICATIONS PRIVACY ACT (ECPA). 18 U.S.C. 2510. DEFINITIONS

As used in this chapter-

(1) "wire communication" means any aural transfer made in whole or in part through the use of facilities for the transmission of communications by the aid of wire, cable, or other like connection between the point of origin and the point of reception (including the use of such connection in a switching station) furnished or operated by any person engaged in providing or operating such facilities for the transmission of interstate or foreign communications or communications affecting interstate or foreign commerce;

(2) "oral communication" means any oral communication uttered by a person exhibiting an expectation that such communication is not subject to interception under circumstances justifying such expectation, but such term does not include any electronic communication;

(3) "State" means any State of the United States, the District of Columbia, the Commonwealth of Puerto Rico, and any territory or possession of the United States;

(4) "intercept" means the aural or other acquisition of the contents of any wire, electronic, or oral communication through the use of any electronic, mechanical, or other device;

(5) "electronic, mechanical, or other device" means any device or apparatus which can be used to intercept a wire, oral, or electronic communication other than-

   (a) any telephone or telegraph instrument, equipment or facility, or any component thereof, (i) furnished to the subscriber or user by a provider of wire or electronic communication service in the ordinary course of its business and being used by the subscriber or user in the ordinary course of its business or furnished by such subscriber or user for connection to the facilities of such service and used in the ordinary course of its business; or (ii) being used by a provider of wire or electronic communication service in the ordinary course of its business, or by an investigative or lawenforcement officer in the ordinary course of his duties;

(b) a hearing aid or similar device being used to correct subnormal hearing to not better than normal;

(6) "person" means any employee, or agent of the United States or any State or political subdivision thereof, and any individual, partnership, association, joint stock company, trust, or corporation;

(7) "Investigative or law enforcement officer" means any officer of the United States or of a State or political subdivision thereof, who is empowered by law to conduct investigations of or to make arrests for offenses enumerated in this chapter, and any attorney authorized by law to prosecute or participate in the prosecution of such offenses;

(8) "contents", when used with respect to any wire, oral, or electronic communication, includes any information concerning the substance, purport, or meaning of that communication;

(9) "Judge of competent jurisdiction" means-

(a) a judge of a United States district court or a United States court of appeals; and

(b) a judge of any court of general criminal jurisdiction of a State who is authorized by a statute of that State to enter orders authorizing interceptions of wire, oral, or electronic communications;

(10)"communication common carrier" has the meaning given the term in section 3 of the Communications Act of 1934;

(11)"aggrieved person" means a person who was a party to any intercepted wire, oral, or electronic communication or a person against whom the interception was directed;

(12)"electronic communication" means any transfer of signs, signals, writing, images, sounds, data, or intelligence of any nature transmitted in whole or in part by a wire, radio, electromagnetic, photoelectronic or photooptical system that affects interstate or foreign commerce, but does not include-

(A) any wire or oral communication;

(B) any communication made through a tone-only paging device;

(C) any communication from a tracking device (as defined in section 3117 of this title); or

(D) electronic funds transfer information stored by a financial institution in a communications system used for the electronic storage and transfer of funds;

(13)"user" means any person or entity who-

(A) uses an electronic communication service; and

(B) is duly authorized by the provider of such service to engage in such use;

(14)"electronic communications system" means any wire, radio, electromagnetic, photooptical or photoelectronic facilities for the transmission of wire or electronic communications, and any computer facilities or related electronic equipment for the electronic storage of such communications;

(15)"electronic communication service" means any service which provides to users thereof the ability to send or receive wire or electronic communications;

(16)"readily accessible to the general public" means, with respect to a radio communication, that such communication is not-

(A) scrambled or encrypted;

(B) transmitted using modulation techniques whose essential parameters have been withheld from the public with the intention of preserving the privacy of such communication;

(C) carried on a subcarrier or other signal subsidiary to a radio transmission;
(D) transmitted over a communication system provided by a common carrier, unless the communication is a tone only paging system communication; or
(E) transmitted on frequencies allocated under part 25, subpart D, E, or F of part 74, or part 94 of the Rules of the Federal Communications Commission, unless, in the case of a communication transmitted on a frequency allocated under part 74 that is not exclusively allocated to broadcast auxiliary services, the communication is a two-way voice communication by radio;

(17)"electronic storage" means-
(A) any temporary, intermediate storage of a wire or electronic communication incidental to the electronic transmission thereof; and
(B) any storage of such communication by an electronic communication service for purposes of backup protection of such communication; and

(18)"aural transfer" means a transfer containing the human voice at any point between and including the point of origin and the point of reception.

(19)"foreign intelligence information", for purposes of section 2517(6) of this title, means –
(A) information, whether or not concerning a United States person, that relates to the ability of the United States to protect against –
(i) actual or potential attack or other grave hostile acts of a foreign power or an agent of a foreign power;
(ii) sabotage or intentional terrorism by a foreign power or an agent of a foreign power; or
(iii) clandestine intelligence activities by and intelligence service or network of a foreign power or by an agent of a foreign power; or
(B) information, whether or not concerning a United States person, with respect to a foreign power or foreign territory that relates to –
(i) the national defense or the security of the United States; or
(ii) the conduct of the foreign affairs of the United States.

(20) "protected computer" has the meaning set forth in section 1030; and

(21) "computer trespasser" –
(A) means a person who accesses a protected computer without authorization and thus has no reasonable expectation of privacy in any communication transmitted to, through, or from the protected computer; and
(B) does not include a person known by the owner or operator of the protected computer to have an existing contractual relationship with the owner or operator of the protected computer for access to all or part of the protected computer.

18 U.S.C. 2511. Interception and Disclosure of Wire, Oral, or Electronic Communications Prohibited

(1) Except as otherwise specifically provided in this chapter any person who-
(a) intentionally intercepts, endeavors to intercept, or procures any other person to intercept or endeavor to intercept, any wire, oral, or electronic communication;
(b) intentionally uses, endeavors to use, or procures any other person to use or endeavor to use any electronic, mechanical, or other device to intercept any oral communication when-

(i) such device is affixed to, or otherwise transmits a signal through, a wire, cable, or other like connection used in wire communication; or

(ii) such device transmits communications by radio, or interferes with the transmission of such communication; or

(iii) such person knows, or has reason to know, that such device or any component thereof has been sent through the mail or transported in interstate or foreign commerce; or

(iv) such use or endeavor to use (A) takes place on the premises of any business or other commercial establishment the operations of which affect interstate or foreign commerce; or (B) obtains or is for the purpose of obtaining information relating to the operations of any business or other commercial establishment the operations of which affect interstate or foreign commerce; or

(v) such person acts in the District of Columbia, the Commonwealth of Puerto Rico, or any territory or possession of the United States;

(c) intentionally discloses, or endeavors to disclose, to any other person the contents of any wire, oral, or electronic communication, knowing or having reason to know that the information was obtained through the interception of a wire, oral, or electronic communication in violation of this subsection;

(d) intentionally uses, or endeavors to use, the contents of any wire, oral, or electronic communication, knowing or having reason to know that the information was obtained through the interception of a wire, oral, or electronic communication in violation of this subsection; or

(e) (i) intentionally discloses, or endeavors to disclose, to any other person the contents of any wire, oral, or electronic communication, intercepted by means authorized by sections 2511(2)(a)(ii), 2511(2)(b)-(c), 2511(2)(e), 2516, and 2518 of this chapter, (ii) knowing or having reason to know that the information was obtained through the interception of such a communication in connection with a criminal investigation, (iii) having obtained or received the information in connection with a criminal investigation, and (iv) with intent to improperly obstruct, impede, or interfere with a duly authorized criminal investigation, shall be punished as provided in subsection (4) or shall be subject to suit as provided in subsection (5).

(2) (a)(i) It shall not be unlawful under this chapter for an operator of a switchboard, or an officer, employee, or agent of a provider of wire or electronic communication service, whose facilities are used in the transmission of a wire or electronic communication, to intercept, disclose, or use that communication in the normal course of his employment while engaged in any activity which is a necessary incident to the rendition of his service or to the protection of the rights or property of the provider of that service, except that a provider of wire communication service to the public shall not utilize service observing or random monitoring except for mechanical or service quality control checks.

(ii) Notwithstanding any other law, providers of wire or electronic communication service, their officers, employees, and agents, landlords, custodians, or other persons, are authorized to provide information, facilities, or technical assistance to persons authorized by law to intercept wire, oral, or electronic communications or to conduct electronic surveillance, as defined in section 101 of the Foreign Intelligence

Surveillance Act of 1978, if such provider, its officers, employees, or agents, landlord, custodian, or other specified person, has been provided with-

[Sec. 101(c)(1)] (A) a court order directing such assistance or a court order pursuant to section 704 of the Foreign Intelligence Surveillance Act of 1978 signed by the authorizing judge,

[Sec.403(b)(2)(C)] Effective December 31, 2012 . . . (C) except as provided in section 404, section 2511(2)(A)(ii)(A) of title 128, United States Code, is amended by striking "or a court order pursuant to section 704 of the Foreign Intelligence Surveillance Act of 1978"

[Sec. 404(b)(3)] *Challenge of directives; protection from liability; use of information* – Notwithstanding any other provision of this Act or of the Foreign Intelligence Surveillance Act of 1978 (50 U.S.C. 1801 et seq.) . . . (E) section 2511(2)(a)(ii)(A) of title 18, United States Code, as amended by section 101(c)(1), shall continue to apply to an order issued pursuant to section 704 of the Foreign Intelligence Surveillance Act of 1978, as added by section 101(a)[50 U.S.C. 1881c]; or

(B) a certification in writing by a person specified in section 2518(7) of this title or the Attorney General of the United States that no warrant or court order is required by law, that all statutory requirements have been met, and that the specified assistance is required, setting forth the period of time during which the provision of the information, facilities, or technical assistance is authorized and specifying the information, facilities, or technical assistance required. No provider of wire or electronic communication service, officer, employee, or agent thereof, or landlord, custodian, or other specified person shall disclose the existence of any interception or surveillance or the device used to accomplish the interception or surveillance with respect to which the person has been furnished a court order or certification under this chapter, except as may otherwise be required by legal process and then only after prior notification to the Attorney General or to the principal prosecuting attorney of a State or any political subdivision of a State, as may be appropriate. Any such disclosure, shall render such person liable for the civil damages provided for in section 2520. No cause of action shall lie in any court against any provider of wire or electronic communication service, its officers, employees, or agents, landlord, custodian, or other specified person for providing information, facilities, or assistance in accordance with the terms of a court order, statutory authorization, or certification under this chapter.

[Sec. 102(c)(1)] (iii) If a certification under subparagraph (ii)(B) for assistance to obtain foreign intelligence information is based on statutory authority, the certification shall identify the specific statutory provision and shall certify that the statutory requirements have been met.

(b) It shall not be unlawful under this chapter for an officer, employee, or agent of the Federal Communications Commission, in the normal course of his employment and in discharge of the monitoring responsibilities exercised by the Commission in the enforcement of chapter 5 of title 47 of the United States Code, to intercept a wire or electronic communication, or oral communication transmitted by radio, or to disclose or use the information thereby obtained.

(c) It shall not be unlawful under this chapter for a person acting under color of law to intercept a wire, oral, or electronic communication, where such person is a party to the communication or one of the parties to the communication has given prior consent to such interception.

(d) It shall not be unlawful under this chapter for a person not acting under color of law to intercept a wire, oral, or electronic communication where such person is a party to the communication or where one of the parties to the communication has given prior consent to such interception unless such communication is intercepted for the purpose of committing any criminal or tortious act in violation of the Constitution or laws of the United States or of any State.

(e) Notwithstanding any other provision of this title or section 705 or 706 of the Communications Act of 1934, it shall not be unlawful for an officer, employee, or agent of the United States in the normal course of his official duty to conduct electronic surveillance, as defined in section 101 of the Foreign Intelligence Surveillance Act of 1978, as authorized by that Act.

(f) Nothing contained in this chapter or chapter 121 or 206 of this title, or section 705 of the Communications Act of 1934, shall be deemed to affect the acquisition by the United States Government of foreign intelligence information from international or foreign communications, or foreign intelligence activities conducted in accordance with otherwise applicable Federal law involving a foreign electronic communications system, utilizing a means other than electronic surveillance as defined in section 101 of the Foreign Intelligence Surveillance Act of 1978, and procedures in this chapter or chapter 121 and the Foreign Intelligence Surveillance Act of 1978 shall be the exclusive means by which electronic surveillance, as defined in section 101 of such Act, and the interception of domestic wire, oral, and electronic communications may be conducted.

(g) It shall not be unlawful under this chapter or chapter 121 of this title for any person-

(i) to intercept or access an electronic communication made through an electronic communication system that is configured so that such electronic communication is readily accessible to the general public;

(ii) to intercept any radio communication which is transmitted-

(I) by any station for the use of the general public, or that relates to ships, aircraft, vehicles, or persons in distress;

(II) by any governmental, law enforcement, civil defense, private land mobile, or public safety communications system, including police and fire, readily accessible to the general public;

(III)by a station operating on an authorized frequency within the bands allocated to the amateur, citizens band, or general mobile radio services; or

(IV) by any marine or aeronautical communications system;

(iii) to engage in any conduct which-

(I) is prohibited by section 633 of the Communications Act of 1934; or

(II) is excepted from the application of section 705(a) of the Communications Act of 1934 by section 705(b) of that Act;

(iv) to intercept any wire or electronic communication the transmission of which is causing harmful interference to any lawfully operating station or consumer electronic equipment, to the extent necessary to identify the source of such interference; or

(v) for other users of the same frequency to intercept any radio communication made through a system that utilizes frequencies monitored by individuals engaged in the provision or the use of such system, if such communication is not scrambled or encrypted.

(h) It shall not be unlawful under this chapter-

  (i) to use a pen register or a trap and trace device (as those terms are defined for the purposes of chapter 206 (relating to pen registers and trap and trace devices) of this title); or

  (ii) for a provider of electronic communication service to record the fact that a wire or electronic communication was initiated or completed in order to protect such provider, another provider furnishing service toward the completion of the wire or electronic communication, or a user of that service, from fraudulent, unlawful or abusive use of such service.

(i) It shall not be unlawful under this chapter for a person acting under color of law to intercept the wire or electronic communications of a computer trespasser transmitted to, through, or from the protected computer, if-

  (I) the owner or operator of the protected computer authorizes the interception of the computer trespasser's communications on the protected computer;

  (II) the person acting under color of law is lawfully engaged in an investigation;

  (III) the person acting under color of law has reasonable grounds to believe that the contents of the computer trespasser's communications will be relevant to the investigation; and

  (IV) such interception does not acquire communications other than those transmitted to or from the computer trespasser.

(3) (a) Except as provided in paragraph (b) of this subsection, a person or entity providing an electronic communication service to the public shall not intentionally divulge the contents of any communication (other than one to such person or entity, or an agent thereof) while in transmission on that service to any person or entity other than an addressee or intended recipient of such communication or an agent of such addressee or intended recipient.

(b) A person or entity providing electronic communication service to the public may divulge the contents of any such communication-

  (i) as otherwise authorized in section 2511(2)(a) or 2517 of this title;

  (ii) with the lawful consent of the originator or any addressee or intended recipient of such communication;

  (iii) to a person employed or authorized, or whose facilities are used, to forward such communication to its destination; or

  (iv) which were inadvertently obtained by the service provider and which appear to pertain to the commission of a crime, if such divulgence is made to a law enforcement agency.

(4) (a) Except as provided in paragraph (b) of this subsection or in subsection (5), whoever violates subsection (1) of this section shall be fined under this title or imprisoned not more than five years, or both.

(b) Conduct otherwise an offense under this subsection that consists of or relates to the interception of a satellite transmission that is not encrypted or scrambled and that is transmitted-

  (i) to a broadcasting station for purposes of retransmission to the general public; or

  (ii) as an audio subcarrier intended for redistribution to facilities open to the public, but not including data transmissions or telephone calls, is not an offense under this subsection unless the conduct is for the purposes of direct or indirect commercial advantage or private financial gain.

(c)[Redesignated (b)]

(5) (a)(i) If the communication is-

(A) a private satellite video communication that is not scrambled or encrypted and the conduct in violation of this chapter is the private viewing of that communication and is not for a tortious or illegal purpose or for purposes of direct or indirect commercial advantage or private commercial gain; or

(B) a radio communication that is transmitted on frequencies allocated under subpart D of part 74 of the rules of the Federal Communications Commission that is not scrambled or encrypted and the conduct in violation of this chapter is not for a tortious or illegal purpose or for purposes of direct or indirect commercial advantage or private commercial gain, then the person who engages in such conduct shall be subject to suit by the Federal Government in a court of competent jurisdiction.

(ii) In an action under this subsection-

(A) if the violation of this chapter is a first offense for the person under paragraph (a) of subsection (4) and such person has not been found liable in a civil action under section 2520 of this title, the Federal Government shall be entitled to appropriate injunctive relief; and

(B) if the violation of this chapter is a second or subsequent offense under paragraph (a) of subsection (4) or such person has been found liable in any prior civil action under section 2520, the person shall be subject to a mandatory $500 civil fine.

(b) The court may use any means within its authority to enforce an injunction issued under paragraph (ii)(A), and shall impose a civil fine of not less than $500 for each violation of such an injunction.

18 U.S.C. 2512. Manufacture, Distribution, Possession, and Advertising of Wire, Oral, or Electronic Communication Intercepting Devices Prohibited

(1) Except as otherwise specifically provided in this chapter, any person who intentionally-

(a) sends through the mail, or sends or carries in interstate or foreign commerce, any electronic, mechanical, or other device, knowing or having reason to know that the design of such device renders it primarily useful for the purpose of the surreptitious interception of wire, oral, or electronic communications;

(b) manufactures, assembles, possesses, or sells any electronic, mechanical, or other device, knowing or having reason to know that the design of such device renders it primarily useful for the purpose of the surreptitious interception of wire, oral, or electronic communications, and that such device or any component thereof has been or will be sent through the mail or transported in interstate or foreign commerce; or

(c) places in any newspaper, magazine, handbill, or other publication or disseminates by electronic means any advertisement of-

(i) any electronic, mechanical, or other device knowing or having reason to know that the design of such device renders it primarily useful for the purpose of the surreptitious interception of wire, oral, or electronic communications; or

(ii) any other electronic, mechanical, or other device, where such advertisement promotes the use of such device for the purpose of the surreptitious interception of wire, oral, or electronic communications, knowing the content of the advertisement and knowing or having reason to know that such advertisement will be sent through the mail or transported in interstate or foreign commerce, shall be fined under this title or imprisoned not more than five years, or both.

(2) It shall not be unlawful under this section for-

(a) a provider of wire or electronic communication service or an officer, agent, or employee of, or a person under contract with, such a provider, in the normal course of the business of providing that wire or electronic communication service, or

(b) an officer, agent, or employee of, or a person under contract with, the United States, a State, or a political subdivision thereof, in the normal course of the activities of the United States, a State, or a political subdivision thereof, to send through the mail, send or carry in interstate or foreign commerce, or manufacture, assemble, possess, or sell any electronic, mechanical, or other device knowing or having reason to know that the design of such device renders it primarily useful for the purpose of the surreptitious interception of wire, oral, or electronic communications.

(3) It shall not be unlawful under this section to advertise for sale a device described in subsection (1) of this section if the advertisement is mailed, sent, or carried in interstate or foreign commerce solely to a domestic provider of wire or electronic communication service or to an agency of the United States, a State, or a political subdivision thereof which is duly authorized to use such device.

18 U.S.C. 2513. Confiscation of Wire, Oral, or Electronic Communication Interception Devices

Any electronic, mechanical, or other device used, sent, carried, manufactured, assembled, possessed, sold, or advertised in violation of section 2511 or section 2512 of this chapter may be seized and forfeited to the United States. All provisions of law relating to (1) the seizure, summary and judicial forfeiture, and condemnation of vessels, vehicles, merchandise, and baggage for violations of the customs laws contained in title 19 of the United States Code, (2) the disposition of such vessels, vehicles, merchandise, and baggage or the proceeds from the sale thereof, (3) the remission or mitigation of such forfeiture, (4) the compromise of claims, and (5) the award of compensation to informers in respect of such forfeitures, shall apply to seizures and forfeitures incurred, or alleged to have been incurred, under the provisions of this section, insofar as applicable and not inconsistent with the provisions of this section; except that such duties as are imposed upon the collector of customs or any other person with respect to the seizure and forfeiture of vessels, vehicles, merchandise, and baggage under the provisions of the customs laws contained in title 19 of the United States Code shall be performed with respect to seizure and forfeiture of electronic, mechanical, or other intercepting devices under this section by such officers, agents, or other persons as may be authorized or designated for that purpose by the Attorney General.

18 U.S.C. 2515. Prohibition of Use as Evidence of Intercepted Wire or Oral Communications

Whenever any wire or oral communication has been intercepted, no part of the contents of such communication and no evidence derived therefrom may be received in evidence in any trial, hearing, or other proceeding in or before any court, grand jury, department, officer, agency, regulatory body, legislative committee, or other authority of the United States, a State, or a political subdivision thereof if the disclosure of that information would be in violation of this chapter.

18 U.S.C. 2516. Authorization for Interception of Wire, Oral, or Electronic Communications

(1) The Attorney General, Deputy Attorney General, Associate Attorney General, or any Assistant Attorney General, any acting Assistant Attorney General, or any Deputy Assistant Attorney General or acting Deputy Assistant Attorney General in the Criminal Division or National Security Division specially designated by the Attorney General, may authorize an application to a Federal judge of competent jurisdiction for, and such judge may grant in conformity with section 2518 of this chapter an order authorizing or approving the interception of wire or oral communications by the Federal Bureau of Investigation, or a Federal agency having responsibility for the investigation of the offense as to which the application is made, when such interception may provide or has provided evidence of-

(a) any offense punishable by death or by imprisonment for more than one year under sections 2122 and 2274 through 2277 of title 42 of the United States Code (relating to the enforcement of the Atomic Energy Act of 1954), section 2284 of title 42 of the United States Code (relating to sabotage of nuclear facilities or fuel), or under the following chapters of this title: chapter 10 (relating to biological weapons) chapter 37 (relating to espionage), chapter 55 (relating to kidnapping), chapter 90 (relating to protection of trade secrets), chapter 105 (relating to sabotage), chapter 115 (relating to treason), chapter 102 (relating to riots), chapter 65 (relating to malicious mischief), chapter 111 (relating to destruction of vessels), or chapter 81 (relating to piracy);

(b) a violation of section 186 or section 501(c) of title 29, United States Code (dealing with restrictions on payments and loans to labor organizations), or any offense which involves murder, kidnapping, robbery, or extortion, and which is punishable under this title;

(c) any offense which is punishable under the following sections of this title: section 37 (relating to violence at international airports), section 43 (relating to animal enterprise terrorism), section 81 (arson within special maritime and territorial jurisdiction), section 201 (bribery of public officials and witnesses), section 215 (relating to bribery of bank officials), section 224 (bribery in sporting contests), subsection (d), (e), (f), (g), (h), or (i) of section 844 (unlawful use of explosives), section 1032 (relating to concealment of assets), section 1084 (transmission of wagering information), section 751 (relating to escape), section 832 (relating to nuclear and weapons of mass destruction threats), section 842 (relating to explosive materials), section 930 (relating to possession of weapons in Federal facilities), section 1014 (relating to loans and credit applications generally; renewals and discounts), section 1114 (relating to officers and employees of the United States), section 1116 (relating to protection of foreign officials), sections 1503, 1512, and 1513 (influencing or injuring an officer, juror, or witness generally), section 1510 (obstruction of criminal investigations), section 1511 (obstruction of State or local law enforcement), section 1591 (sex trafficking of children by force, fraud, or coercion), section 1751 (Presidential and Presidential staff assassination, kidnapping, and assault), section 1951 (interference with commerce by threats or violence), section 1952 (interstate and foreign travel or transportation in aid of racketeering enterprises), section 1958 (relating to use of interstate commerce facilities in the commission of murder for hire), section 1959 (relating to violent crimes in aid of racketeering activity), section 1954 (offer, acceptance, or solicitation to influence operations of employee benefit plan), section 1955 (prohibition of business enterprises of gambling), section 1956 (laundering of monetary instruments), section 1957 (relating to engaging in monetary transactions in property derived from specified unlawful activity), section 659 (theft from interstate shipment), section 664 (embezzlement from pension and welfare funds), section 1343 (fraud by wire, radio, or television), section 1344 (relating to bank fraud), section 1992 (relating to terrorist attacks against mass transportation), sections 2251 and 2252 (sexual exploitation of children), section 2251A (selling or buying of children), section 2252A (relating to material constituting or containing child pornography), section 1466A (relating to child obscenity), section 2260 (production of sexually explicit depictions of a minor for importation into the United States), sections 2421, 2422, 2423, and 2425 (relating to transportation for illegal sexual activity and related crimes), sections 2312, 2313, 2314, and 2315 (interstate transportation of stolen property), section 2321 (relating to trafficking in certain motor vehicles or motor vehicle parts), section 2340A (relating to torture), section 1203 (relating to hostage taking), section 1029 (relating to fraud and related activity in connection with access devices), section 3146 (relating to penalty for failure to appear), section 3521(b)(3) (relating to witness relocation and assistance), section 32 (relating to destruction of aircraft or aircraft facilities), section 38 (relating to aircraft parts fraud), section 1963 (violations with respect to racketeer influenced and corrupt organizations), section 115 (relating to threatening or retaliating against a Federal official), section 1341 (relating to mail fraud), a felony violation of section 1030 (relating to computer fraud and abuse), section 351 (violations with respect to congressional, Cabinet, or Supreme Court assassinations, kidnapping, and assault), section 831 (relating to prohibited transactions involving nuclear materials), section 33 (relating to destruction of motor vehicles or motor vehicle facilities), section 175 (relating to biological weapons), section 175c (relating to variola virus), section 956 (conspiracy to harm persons or property overseas), section a felony violation of section 1028 (relating to production of false identification documentation), section 1425 (relating to the procurement of citizenship or nationalization unlawfully), section 1426 (relating to the reproduction of naturalization or citizenship papers), section 1427 (relating to the sale of naturalization or citizenship papers), section 1541 (relating to passport issuance without authority), section 1542 (relating to false statements in passport applications), section 1543 (relating to forgery or false use of passports), section 1544 (relating to misuse of passports), or section 1546 (relating to fraud and misuse of visas, permits, and other documents);

(d) any offense involving counterfeiting punishable under section 471, 472, or 473 of this title;

(e) any offense involving fraud connected with a case under title 11 or the manufacture, importation, receiving, concealment, buying, selling, or otherwise dealing in narcotic drugs, marihuana, or other dangerous drugs, punishable under any law of the United States;

(f) any offense including extortionate credit transactions under sections 892, 893, or 894 of this title;

(g) a violation of section 5322 of title 31, United States Code (dealing with the reporting of currency transactions), or section 5324 of title 31, United States Code (relating to structuring transactions to evade reporting requirement prohibited);

(h) any felony violation of sections 2511 and 2512 (relating to interception and disclosure of certain communications and to certain intercepting devices) of this title;

(i) any felony violation of chapter 71 (relating to obscenity) of this title;

(j) any violation of section 60123(b) (relating to destruction of a natural gas pipeline), section 46502 (relating to aircraft piracy), the second sentence of section 46504 (relating to assault on a flight crew with dangerous weapon), or section 46505(b)(3) or (c) (relating to explosive or incendiary devices, or endangerment of human life, by means of weapons on aircraft) of title 49;

(k) any criminal violation of section 2778 of title 22 (relating to the Arms Export Control Act);

(l) the location of any fugitive from justice from an offense described in this section;

(m) a violation of section 274, 277, or 278 of the Immigration and Nationality Act (8 U.S.C. 1324, 1327, or 1328) (relating to the smuggling of aliens);

(n) any felony violation of sections 922 and 924 of title 18, United States Code (relating to firearms);

(o) any violation of section 5861 of the Internal Revenue Code of 1986 (relating to firearms);

(p) a felony violation of section 1028 (relating to production of false identification documents), section 1542 (relating to false statements in passport applications), section 1546 (relating to fraud and misuse of visas, permits, and other documents, section 1028A (relating to aggravated identity theft)) of this title or a violation of section 274, 277, or 278 of the Immigration and Nationality Act (relating to the smuggling of aliens); or

(q) any criminal violation of section 229 (relating to chemical weapons): or sections 2332, 2332a, 2332b, 2332d, 2332f, 2332g, 2332h 2339, 2339A, 2339B, 2339C, or 2339D of this title (relating to terrorism);

(r) any criminal violation of section 1 (relating to illegal restraints of trade or commerce), 2 (relating to illegal monopolizing of trade or commerce), or 3 (relating to illegal restraints of trade or commerce in territories or the District of Columbia) of the Sherman Act (15 U.S.C. 1, , 3); or

(s) any conspiracy to commit any offense described in any subparagraph of this paragraph.

(2) The principal prosecuting attorney of any State, or the principal prosecuting attorney of any political subdivision thereof, if such attorney is authorized by a statute of that State to make application to a State court judge of competent jurisdiction for an order authorizing or approving the interception of wire, oral, or electronic communications, may apply to such judge for, and such judge may grant in conformity with section 2518 of this chapter and with the applicable State statute an order authorizing, or approving the interception of wire, oral, or electronic communications by investigative or law enforcement officers having responsibility for the investigation of the offense as to which the application is made, when such interception may provide or has provided evidence of the commission of the offense of murder, kidnapping, gambling, robbery, bribery, extortion, or dealing in narcotic drugs, marihuana or other dangerous drugs, or other crime dangerous to life, limb, or property, and punishable by imprisonment for more than one year, designated in any applicable State statute authorizing such interception, or any conspiracy to commit any of the foregoing offenses.

(3) Any attorney for the Government (as such term is defined for the purposes of the Federal Rules of Criminal Procedure) may authorize an application to a Federal judge of competent jurisdiction for, and such judge may grant, in conformity with section 2518 of this title, an order authorizing or approving the interception of electronic communications by an investigative or law enforcement officer having responsibility for the investigation of the offense as to which the application is made, when such interception may provide or has provided evidence of any Federal felony.

18 U.S.C. 2517. Authorization for Disclosure and Use of Intercepted Wire, Oral, or Electronic Communications

(1) Any investigative or law enforcement officer who, by any means authorized by this chapter, has obtained knowledge of the contents of any wire, oral, or electronic communication, or evidence derived therefrom, may disclose such contents to another investigative or law enforcement officer to the extent that such disclosure is appropriate to the proper performance of the official duties of the officer making or receiving the disclosure.

(2) Any investigative or law enforcement officer who, by any means authorized by this chapter, has obtained knowledge of the contents of any wire, oral, or electronic communication or evidence derived therefrom may use such contents to the extent such use is appropriate to the proper performance of his official duties.

(3) Any person who has received, by any means authorized by this chapter, any information concerning a wire, oral, or electronic communication, or evidence derived therefrom intercepted in accordance with the provisions of this chapter may disclose the contents of that communication or such derivative evidence while giving

testimony under oath or affirmation in any proceeding held under the authority of the United States or of any State or political subdivision thereof.

(4) No otherwise privileged wire, oral, or electronic communication intercepted in accordance with, or in violation of, the provisions of this chapter shall lose its privileged character.

(5) When an investigative or law enforcement officer, while engaged in intercepting wire, oral, or electronic communications in the manner authorized herein, intercepts wire, oral, or electronic communications relating to offenses other than those specified in the order of authorization or approval, the contents thereof, and evidence derived therefrom, may be disclosed or used as provided in subsections (1) and (2) of this section. Such contents and any evidence derived therefrom may be used under subsection (3) of this section when authorized or approved by a judge of competent jurisdiction where such judge finds on subsequent application that the contents were otherwise intercepted in accordance with the provisions of this chapter. Such application shall be made as soon as practicable.

(6) Any investigative or law enforcement officer, or attorney for the Government, who by any means authorized by this chapter, has obtained knowledge of the contents of any wire, oral, or electronic communication, or evidence derived therefrom, may disclose such contents to any Federal law enforcement, intelligence, protective, immigration, national defense, or national security official to the extent that such contents include foreign intelligence or counterintelligence (as defined in section 3 of the National Security act of 1947 (50 U.S.C. 401a), or foreign intelligence information (as defined in subsection (19) of section 2510 of this title), to assist the official who is to receive that information in the performance of his official duties. Any Federal official who receives information pursuant to this provision may use that information only as necessary in the conduct of that person's official duties subject to any limitations on the unauthorized disclosure of such information.

(7) Any investigative or law enforcement officer, or other Federal official in carrying out official duties as such Federal official, who by any means authorized by this chapter, has obtained knowledge of the contents of any wire, oral, or electronic communication, or evidence derived therefrom, may disclose such contents or derivative evidence to a foreign investigative or law enforcement officer to the extent that such disclosure is appropriate to the proper performance of the official duties of the officer making or receiving the disclosure, and foreign investigative or law enforcement officers may use or disclose such contents or derivative evidence to the extent such use or disclosure is appropriate to the proper performance of their official duties.

(8) Any investigative or law enforcement officer, or other Federal official in carrying out official duties as such Federal official, who by any means authorized by this chapter, has obtained knowledge of the contents of any wire, oral, or electronic communication, or evidence derived therefrom, may disclose such contents or derivative evidence to any appropriate Federal, State, local, or foreign government official to the extent that such contents or derivative evidence reveals a threat of actual or potential attack or other grave hostile acts of a foreign power of an agent of as foreign power, domestic or international sabotage, domestic or international terrorism, or clandestine intelligence gathering activities by an intelligence service or

network of a foreign power or by an agent of a foreign power, within the United States or elsewhere, for the purpose of preventing or responding to such a threat. Any official who receives information pursuant to this provision may use that information only as necessary in the conduct of that person's official duties subject to any limitations on the unauthorized disclosure of such information, and any State, local, or foreign official who receives information pursuant to this provision may use that information only consistent with such guidelines as the Attorney General and Director of Central Intelligence shall jointly issue.

18 U.S.C. 2518. Procedure for Interception of Wire, Oral, or Electronic Communications

(1) Each application for an order authorizing or approving the interception of a wire, oral, or electronic communication under this chapter shall be made in writing upon oath or affirmation to a judge of competent jurisdiction and shall state the applicant's authority to make such application. Each application shall include the following information:

- (a) the identity of the investigative or law enforcement officer making the application, and the officer authorizing the application;
- (b) a full and complete statement of the facts and circumstances relied upon by the applicant, to justify his belief that an order should be issued, including (i) details as to the particular offense that has been, is being, or is about to be committed, (ii) except as provided in subsection (11), a particular description of the nature and location of the facilities from which or the place where the communication is to be intercepted, (iii) a particular description of the type of communications sought to be intercepted, (iv) the identity of the person, if known, committing the offense and whose communications are to be intercepted;
- (c) a full and complete statement as to whether or not other investigative procedures have been tried and failed or why they reasonably appear to be unlikely to succeed if tried or to be too dangerous;
- (d) a statement of the period of time for which the interception is required to be maintained. If the nature of the investigation is such that the authorization for interception should not automatically terminate when the described type of communication has been first obtained, a particular description of facts establishing probable cause to believe that additional communications of the same type will occur thereafter;
- (e) a full and complete statement of the facts concerning all previous applications known to the individual authorizing and making the application, made to any judge for authorization to intercept, or for approval of interceptions of, wire, oral, or electronic communications involving any of the same persons, facilities or places specified in the application, and the action taken by the judge on each such application; and
- (f) where the application is for the extension of an order, a statement setting forth the results thus far obtained from the interception, or a reasonable explanation of the failure to obtain such results.

(2) The judge may require the applicant to furnish additional testimony or documentary evidence in support of the application.

(3) Upon such application the judge may enter an ex parte order, as requested or as modified, authorizing or approving interception of wire, oral, or electronic communications within the territorial jurisdiction of the court in which the judge is sitting (and outside that jurisdiction but within the United States in the case of a mobile interception device authorized by a Federal court within such jurisdiction), if the judge determines on the basis of the facts submitted by the applicant that-
   (a) there is probable cause for belief that an individual is committing, has committed, or is about to commit a particular offense enumerated in section 2516 of this chapter;
   (b) there is probable cause for belief that particular communications concerning that offense will be obtained through such interception;
   (c) normal investigative procedures have been tried and have failed or reasonably appear to be unlikely to succeed if tried or to be too dangerous;
   (d) except as provided in subsection (11), there is probable cause for belief that the facilities from which, or the place where, the wire, oral, or electronic communications are to be intercepted are being used, or are about to be used, in connection with the commission of such offense, or are leased to, listed in the name of, or commonly used by such person.

(4) Each order authorizing or approving the interception of any wire, oral, or electronic communication under this chapter shall specify-
   (a) the identity of the person, if known, whose communications are to be intercepted;
   (b) the nature and location of the communications facilities as to which, or the place where, authority to intercept is granted;
   (c) a particular description of the type of communication sought to be intercepted, and a statement of the particular offense to which it relates;
   (d) the identity of the agency authorized to intercept the communications, and of the person authorizing the application; and
   (e) the period of time during which such interception is authorized, including a statement as to whether or not the interception shall automatically terminate when the described communication has been first obtained.

   An order authorizing the interception of a wire, oral, or electronic communication under this chapter shall, upon request of the applicant, direct that a provider of wire or electronic communication service, landlord, custodian or other person shall furnish the applicant forthwith all information, facilities, and technical assistance necessary to accomplish the interception unobtrusively and with a minimum of interference with the services that such service provider, landlord, custodian, or person is according the person whose communications are to be intercepted. Any provider of wire or electronic communication service, landlord, custodian or other person furnishing such facilities or technical assistance shall be compensated therefor by the applicant for reasonable expenses incurred in providing such facilities or assistance. Pursuant to section 2522 of this chapter, an order may also be issued to enforce the assistance capability and capacity requirements under the Communications Assistance for Law Enforcement Act.

(5) No order entered under this section may authorize or approve the interception of any wire, oral, or electronic communication for any period longer than is necessary to achieve the objective of the authorization, nor in any event longer than thirty days. Such thirty-day period begins on the earlier of the day on which the investigative or

law enforcement officer first begins to conduct an interception under the order or ten days after the order is entered. Extensions of an order may be granted, but only upon application for an extension made in accordance with subsection (1) of this section and the court making the findings required by subsection (3) of this section. The period of extension shall be no longer than the authorizing judge deems necessary to achieve the purposes for which it was granted and in no event for longer than thirty days. Every order and extension thereof shall contain a provision that the authorization to intercept shall be executed as soon as practicable, shall be conducted in such a way as to minimize the interception of communications not otherwise subject to interception under this chapter, and must terminate upon attainment of the authorized objective, or in any event in thirty days. In the event the intercepted communication is in a code or foreign language, and an expert in that foreign language or code is not reasonably available during the interception period, minimization may be accomplished as soon as practicable after such interception. An interception under this chapter may be conducted in whole or in part by Government personnel, or by an individual operating under a contract with the Government, acting under the supervision of an investigative or law enforcement officer authorized to conduct the interception.

(6) Whenever an order authorizing interception is entered pursuant to this chapter, the order may require reports to be made to the judge who issued the order showing what progress has been made toward achievement of the authorized objective and the need for continued interception. Such reports shall be made at such intervals as the judge may require.

(7) Notwithstanding any other provision of this chapter, any investigative or law enforcement officer, specially designated by the Attorney General, the Deputy Attorney General, the Associate Attorney General, or by the principal prosecuting attorney of any State or subdivision thereof acting pursuant to a statute of that State, who reasonably determines that-

(a) an emergency situation exists that involves-

(i) immediate danger of death or serious physical injury to any person,

(ii) conspiratorial activities threatening the national security interest, or

(iii) conspiratorial activities characteristic of organized crime, that requires a wire, oral, or electronic communication to be intercepted before an order authorizing such interception can, with due diligence, be obtained, and

(b) there are grounds upon which an order could be entered under this chapter to authorize such interception, may intercept such wire, oral, or electronic communication if an application for an order approving the interception is made in accordance with this section within forty-eight hours after the interception has occurred, or begins to occur. In the absence of an order, such interception shall immediately terminate when the communication sought is obtained or when the application for the order is denied, whichever is earlier. In the event such application for approval is denied, or in any other case where the interception is terminated without an order having been issued, the contents of any wire, oral, or electronic communication intercepted shall be treated as having been obtained in violation of this chapter, and an inventory shall be served as provided for in subsection (d) of this section on the person named in the application.

(8) (a) The contents of any wire, oral, or electronic communication intercepted by any means authorized by this chapter shall, if possible, be recorded on tape or wire or other comparable device. The recording of the contents of any wire, oral, or electronic communication under this subsection shall be done in such way as will protect the recording from editing or other alterations. Immediately upon the expiration of the period of the order, or extensions thereof, such recordings shall be made available to the judge issuing such order and sealed under his directions. Custody of the recordings shall be wherever the judge orders. They shall not be destroyed except upon an order of the issuing or denying judge and in any event shall be kept for ten years. Duplicate recordings may be made for use or disclosure pursuant to the provisions of subsections (1) and (2) of section 2517 of this chapter for investigations. The presence of the seal provided for by this subsection, or a satisfactory explanation for the absence thereof, shall be a prerequisite for the use or disclosure of the contents of any wire, oral, or electronic communication or evidence derived therefrom under subsection (3) of section 2517.

(b) Applications made and orders granted under this chapter shall be sealed by the judge. Custody of the applications and orders shall be wherever the judge directs. Such applications and orders shall be disclosed only upon a showing of good cause before a judge of competent jurisdiction and shall not be destroyed except on order of the issuing or denying judge, and in any event shall be kept for ten years.

(c) Any violation of the provisions of this subsection may be punished as contempt of the issuing or denying judge.

(d) Within a reasonable time but not later than ninety days after the filing of an application for an order of approval under section 2518(7)(b) which is denied or the termination of the period of an order or extensions thereof, the issuing or denying judge shall cause to be served, on the persons named in the order or the application, and such other parties to intercepted communications as the judge may determine in his discretion that is in the interest of justice, an inventory which shall include notice of-

(1) the fact of the entry of the order or the application;
(2) the date of the entry and the period of authorized, approved or disapproved interception, or the denial of the application; and
(3) the fact that during the period wire, oral, or electronic communications were or were not intercepted. The judge, upon the filing of a motion, may in his discretion make available to such person or his counsel for inspection such portions of the intercepted communications, applications and orders as the judge determines to be in the interest of justice. On an ex parte showing of good cause to a judge of competent jurisdiction the serving of the inventory required by this subsection may be postponed.

(9) The contents of any wire, oral, or electronic communication intercepted pursuant to this chapter or evidence derived therefrom shall not be received in evidence or otherwise disclosed in any trial, hearing, or other proceeding in a Federal or State court unless each party, not less than ten days before the trial, hearing, or proceeding, has been furnished with a copy of the court order, and accompanying application, under which the interception was authorized or approved. This ten-day period may be waived by the judge if he finds that it was not possible to furnish the party with

the above information ten days before the trial, hearing, or proceeding and that the party will not be prejudiced by the delay in receiving such information.

(10)(a) Any aggrieved person in any trial, hearing, or proceeding in or before any court, department, officer, agency, regulatory body, or other authority of the United States, a State, or a political subdivision thereof, may move to suppress the contents of any wire or oral communication intercepted pursuant to this chapter, or evidence derived therefrom, on the grounds that-

(i) the communication was unlawfully intercepted;

(ii) the order of authorization or approval under which it was intercepted is insufficient on its face; or

(iii) the interception was not made in conformity with the order of authorization or approval. Such motion shall be made before the trial, hearing, or proceeding unless there was no opportunity to make such motion or the person was not aware of the grounds of the motion. If the motion is granted, the contents of the intercepted wire or oral communication, or evidence derived therefrom, shall be treated as having been obtained in violation of this chapter. The judge, upon the filing of such motion by the aggrieved person, may in his discretion make available to the aggrieved person or his counsel for inspection such portions of the intercepted communication or evidence derived therefrom as the judge determines to be in the interests of justice.

(b) In addition to any other right to appeal, the United States shall have the right to appeal from an order granting a motion to suppress made under paragraph (a) of this subsection, or the denial of an application for an order of approval, if the United States attorney shall certify to the judge or other official granting such motion or denying such application that the appeal is not taken for purposes of delay. Such appeal shall be taken within thirty days after the date the order was entered and shall be diligently prosecuted.

(c) The remedies and sanctions described in this chapter with respect to the interception of electronic communications are the only judicial remedies and sanctions for nonconstitutional violations of this chapter involving such communications.

(11)The requirements of subsections (1)(b)(ii) and (3)(d) of this section relating to the specification of the facilities from which, or the place where, the communication is to be intercepted do not apply if-

(a) in the case of an application with respect to the interception of an oral communication-

(i) the application is by a Federal investigative or law enforcement officer and is approved by the Attorney General, the Deputy Attorney General, the Associate Attorney General, an Assistant Attorney General, or an acting Assistant Attorney General;

(ii) the application contains a full and complete statement as to why such specification is not practical and identifies the person committing the offense and whose communications are to be intercepted; and

(iii) the judge finds that such specification is not practical; and

(b) in the case of an application with respect to a wire or electronic communication-

(i) the application is by a Federal investigative or law enforcement officer and is approved by the Attorney General, the Deputy Attorney General, the

Associate Attorney General, an Assistant Attorney General, or an acting Assistant Attorney General;

(ii) the application identifies the person believed to be committing the offense and whose communications are to be intercepted and the applicant makes a showing that there is probable cause to believe that the person's actions could have the effect of thwarting interception from a specified facility;

(iii) the judge finds that such showing has been adequately made; and

(iv) the order authorizing or approving the interception is limited to interception only for such time as it is reasonable to presume that the person identified in the application is or was reasonably proximate to the instrument through which such communication will be or was transmitted.

(12) An interception of a communication under an order with respect to which the requirements of subsections (1)(b)(ii) and (3)(d) of this section do not apply by reason of subsection (11)(a) shall not begin until the place where the communication is to be intercepted is ascertained by the person implementing the interception order. A provider of wire or electronic communications service that has received an order as provided for in subsection (11)(b) may move the court to modify or quash the order on the ground that its assistance with respect to the interception cannot be performed in a timely or reasonable fashion. The court, upon notice to the government, shall decide such a motion expeditiously.

18 U.S.C. 2519. Reports Concerning Intercepted Wire, Oral, Or Electronic Communications

(1) Within thirty days after the expiration of an order (or each extension thereof) entered under section 2518, or the denial of an order approving an interception, the issuing or denying judge shall report to the Administrative Office of the United States Courts-

(a) the fact that an order or extension was applied for;

(b) the kind of order or extension applied for (including whether or not the order was an order with respect to which the requirements of sections 2518(1)(b)(ii) and 2518(3)(d) of this title did not apply by reason of section 2518(11) of this title);

(c) the fact that the order or extension was granted as applied for, was modified, or was denied;

(d) the period of interceptions authorized by the order, and the number and duration of any extensions of the order;

(e) the offense specified in the order or application, or extension of an order;

(f) the identity of the applying investigative or law enforcement officer and agency making the application and the person authorizing the application; and

(g) the nature of the facilities from which or the place where communications were to be intercepted.

(2) In January of each year the Attorney General, an Assistant Attorney General specially designated by the Attorney General, or the principal prosecuting attorney of a State, or the principal prosecuting attorney for any political subdivision of a State, shall report to the Administrative Office of the United States Courts-

(a) the information required by paragraphs (a) through (g) of subsection (1) of this section with respect to each application for an order or extension made during the preceding calendar year;
(b) a general description of the interceptions made under such order or extension, including (i) the approximate nature and frequency of incriminating communications intercepted, (ii) the approximate nature and frequency of other communications intercepted, (iii) the approximate number of persons whose communications were intercepted, (iv) the number of orders in which encryption was encountered and whether such encryption prevented law enforcement from obtaining the plain text of communications intercepted pursuant to such order, and (v) the approximate nature, amount, and cost of the manpower and other resources used in the interceptions;
(c) the number of arrests resulting from interceptions made under such order or extension, and the offenses for which arrests were made;
(d) the number of trials resulting from such interceptions;
(e) the number of motions to suppress made with respect to such interceptions, and the number granted or denied;
(f) the number of convictions resulting from such interceptions and the offenses for which the convictions were obtained and a general assessment of the importance of the interceptions; and
(g) the information required by paragraphs (b) through (f) of this subsection with respect to orders or extensions obtained in a preceding calendar year.

(3) In April of each year the Director of the Administrative Office of the United States Courts shall transmit to the Congress a full and complete report concerning the number of applications for orders authorizing or approving the interception of wire, oral, or electronic communications pursuant to this chapter and the number of orders and extensions granted or denied pursuant to this chapter during the preceding calendar year. Such report shall include a summary and analysis of the data required to be filed with the Administrative Office by subsections (1) and (2) of this section. The Director of the Administrative Office of the United States Courts is authorized to issue binding regulations dealing with the content and form of the reports required to be filed by subsections (1) and (2) of this section.

18 U.S.C. 2520. Recovery of Civil Damages Authorized

(a) In general.—Except as provided in section 2511(2)(a)(ii), any person whose wire, oral, or electronic communication is intercepted, disclosed, or intentionally used in violation of this chapter may in a civil action recover from the person or entity other than the United States which engaged in that violation such relief as may be appropriate.

(b) Relief.—In an action under this section, appropriate relief includes-
(1) such preliminary and other equitable or declaratory relief as may be appropriate;
(2) damages under subsection (c) and punitive damages in appropriate cases; and
(3) a reasonable attorney's fee and other litigation costs reasonably incurred.

(c) Computation of damages.—(1) In an action under this section, if the conduct in violation of this chapter is the private viewing of a private satellite video communication that is not scrambled or encrypted or if the communication is a radio communication that is transmitted on frequencies allocated under subpart D of part 74 of the rules of the Federal Communications Commission that is not scrambled or encrypted and the conduct is not for a tortious or illegal purpose or for purposes of direct or indirect commercial advantage or private commercial gain, then the court shall assess damages as follows:

(A) If the person who engaged in that conduct has not previously been enjoined under section 2511(5) and has not been found liable in a prior civil action under this section, the court shall assess the greater of the sum of actual damages suffered by the plaintiff, or statutory damages of not less than $50 and not more than $500.

(B) If, on one prior occasion, the person who engaged in that conduct has been enjoined under section 2511(5) or has been found liable in a civil action under this section, the court shall assess the greater of the sum of actual damages suffered by the plaintiff, or statutory damages of not less than $100 and not more than $1000.

(2) In any other action under this section, the court may assess as damages whichever is the greater of-

(A) the sum of the actual damages suffered by the plaintiff and any profits made by the violator as a result of the violation; or

(B) statutory damages of whichever is the greater of $100 a day for each day of violation or $10,000.

(d) Defense.—A good faith reliance on-

(1) a court warrant or order, a grand jury subpoena, a legislative authorization, or a statutory authorization;

(2) a request of an investigative or law enforcement officer under section 2518(7) of this title; or

(3) a good faith determination that section 2511(3) or 2511(2)(i) of this title permitted the conduct complained of; is a complete defense against any civil or criminal action brought under this chapter or any other law.

(e) Limitation.—A civil action under this section may not be commenced later than two years after the date upon which the claimant first has a reasonable opportunity to discover the violation.

(f) Administrative Discipline. – If a court or appropriate department or agency determines that the United States or any of its departments or agencies has violated any provision of this chapter, and the court finds that the circumstances surrounding the violation raise serious questions about whether or not an officer or employee of the Untied States acted willfully or intentionally with respect to the possible violation, the department or agency shall, upon receipt of a true and correct copy of the decision and findings of the court or appropriate department or agency promptly initiate a proceeding to determine whether disciplinary action against the officer or employee is warranted. If the head of the department or agency involved determines that disciplinary action is not warranted, he or she shall notify the Inspector General with jurisdiction over the department or agency concerned and shall provide the Inspector General with the reasons for such determination.

(g) Improper Disclosure Is Violation. – Any willful disclosure or use by an investigative or law enforcement officer or governmental entity of information beyond the extent permitted by section 2517 is a violation of this chapter for purposes of section 2510(a).

18 U.S.C. 2521. Injunction Against Illegal Interception

Whenever it shall appear that any person is engaged or is about to engage in any act which constitutes or will constitute a felony violation of this chapter, the Attorney General may initiate a civil action in a district court of the United States to enjoin such violation. The court shall proceed as soon as practicable to the hearing and determination of such an action, and may, at any time before final determination, enter such a restraining order or prohibition, or take such other action, as is warranted to prevent a continuing and substantial injury to the United States or to any person or class of persons for whose protection the action is brought. A proceeding under this section is governed by the Federal Rules of Civil Procedure, except that, if an indictment has been returned against the respondent, discovery is governed by the Federal Rules of Criminal Procedure.

18 U.S.C. 2522. Enforcement of the Communications Assistance for Law Enforcement Act

(a) Enforcement by court issuing surveillance order.—If a court authorizing an interception under this chapter, a State statute, or the Foreign Intelligence Surveillance Act of 1978 (50 U.S.C. 1801 et seq.) or authorizing use of a pen register or a trap and trace device under chapter 206 or a State statute finds that a telecommunications carrier has failed to comply with the requirements of the Communications Assistance for Law Enforcement Act, the court may, in accordance with section 108 of such Act, direct that the carrier comply forthwith and may direct that a provider of support services to the carrier or the manufacturer of the carrier's transmission or switching equipment furnish forthwith modifications necessary for the carrier to comply.

(b) Enforcement upon application by Attorney General.—The Attorney General may, in a civil action in the appropriate United States district court, obtain an order, in accordance with section 108 of the Communications Assistance for Law Enforcement Act, directing that a telecommunications carrier, a manufacturer of telecommunications transmission or switching equipment, or a provider of telecommunications support services comply with such Act.

(c) Civil penalty.—

(1) In general.—A court issuing an order under this section against a telecommunications carrier, a manufacturer of telecommunications transmission or switching equipment, or a provider of telecommunications support services may impose a civil penalty of up to $10,000 per day for each day in violation after the issuance of the order or after such future date as the court may specify.

(2) Considerations.—In determining whether to impose a civil penalty and in determining its amount, the court shall take into account-

(A) the nature, circumstances, and extent of the violation;

(B) the violator's ability to pay, the violator's good faith efforts to comply in a timely manner, any effect on the violator's ability to continue to do business, the degree of culpability, and the length of any delay in undertaking efforts to comply; and

(c) such other matters as justice may require.

(d) Definitions.—As used in this section, the terms defined in section 102 of the Communications Assistance for Law Enforcement Act have the meanings provided, respectively, in such section.

18 U.S.C. 2701. Unlawful Access to Stored Communications

(a) *Offense.*—Except as provided in subsection (c) of this section whoever-

(1) intentionally accesses without authorization a facility through which an electronic communication service is provided; or

(2) intentionally exceeds an authorization to access that facility; and thereby obtains, alters, or prevents authorized access to a wire or electronic communication while it is in electronic storage in such system shall be punished as provided in subsection (b) of this section.

(b) *Punishment.*—The punishment for an offense under subsection (a) of this section is-

(1) if the offense is committed for purposes of commercial advantage, malicious destruction or damage, or private commercial gain, or in furtherance of any criminal or tortious act in violation of the constitution and laws of the United States or any state -

(A) a fine under this title or imprisonment for not more than 5 years, or both, in the case of a first offense under this subparagraph; and

(B) a fine under this title or imprisonment for not more than 10 years, or both, for any subsequent offense under this subparagraph; and

(2) (A) a fine under this title or imprisonment for not more than 1 year or both, in the case of a first offense under this paragraph; and

(B) a fine under this title or imprisonment for not more than 5 years, or both, in the case of an offense under this subparagraph that occurs after a conviction of another offense under this section.

(c) *Exceptions.*—Subsection (a) of this section does not apply with respect to conduct authorized-

(1) by the person or entity providing a wire or electronic communications service;

(2) by a user of that service with respect to a communication of or intended for that user; or

(3) in section 2703, 2704 or 2518 of this title.

18 U.S.C. 2702. Voluntary Disclosure of Customer Communications or Records

(a) *Prohibitions.*--Except as provided in subsection (b) or (c)-

(1) a person or entity providing an electronic communication service to the public shall not knowingly divulge to any person or entity the contents of a communication while in electronic storage by that service; and

(2) a person or entity providing remote computing service to the public shall not knowingly divulge to any person or entity the contents of any communication which is carried or maintained on that service-

(A) on behalf of, and received by means of electronic transmission from (or created by means of computer processing of communications received by means of electronic transmission from), a subscriber or customer of such service;

(B) solely for the purpose of providing storage or computer processing services to such subscriber or customer, if the provider is not authorized to access the contents of any such communications for purposes of providing any services other than storage or computer processing; and

(3) a provider of remote computing service or electronic communication service to the public shall not knowingly divulge a record or other information pertaining to a subscriber to or customer of such service (not including the contents of communications covered by paragraph (1) or (2)) to any governmental entity.

(b) *Exceptions for disclosure of communications.*— A provider described in subsection (a) may divulge the contents of a communication-

(1) to an addressee or intended recipient of such communication or an agent of such addressee or intended recipient;

(2) as otherwise authorized in section 2517, 2511(2)(a), or 2703 of this title;

(3) with the lawful consent of the originator or an addressee or intended recipient of such communication, or the subscriber in the case of remote computing service;

(4) to a person employed or authorized or whose facilities are used to forward such communication to its destination;

(5) as may be necessarily incident to the rendition of the service or to the protection of the rights or property of the provider of that service;

(6) to the National Center for Missing and Exploited Children, in connection with a report submitted thereto under section 227 of the Victims of Child Abuse Act of 1990 (42 U.S.C. 13032);

(7) to a law enforcement agency-

(A) if the contents-

(i) were inadvertently obtained by the service provider; and

(ii) appear to pertain to the commission of a crime; or

[(B) Repealed. Publ. 108-21, Title V, § 508(b)(1)(A), Apr. 30, 2003, 117 Stat. 684]

[(C) Repealed. Publ. 107-296, Title II, § 225(d)(1)(C), Nov. 25, 2002, 116 Stat. 2157]

(8) to a governmental entity, if the provider, in good faith, believes that an emergency involving danger of death or serious physical injury to any person requires disclosure without delay of communications relating to the emergency.

(C) *Exceptions for disclosure of customer records.*—A provider described in subsection (a) may divulge a record or other information pertaining to a subscriber to or customer of such service (not including the contents of communications covered by subsection (a)(1) or (a)(2))-

(1) as otherwise authorized in section 2703;

(2) with the lawful consent of the customer or subscriber;

(3) as may be necessarily incident to the rendition of the service or to the protection of the rights or property of the provider of that service;

(4) to a governmental entity, if the provider, in good faith, believes that an emergency involving danger of death or serious physical injury to any person requires disclosure without delay of information relating to the emergency;
(5) to the National Center for Missing and Exploited Children, in connection with a report submitted thereto under section 227 of the Victims of Child Abuse Act of 1990 (42 U.S.C. 13032); or
(6) to any person other than a governmental entity.

(d) *Reporting of emergency disclosures.*—On an annual basis, the Attorney General shall submit to the Committee on the Judiciary of the House of Representatives and the Committee on the Judiciary of the Senate a report containing-
(1) the number of accounts from which the Department of Justice has received voluntary disclosures under subsection (b)(8); and
(2) a summary of the basis for disclosure in those instances where-
(A) voluntary disclosures under subsection (b)(8) were made to the Department of Justice; and
(B) the investigation pertaining to those disclosures was closed without the filing of criminal charges.

18 U.S.C. 2703. Required Disclosure of Customer Communications or Records

(a) *Contents of wire or electronic communications in electronic storage.*—A governmental entity may require the disclosure by a provider of electronic communication service of the contents of a wire or electronic communication, that is in electronic storage in a wire or electronic communications system for one hundred and eighty days or less, only pursuant to a warrant issued using the procedures described in the Federal Rules of Criminal Procedure by a court with jurisdiction over the offense under investigation or equivalent State warrant. A governmental entity may require the disclosure by a provider of electronic communications services of the contents of a wire or electronic communication that has been in electronic storage in an electronic communications system for more than one hundred and eighty days by the means available under subsection (b) of this section.

(b) (1) *Contents of electronic communications in a remote computing service.*—(1) A governmental entity may require a provider of remote computing service to disclose the contents of any wire or electronic communication to which this paragraph is made applicable by paragraph (2) of this subsection-
(A) without required notice to the subscriber or customer, if the governmental entity obtains a warrant issued using the procedures described in the Federal Rules of Criminal Procedure by a court with jurisdiction over the offense under investigation or equivalent State warrant; or
(B) with prior notice from the governmental entity to the subscriber or customer if the governmental entity-
(i) uses an administrative subpoena authorized by a Federal or State statute or a Federal or State grand jury or trial subpoena; or

(ii) obtains a court order for such disclosure under subsection (d) of this section; except that delayed notice may be given pursuant to section 2705 of this title.

(2) Paragraph (1) is applicable with respect to any wire or electronic communication that is held or maintained on that service-

(A) on behalf of, and received by means of electronic transmission from (or created by means of computer processing of communications received by means of electronic transmission from), a subscriber or customer of such remote computing service; and

(B) solely for the purpose of providing storage or computer processing services to such subscriber or customer, if the provider is not authorized to access the contents of any such communications for purposes of providing any services other than storage or computer processing.

(c) *Records concerning electronic communication service or remote computing service.*—(1)(A) A government entity may require a provider of electronic communication service or remote computing service to disclose a record or other information pertaining to a subscriber to or customer of such service (not including the contents of communications).

(B) A provider of electronic communication service or remote computing service shall disclose a record or other information pertaining to a subscriber to or customer of such service (not including the contents of communications covered by subsection (a) or (b) of this section) to a governmental entity only when the governmental entity-

(A) obtains a warrant issued using the procedures described in the Federal Rules of Criminal Procedure by a court with jurisdiction over the offense under investigation or equivalent State warrant;

(B) obtains a court order for such disclosure under subsection (d) of this section;

(C) has the consent of the subscriber or customer to such disclosure; or

(D) submits a formal written request relevant to a law enforcement investigation concerning telemarketing fraud for the name, address, and place of business of a subscriber or customer of such provider, which subscriber or customer is engaged in telemarketing (as such term is defined in section 2325 of this title); or

(E) seeks information under paragraph (2).

(2) A provider of electronic communication service or remote computing service shall disclose to a governmental entity the (A) name; (B) address; (C) local and long distance telephone connection records, or records of session times and durations; (D) length of service (including start date) and types of service utilized; (E) telephone or instrument number or other subscriber number or identity, including any temporarily assigned network address; and (F) means and source of payment (including any credit car or bank account number), of a subscriber to or customer of such service, when the governmental entity uses an administrative subpoena authorized by a Federal or State statute or a Federal or State grand jury or trial subpoena or any means available under paragraph (1).

(3) A governmental entity receiving records or information under this subsection is not required to provide notice to a subscriber or customer.

(d) *Requirements for court order.*—A court order for disclosure under subsection (b) or (c) may be issued by any court that is a court of competent jurisdiction and shall issue only if the governmental entity offers specific and articulable facts showing that there are reasonable grounds to believe that the contents of a wire or electronic communication, or the records or other information sought, are relevant and material to an ongoing criminal investigation. In the case of a State governmental authority, such a court order shall not issue if prohibited by the law of such State. A court issuing an order pursuant to this section, on a motion made promptly by the service provider, may quash or modify such order, if the information or records requested are unusually voluminous in nature or compliance with such order otherwise would cause an undue burden on such provider.

(e) *No cause of action against a provider disclosing information under this chapter.*— No cause of action shall lie in any court against any provider of wire or electronic communication service, its officers, employees, agents, or other specified persons for providing information, facilities, or assistance in accordance with the terms of a court order, warrant, subpoena *, statutory authorization*, or certification under this chapter.

(f) *Requirement to preserve evidence*.-
  (1) In general.—A provider of wire or electronic communication services or a remote computing service, upon the request of a governmental entity, shall take all necessary steps to preserve records and other evidence in its possession pending the issuance of a court order or other process.
  (2) Period of retention.—Records referred to in paragraph (1) shall be retained for a period of 90 days, which shall be extended for an additional 90-day period upon a renewed request by the governmental entity.

(g) *Presence of Officer not Required.*—Notwithstanding section 3105 of this title, the presence of an officer shall not be required for service or execution of a search warrant issued in accordance with this chapter requiring disclosure by a provider of electronic communications service or remote computing service of the contents of communications or records or other information pertaining to a subscriber to or customer of such service.

18 U.S.C. 2704. BACKUP PRESERVATION

(a) *Backup preservation.*—(1) A governmental entity acting under section 2703(b)(2) may include in its subpoena or court order a requirement that the service provider to whom the request is directed create a backup copy of the contents of the electronic communications sought in order to preserve those communications. Without notifying the subscriber or customer of such subpoena or court order, such service provider shall create such backup copy as soon as practicable consistent with its regular business practices and shall confirm to the governmental entity that such backup copy has been made. Such backup copy shall be created within two business days after receipt by the service provider of the subpoena or court order.

(2) Notice to the subscriber or customer shall be made by the governmental entity within three days after receipt of such confirmation, unless such notice is delayed pursuant to section 2705(a).

(3) The service provider shall not destroy such backup copy until the later of-
  (A) the delivery of the information; or
  (B) the resolution of any proceedings (including appeals of any proceeding) concerning the government's subpoena or court order.

(4) The service provider shall release such backup copy to the requesting governmental entity no sooner than fourteen days after the governmental entity's notice to the subscriber or customer if such service provider-

(A) has not received notice from the subscriber or customer that the subscriber or customer has challenged the governmental entity's request; and

(B) has not initiated proceedings to challenge the request of the governmental entity.

(5) A governmental entity may seek to require the creation of a backup copy under subsection

(a) (1) of this section if in its sole discretion such entity determines that there is reason to believe that notification under section 2703 of this title of the existence of the subpoena or court order may result in destruction of or tampering with evidence. This determination is not subject to challenge by the subscriber or customer or service provider.

(b) *Customer challenges.*—(1) Within fourteen days after notice by the governmental entity to the subscriber or customer under subsection (a)(2) of this section, such subscriber or customer may file a motion to quash such subpoena or vacate such court order, with copies served upon the governmental entity and with written notice of such challenge to the service provider. A motion to vacate a court order shall be filed in the court which issued such order. A motion to quash a subpoena shall be filed in the appropriate United States district court or State court. Such motion or application shall contain an affidavit or sworn statement-

(A) stating that the applicant is a customer or subscriber to the service from which the contents of electronic communications maintained for him have been sought; and

(B) stating the applicant's reasons for believing that the records sought are not relevant to a legitimate law enforcement inquiry or that there has not been substantial compliance with the provisions of this chapter in some other respect.

(2) Service shall be made under this section upon a governmental entity by delivering or mailing by registered or certified mail a copy of the papers to the person, office, or department specified in the notice which the customer has received pursuant to this chapter. For the purposes of this section, the term "delivery" has the meaning given that term in the Federal Rules of Civil Procedure.

(3) If the court finds that the customer has complied with paragraphs (1) and (2) of this subsection, the court shall order the governmental entity to file a sworn response, which may be filed in camera if the governmental entity includes in its response the reasons which make in camera review appropriate. If the court is unable to determine the motion or application on the basis of the parties' initial allegations and response, the court may conduct such additional proceedings as it deems appropriate. All such proceedings shall be completed and the motion or application decided as soon as practicable after the filing of the governmental entity's response.

(4) If the court finds that the applicant is not the subscriber or customer for whom the communications sought by the governmental entity are maintained, or that there is a reason to believe that the law enforcement inquiry is legitimate and that the communications sought are relevant to that inquiry, it shall deny the motion or application and order such process enforced. If the court finds that the applicant is

the subscriber or customer for whom the communications sought by the governmental entity are maintained, and that there is not a reason to believe that the communications sought are relevant to a legitimate law enforcement inquiry, or that there has not been substantial compliance with the provisions of this chapter, it shall order the process quashed.

(5) A court order denying a motion or application under this section shall not be deemed a final order and no interlocutory appeal may be taken therefrom by the customer.

18 U.S.C. 2705. Delayed Notice

(a) *Delay of notification.*—(1) A governmental entity acting under section 2703(b) of this title may-
  (A) where a court order is sought, include in the application a request, which the court shall grant, for an order delaying the notification required under section 2703(b) of this title for a period not to exceed ninety days, if the court determines that there is reason to believe that notification of the existence of the court order may have an adverse result described in paragraph (2) of this subsection; or
  (B) where an administrative subpoena authorized by a Federal or State statute or a Federal or State grand jury subpoena is obtained, delay the notification required under section 2703(b) of this title for a period not to exceed ninety days upon the execution of a written certification of a supervisory official that there is reason to believe that notification of the existence of the subpoena may have an adverse result described in paragraph (2) of this subsection.

(2) An adverse result for the purposes of paragraph (1) of this subsection is-
  (A) endangering the life or physical safety of an individual;
  (B) flight from prosecution;
  (C) destruction of or tampering with evidence;
  (D) intimidation of potential witnesses; or
  (E) otherwise seriously jeopardizing an investigation or unduly delaying a trial.

(3) The governmental entity shall maintain a true copy of certification under paragraph (1)(B).

(4) Extensions of the delay of notification provided in section 2703 of up to ninety days each may be granted by the court upon application, or by certification by a governmental entity, but only in accordance with subsection (b) of this section.

(5) Upon expiration of the period of delay of notification under paragraph (1) or (4) of this subsection, the governmental entity shall serve upon, or deliver by registered or first-class mail to, the customer or subscriber a copy of the process or request together with notice that-
  (A) states with reasonable specificity the nature of the law enforcement inquiry; and
  (B) informs such customer or subscriber-
    (i) that information maintained for such customer or subscriber by the service provider named in such process or request was supplied to or requested by that governmental authority and the date on which the supplying or request took place;
    (ii) that notification of such customer or subscriber was delayed;

(iii) what governmental entity or court made the certification or determination pursuant to which that delay was made; and

(iv) which provision of this chapter allowed such delay.

(6) As used in this subsection, the term "supervisory official" means the investigative agent in charge or assistant investigative agent in charge or an equivalent of an investigating agency's headquarters or regional office, or the chief prosecuting attorney or the first assistant prosecuting attorney or an equivalent of a prosecuting attorney's headquarters or regional office.

(b) *Preclusion of notice to subject of governmental access.*—A governmental entity acting under section 2703, when it is not required to notify the subscriber or customer under section 2703(b)(1), or to the extent that it may delay such notice pursuant to subsection (a) of this section, may apply to a court for an order commanding a provider of electronic communications service or remote computing service to whom a warrant, subpoena, or court order is directed, for such period as the court deems appropriate, not to notify any other person of the existence of the warrant, subpoena, or court order. The court shall enter such an order if it determines that there is reason to believe that notification of the existence of the warrant, subpoena, or court order will result in-

(1) endangering the life or physical safety of an individual;

(2) flight from prosecution;

(3) destruction of or tampering with evidence;

(4) intimidation of potential witnesses; or

(5) otherwise seriously jeopardizing an investigation or unduly delaying a trial.

18 U.S.C. 2706. Cost Reimbursement

(a) *Payment.*—Except as otherwise provided in subsection (c), a governmental entity obtaining the contents of communications, records, or other information under section 2702, 2703, or 2704 of this title shall pay to the person or entity assembling or providing such information a fee for reimbursement for such costs as are reasonably necessary and which have been directly incurred in searching for, assembling, reproducing, or otherwise providing such information. Such reimbursable costs shall include any costs due to necessary disruption of normal operations of any electronic communication service or remote computing service in which such information may be stored.

(b) *Amount.*—The amount of the fee provided by subsection (a) shall be as mutually agreed by the governmental entity and the person or entity providing the information, or, in the absence of agreement, shall be as determined by the court which issued the order for production of such information (or the court before which a criminal prosecution relating to such information would be brought, if no court order was issued for production of the information).

(c) *Exception.*—The requirement of subsection (a) of this section does not apply with respect to records or other information maintained by a communications common carrier that relate to telephone toll records and telephone listings obtained under section 2703 of this title. The court may, however, order a payment as described in subsection (a) if the court determines the information required is unusually voluminous in nature or otherwise caused an undue burden on the provider.

18 U.S.C. 2707. Civil Action

(a) *Cause of action.*—Except as provided in section 2703(e), any provider of electronic communication service, subscriber, or other person aggrieved by any violation of this chapter in which the conduct constituting the violation is engaged in with a knowing or intentional state of mind may, in a civil action, recover from the person or entity other than the United States which engaged in that violation such relief as may be appropriate.

(b) *Relief.*—In a civil action under this section, appropriate relief includes-

(1) such preliminary and other equitable or declaratory relief as may be appropriate;
(2) damages under subsection (c); and
(3) a reasonable attorney's fee and other litigation costs reasonably incurred.

(c) *Damages.*—The court may assess as damages in a civil action under this section the sum of the actual damages suffered by the plaintiff and any profits made by the violator as a result of the violation, but in no case shall a person entitled to recover receive less than the sum of $1,000. If the violation is willful or intentional, the court may assess punitive damages. In the case of a successful action to enforce liability under this section, the court may assess the costs of the action, together with reasonable attorney fees determined by the court.

(d) *Administrative Discipline.*—If a court or appropriate department or agency determines that the United States or any of its departments or agencies has violated any provision of this chapter, and the court or appropriate department or agency finds that the circumstances surrounding the violation raise serious questions about whether or not an officer or employee of the United States acted willfully or intentionally with respect to the possible violation, the department or agency shall, upon receipt of a true and correct copy of the decision and findings of the court or appropriate department or agency promptly initiate a proceeding to determine whether disciplinary action against the officer or employee is warranted. If the head of the department or agency involved determines that disciplinary action is not warranted, he or she shall notify the Inspector General with jurisdiction over the department or agency concerned and shall provide the Inspector General with the reasons for such determination.

(e) *Defense.*—A good faith reliance on-

(1) a court warrant or order, a grand jury subpoena, a legislative authorization, or a statutory authorization (including a request of a governmental entity under section 2703(f) of this title);
(2) a request of an investigative or law enforcement officer under section 2518(7) of this title; or
(3) a good faith determination that section 2511(3) of this title permitted the conduct complained of; is a complete defense to any civil or criminal action brought under this chapter or any other law.

(f) *Limitation.*—A civil action under this section may not be commenced later than two years after the date upon which the claimant first discovered or had a reasonable opportunity to discover the violation.

(g) *Improper Disclosure Is Violation.* —Any willful disclosure of a "record", as that term is defined in section 552a(a) of title 5, United States Code, obtained by an investigative or law enforcement officer, or governmental entity, pursuant to section 2703 of this title, or from a device installed pursuant to section 3123 or 3125 of this title, that is not a disclosure made in the proper performance of the official duties of the officer or governmental entity making the disclosure, is a violation of this chapter. This provision shall not apply to information previously lawfully disclosed (prior to the commencement of any civil or administrative proceeding under this chapter) to the public by a Federal, State, or local governmental entity or by the plaintiff in a civil action under this chapter.

18 U.S.C. 2708. Exclusivity of Remedies

The remedies and sanctions described in this chapter are the only judicial remedies and sanctions for nonconstitutional violations of this chapter.

18 U.S.C. 2709. Counterintelligence Access to Telephone Toll and Transactional Records

(a) *Duty to provide.*—A wire or electronic communication service provider shall comply with a request for subscriber information and toll billing records information, or electronic communication transactional records in its custody or possession made by the Director of the Federal Bureau of Investigation under subsection (b) of this section.

(b) *Required certification.*—The Director of the Federal Bureau of Investigation, or his designee in a position not lower than Deputy Assistant Director at Bureau headquarters or a Special Agent in Charge in a Bureau field office designated by the Director, may-

(1) request the name, address, length of service, and local and long distance toll billing records of a person or entity if the Director (or his designee) certifies in writing to the wire or electronic communication service provider to which the request is made that the name, address, length of service, and toll billing records sought are relevant to an authorized investigation to protect against international terrorism or clandestine intelligence activities, provided that such an investigation of a United States person is not conducted solely on the basis of activities protected by the first amendment to the Constitution of the United States; and

(2) request the name, address, and length of service of a person or entity if the Director (or his designee) certifies in writing to the wire or electronic communication service provider to which the request is made that the information sought is relevant to an authorized investigation to protect against international terrorism or clandestine intelligence activities, provided that such

an investigation of a United States person is not conducted solely upon the basis of activities protected by the first amendment to the Constitution of the United States.

(c) *Prohibition of certain disclosure.*—

(1) If the Director of the Federal Bureau of Investigation, or his designee in a position not lower than Deputy Assistant Director at Bureau headquarters or a Special Agent in Charge in a Bureau field office designated by the Director, certifies that otherwise there may result a danger to the national security of the United States, interference with a criminal, counter terrorism, or counterintelligence investigation, interference with diplomatic relations, or danger to the life or physical safety of any person, no wire or electronic communications service provider, or officer, employee, or agent thereof, shall disclose to any person (other than those to whom such disclosure is necessary to comply with the request or an attorney to obtain legal advice or legal assistance with respect to the request) that the Federal Bureau of Investigation has sought or obtained access to information or records under this section.

(2) The request shall notify the person or entity to whom the request is directed of the nondisclosure requirement under paragraph (1).

(3) Any recipient disclosing to those persons necessary to comply with the request or to an attorney to obtain legal advice or legal assistance with respect to the request shall inform such person of any applicable nondisclosure requirement. Any person who receives a disclosure under this subsection shall be subject to the same prohibitions on disclosure under paragraph (1).

(4) At the request of the Director of the Federal Bureau of Investigation or the designee of the Director, any person making or intending to make a disclosure under this section shall identify to the Director or such designee the person to whom such disclosure will be made or to whom such disclosure was made prior to the request, except that nothing in this section shall require a person to inform the Director or such designee of the identity of an attorney to whom disclosure was made or will be made to obtain legal advice or legal assistance with respect to the request under subsection (a).

(d) *Dissemination by bureau.*—The Federal Bureau of Investigation may disseminate information and records obtained under this section only as provided in guidelines approved by the Attorney General for foreign intelligence collection and foreign counterintelligence investigations conducted by the Federal Bureau of Investigation, and, with respect to dissemination to an agency of the United States, only if such information is clearly relevant to the authorized responsibilities of such agency.

(e) *Requirement that certain congressional bodies be informed.*—On a semiannual basis the Director of the Federal Bureau of Investigation shall fully inform the Permanent Select Committee on Intelligence of the House of Representatives and the Select Committee on Intelligence of the Senate, and the Committee on the Judiciary of the House of Representatives and the Committee on the Judiciary of the Senate, concerning all requests made under subsection (b) of this section.

(f) *Libraries.*—A library (as that term is defined in section 213(1) of the Library Services and Technology Act (20 U.S.C. 9122(1)), the services of which include access to the Internet, books, journals, magazines, newspapers, or other similar forms of communication in print or digitally by patrons for their use, review, examination, or circulation, is not a wire or electronic communication service provider for purposes of this section, unless the library is providing the services defined in section 2510(15) ("electronic communication service") of this title.

18 U.S.C. 2711. Definitions for Chapter

As used in this chapter-

(1) the terms defined in section 2510 of this title have, respectively, the definitions given such terms in that section;

(2) the term "remote computing service" means the provision to the public of computer storage or processing services by means of an electronic communications system;

(3) the term "court of competent jurisdiction" has the meaning assigned by section 3127, and includes any Federal court within that definition, without geographic limitation.

(4) the term "governmental entity" means a department or agency of the United States or State or political subdivision thereof.

18 U.S.C. 2712. Civil Action against the United States

(a) *In General.*– Any person who is aggrieved by any willful violation of this chapter or of chapter 119 of this title or of sections 106(a), 305(a), or 405(a) of the Foreign Intelligence Surveillance Act (50 U.S.C. 1801 et seq.) may commence an action in United States District Court against the United States to recover money damages. In any such action, if a person who is aggrieved successfully establishes a violation of this chapter or of chapter 119 of this title or of the above special provisions of title 50, the Court may assess as damages–

  (1) actual damages, but not less than $10,000, whichever amount is greater; and

  (2) litigation costs, reasonably incurred.

(b) *Procedures.* –

  (1) Any action against the United States under this section may be commenced only after a claim is presented to the appropriate department or agency under the procedures of the Federal Tort Claims Act, as set forth in title 28, United States Code.

  (2) Any action against the United States under this section shall be forever barred unless it is presented in writing to the appropriate Federal agency within 2 years after such claim accrues or unless action is begun within 6 months after the date of mailing, by certified or registered mail, of notice of final denial of the claim by the agency to which it was presented. The claim shall accrue on the date upon which the claimant first has a reasonable opportunity to discover the violation.

  (3) Any action under this section shall be tried in the court without a jury.

  (4) Notwithstanding any other provision of law, the procedures set forth in section 106(f), 305(g), or 405(f) of the Foreign Intelligence Surveillance Act of 1978 (50 U.S.C. 1801 et seq.) shall be the exclusive means by which materials governed by those sections may be reviewed.

  (5) An amount equal to any award against the United States under this section shall be reimbursed by the department or agency concerned to the fund described in

section 1304 of title 31, United States Code, out of any appropriation, fund, or other account (excluding any part of such appropriation, fund, or account that is available for the enforcement of any Federal law) that is available for the operating expenses of the department or agency concerned.

(c) *Administrative Discipline.* – If a court or appropriate department or agency determines that the United States or any of the departments or agencies has violated any provision of this chapter, and the court or appropriate department or agency finds that the circumstances surrounding the violation raise serious questions about whether or not an officer or employee of the Untied States acted willfully or intentionally with respect to the possible violation, the department or agency shall, upon receipt of a true and correct copy of the decision and findings of the court or appropriate department or agency promptly initiate a proceeding to determine whether disciplinary action against the officer or employee is warranted. If the head of the department or agency involved determines that disciplinary action is not warranted, he or she shall notify the Inspector General with jurisdiction over the department or agency concerned and shall provide the Inspector General with the reasons for such determination.

(d) *Exclusive Remedy.* – Any action against the United States under this subsection shall be the exclusive remedy against the United States for any claims within the purview of this section.

(e) *Stay of Proceedings.* –

(1) Upon the motion of the united States, the curt shall stay any action commenced under this section f the court determines that civil discovery will adversely affect the ability of the Government to conduct a related investigation or the prosecution of a related criminal case. Such a stay shall toll the limitations periods of paragraph (2) of subsection (b).

(2) In this subsection, the terms "related criminal case" and "related investigation" means an actual prosecution or investigation in progress at the time at which the request for the stay or any subsequent motion to lift the stay is made. In determining whether any investigation or a criminal case is related to an action commenced under this section, the court shall consider the degree of similarity between the parties, witnesses, facts, and circumstances involved in the 2 proceedings, without requiring that nay one or more factors be identical.

(3) In requesting a stay under paragraph (1), the Government may, in appropriate cases submit evidence ex parte in order to avoid disclosing any matter that may adversely affect a related investigation or a related criminal case. If the Government makes such an ex parte submission, the plaintiff shall be given an opportunity to make a submission to the court, not ex parte, and the court may, in its discretion, request further information from either party.

18 U.S.C. 3121. General Prohibition on Pen Register and Tape and Trace Device Use; Exception

(a) *In general.*—Except as provided in this section, no person may install or use a pen register or a trap and trace device without first obtaining a court order under section

3123 of this title or under the Foreign Intelligence Surveillance Act of 1978 (50 U.S.C. 1801 et seq.).

(b) *Exception.*—The prohibition of subsection (a) does not apply with respect to the use of a pen register or a trap and trace device by a provider of electronic or wire communication service-

(1) relating to the operation, maintenance, and testing of a wire or electronic communication service or to the protection of the rights or property of such provider, or to the protection of users of that service from abuse of service or unlawful use of service; or

(2) to record the fact that a wire or electronic communication was initiated or completed in order to protect such provider, another provider furnishing service toward the completion of the wire communication, or a user of that service, from fraudulent, unlawful or abusive use of service; or (3) where the consent of the user of that service has been obtained.

(c) *Limitation.*—A government agency authorized to install and use a pen register or trap and trace device under this chapter or under State law shall use technology reasonably available to it that restricts the recording or decoding of electronic or other impulses to the dialing, routing, addressing, and signaling information utilized in identifying the origination or destination of wire or electronic communications.

(d) *Penalty.*—Whoever knowingly violates subsection (a) shall be fined under this title or imprisoned not more than one year, or both.

18 U.S.C. 3122. Application for an Order for a Pen Register or a Trap and Trace Device

(a) *Application.*—

(1) An attorney for the Government may make application for an order or an extension of an order under section 3123 of this title authorizing or approving the installation and use of a pen register or a trap and trace device under this chapter, in writing under oath or equivalent affirmation, to a court of competent jurisdiction.

(2) Unless prohibited by State law, a State investigative or law enforcement officer may make application for an order or an extension of an order under section 3123 of this title authorizing or approving the installation and use of a pen register or a trap and trace device under this chapter, in writing under oath or equivalent affirmation, to a court of competent jurisdiction of such State.

(b) *Contents of application.*—An application under subsection (a) of this section shall include-

(1) the identity of the attorney for the Government or the State law enforcement or investigative officer making the application and the identity of the law enforcement agency conducting the investigation; and

(2) a certification by the applicant that the information likely to be obtained is relevant to an ongoing criminal investigation being conducted by that agency.

18 U.S.C. 3123. Issuance of an Order for a Pen Register or a Trap and Trace Device

(a) *In general.-*

(1) Upon an application made under section 3122(a)(1) of this title, the court shall enter an ex parte order authorizing the installation and use of a pen register or a trap and trace device if the court finds, based on facts contained in the application, that the information likely to be obtained by such installation and use is relevant to an ongoing criminal investigation. Such order shall, upon service of such order, apply to any entity providing wire or electronic communication service in the United States whose assistance may facilitate the execution of the order.

(2) Upon an application made under section 3122(a)(2) of this title, the court shall enter an ex parte order authorizing the installation and use of a pen register or a trap and trace device within the jurisdiction of the court if the court finds, based on facts contained in the application, that the information likely to be obtained by such installation and use is relevant to an ongoing criminal investigation.

(3) (A) Where the law enforcement agency implementing an ex part order under this subsection seeks to do so by installing and using its own pen register or trap and trace device on a packet-switched data network of a provider of electronic communication service to the public the agency shall ensure that a record will be maintained which will identify –

(i) any officer or officers who installed the device and any officer or officers who accessed the device to obtain information from the network;

(ii) the date and time the device was installed, the date and time the device was uninstalled, and the date, time, and duration of each time the device is accessed to obtain information;

(iii) the configuration of the device at the time of its installation and anysubsequent modification thereof; and

(iv) any information which has been collected by the device.

To the extent that the pen register or trap and trace device can be set automatically to record this information electronically, the record shall be maintained electronically throughout the installation and use of the such device.

(B) The record maintained under subparagraph (A) shall be provided ex parte and under seal to the court which entered the ex parte order authorizing the installation and use of the device within 30 days after termination of the order (including any extensions thereof).

(b) *Contents of order.*—An order issued under this section-

(1) shall specify-

(A) the identity, if known, of the person to whom is leased or in whose name is listed the telephone line or other facility to which the pen register or trap and trace device is to be attached or applied;

(B) the identity, if known, of the person who is the subject of the criminal investigation;

(C) the attributes of the communications to which the order applies, including the number or other identifier and, if known, the location of the telephone line or other facility to which the pen register or trap and trace device is to be attached or applied, and, in the case of an order authorizing installation and use of a trap and trace device under subsection (a)(2), the geographic limits of the order; and

(D) a statement of the offense to which the information likely to be obtained by the pen register or trap and trace device relates; and

(2) shall direct, upon the request of the applicant, the furnishing of information, facilities, and technical assistance necessary to accomplish the installation of the pen register or trap and trace device under section 3124 of this title.

(c) *Time period and extensions.*—

(1) An order issued under this section shall authorize the installation and use of a pen register or a trap and trace device for a period not to exceed sixty days.

(2) Extensions of such an order may be granted, but only upon an application for an order under section 3122 of this title and upon the judicial finding required by subsection (a) of this section. The period of extension shall be for a period not to exceed sixty days.

(d) *Nondisclosure of existence of pen register or a trap and trace device.*—An order authorizing or approving the installation and use of a pen register or a trap and trace device shall direct that-

(1) the order be sealed until otherwise ordered by the court; and

(2) the person owning or leasing the line or other facility to which the pen register or a trap and trace device is attached, or applied, or who is obligated by the order to provide assistance to the applicant, not disclose the existence of the pen register or trap and trace device or the existence of the investigation to the listed subscriber, or to any other person, unless or until otherwise ordered by the court.

18 U.S.C. 3124. Assistance in Installation and Use of a Pen Register or a Trap and Trace Device

(a) *Pen registers.*—Upon the request of an attorney for the Government or an officer of a law enforcement agency authorized to install and use a pen register under this chapter, a provider of wire or electronic communication service, landlord, custodian, or other person shall furnish such investigative or law enforcement officer forthwith all information, facilities, and technical assistance necessary to accomplish the installation of the pen register unobtrusively and with a minimum of interference with the services that the person so ordered by the court accords the party with respect to whom the installation and use is to take place, if such assistance is directed by a court order as provided in section 3123(b)(2) of this title.

(b) *Trap and trace device.*—Upon the request of an attorney for the Government or an officer of a law enforcement agency authorized to receive the results of a trap and trace device under this chapter, a provider of a wire or electronic communication service, landlord, custodian, or other person shall install such device forthwith on the appropriate line or other facility and shall furnish such investigative or law enforcement officer all additional information, facilities and technical assistance including installation and operation of the device unobtrusively and with a minimum of interference with the services that the person so ordered by the court accords the party with respect to whom the installation and use is to take place, if such installation and assistance is directed by a court order as provided in section 3123(b)(2) of this title. Unless otherwise ordered by the court, the results of the trap and trace device shall be furnished, pursuant to section 3123(b) or section 3125 of this title, to the officer of a law enforcement agency, designated in the court order, at reasonable intervals during regular business hours for the duration of the order.

(c) *Compensation.*—A provider of a wire or electronic communication service, landlord, custodian, or other person who furnishes facilities or technical assistance pursuant to this section shall be reasonably compensated for such reasonable expenses incurred in providing such facilities and assistance.

(d) *No cause of action against a provider disclosing information under this chapter.*—No cause of action shall lie in any court against any provider of a wire or electronic communication service, its officers, employees, agents, or other specified persons for providing information, facilities, or assistance in accordance with a court order under this chapter or request pursuant to section 3125 of this title.

(e) *Defense.*—A good faith reliance on a court order under this chapter, a request pursuant to section 3125 of this title, a legislative authorization, or a statutory authorization is a complete defense against any civil or criminal action brought under this chapter or any other law.

(f) *Communications assistance enforcement orders.*—Pursuant to section 2522, an order may be issued to enforce the assistance capability and capacity requirements under the Communications Assistance for Law Enforcement Act.

18 U.S.C. 3125. Emergency Pen Register and Trap and Trace Device Installation

(a) Notwithstanding any other provision of this chapter, any investigative or law enforcement officer, specially designated by the Attorney General, the Deputy Attorney General, the Associate Attorney General, any Assistant Attorney General, any acting Assistant Attorney General, or any Deputy Assistant Attorney General, or by the principal prosecuting attorney of any State or subdivision thereof acting pursuant to a statute of that State, who reasonably determines that-

(1) an emergency situation exists that involves-

(A) immediate danger of death or serious bodily injury to any person; ~~or~~

(B) conspiratorial activities characteristic of organized crime;

(C) an immediate threat to a national security interest; or

(D) an ongoing attack on a protected computer (as defined in section 1030) that constitutes a crime punishable by a term of imprisonment greater than one year; that requires the installation and use of a pen register or a trap and trace device before an order authorizing such installation and use can, with due diligence, be obtained, and

(2) there are grounds upon which an order could be entered under this chapter to authorize such installation and use; may have installed and use a pen register or trap and trace device if, within forty-eight hours after the installation has

occurred, or begins to occur, an order approving the installation or use is issued in accordance with section 3123 of this title.

(b) In the absence of an authorizing order, such use shall immediately terminate when the information sought is obtained, when the application for the order is denied or when forty-eight hours have lapsed since the installation of the pen register or trap and trace device, whichever is earlier.

(c) The knowing installation or use by any investigative or law enforcement officer of a pen register or trap and trace device pursuant to subsection (a) without application for the authorizing order within forty-eight hours of the installation shall constitute a violation of this chapter.

(d) A provider of a wire or electronic service, landlord, custodian, or other person who furnished facilities or technical assistance pursuant to this section shall be reasonably compensated for such reasonable expenses incurred in providing such facilities and assistance.

18 U.S.C. 3126. Reports Concerning Pen Registers and Trap and Trace Devices

The Attorney General shall annually report to Congress on the number of pen register orders and orders for trap and trace devices applied for by law enforcement agencies of the Department of Justice, which report shall include information concerning-

(1) the period of interceptions authorized by the order, and the number and duration of any extensions of the order;
(2) the offense specified in the order or application, or extension of an order;
(3) the number of investigations involved;
(4) the number and nature of the facilities affected; and
(5) the identity, including district, of the applying investigative or law enforcement agency making the application and the person authorizing the order.

18 U.S.C. 3127. Definitions for Chapter

As used in this chapter-

(1) the terms "wire communication", "electronic communication", "electronic communication service" and "contents" have the meanings set forth for such terms in section 2510 of this title;
(2) the term "court of competent jurisdiction" means-
    (A) any district court of the United States (including a magistrate of such a court) or a United States Court of Appeals having jurisdiction over the offense being investigated; or
    (B) a court of general criminal jurisdiction of a State authorized by the law of that State to enter orders authorizing the use of a pen register or a trap and trace device;

(3) the term "pen register" means a device or process which records or decodes or other dialing, routing, addressing, and signaling information reasonably likely to identify the source of a wire or electronic communication, provided, however, that such information shall not include the contents of any communication, but such term does not include any device or process used by a provider or customer of a wire or electronic communication service for billing, or recording as an incident to billing, for communications services provided by such provider or any device or process used by a provider or customer of a wire communication service for cost accounting or other like purposes in the ordinary course of its business;
(4) the term "trap and trace device" means a device or process which captures the incoming electronic or other impulses which identify the originating number or other dialing, routing, addressing, and signaling information reasonably likely to identify the source of a wire or electronic communication, provided, however, that such information shall not include the contents of any communication;
(5) the term "attorney for the Government" has the meaning given such term for the purposes of the Federal Rules of Criminal Procedure; and
(6) the term "State" means a State, the District of Columbia, Puerto Rico, and any other possession or territory of the United States.

FOREIGN INTELLIGENCE SURVEILLANCE ACT (FISA)

50 U.S.C. 1801. Definitions

As used in this subchapter:
(a) 'Foreign power' means–
  (1) a foreign government or any component thereof, whether or not recognized by the United States;
  (2) a faction of a foreign nation or nations, not substantially composed of United States persons;
  (3) an entity that is openly acknowledged by a foreign government or governments to be directed and controlled by such foreign government or governments;
  (4) a group engaged in international terrorism or activities in preparation therefor;
  (5) a foreign-based political organization, not substantially composed of United States persons;
  (6) an entity that is directed and controlled by a foreign government or governments; or
  [Sec. 110(a)(1)(C)] (7) an entity not substantially composed of United States persons that is engaged in the international proliferation of weapons of mass destruction.
(b) 'Agent of a foreign power' means–
  (1) any person other than a United States person, who–
    (A) acts in the United States as an officer or employee of a foreign power, or as a member of a foreign power as defined in subsection (a)(4) of this section;
    (B) acts for or on behalf of a foreign power which engages in clandestine intelligence activities in the United States contrary to the interests of the United States, when the circumstances of such person's presence in the

United States indicate that such person may engage in such activities in the United States, or when such person knowingly aids or abets any person in the conduct of such activities or knowingly conspires with any person to engage in such activities;

(C) engages in international terrorism or activities in preparation therefore;

[Sec. 110(a)(2)(C)] (D) engages in the international proliferation of weapons of mass destruction, or activities in preparation therefor; or

(E) engages in the international proliferation of weapons of mass destruction, or activities in preparation therefor for or on behalf of a foreign power;

or

(2) any person who–

(A) knowingly engages in clandestine intelligence gathering activities for or on behalf of a foreign power, which activities involve or may involve a violation of the criminal statutes of the United States;

(B) pursuant to the direction of an intelligence service or network of a foreign power, knowingly engages in any other clandestine intelligence activities for or on behalf of such foreign power, which activities involve or are about to involve a violation of the criminal statutes of the United States;

(C) knowingly engages in sabotage or international terrorism, or activities that are in preparation therefor, or on behalf of a foreign power;

(D) knowingly enters the United States under a false or fraudulent identity for or on behalf of a foreign power or, while in the United States, knowingly assumes a false or fraudulent identity for or on behalf of a foreign power; or

(E) knowingly aids or abets any person in the conduct of activities described in subparagraph (A), (B), or (C) or knowingly conspires with any person to engage in activities described in subparagraph (A), (B), or (C).

(c) 'International terrorism' means activities that–

(1) involve violent acts or acts dangerous to human life that are a violation of the criminal laws of the United States or of any State, or that would be a criminal violation if committed within the jurisdiction of the United States or any State;

(2) appear to be intended–

(A) to intimidate or coerce a civilian population;

(B) to influence the policy of a government by intimidation or coercion; or

(C) to affect the conduct of a government by assassination or kidnapping; and

(3) occur totally outside the United States, or transcend national boundaries in terms of the means by which they are accomplished, the persons they appear intended to coerce or intimidate, or the locale in which their perpetrators operate or seek asylum.

(d) 'Sabotage' means activities that involve a violation of chapter 105 of Title 18, or that would involve such a violation if committed against the United States.

(e) 'Foreign intelligence information' means–

(1) information that relates to, and if concerning a United States person is necessary to, the ability of the United States to protect against–

(A) actual or potential attack or other grave hostile acts of a foreign power or an agent of a foreign power;

[Sec. 110(a)(3)]

(B) sabotage, international terrorism, or the international proliferation of weapons of mass destruction by a foreign power or an agent of a foreign power; or

(C) clandestine intelligence activities by an intelligence service or network of a foreign power or by an agent of a foreign power; or

(2) information with respect to a foreign power or foreign territory that relates to, and if concerning a United States person is necessary to–

(A) the national defense or the security of the United States; or

(B) the conduct of the foreign affairs of the United States.

(f) 'Electronic surveillance' means–

(1) the acquisition by an electronic, mechanical, or other surveillance device of the contents of any wire or radio communication sent by or intended to be received by a particular, known United States person who is in the United States, if the contents are acquired by intentionally targeting that United States person, under circumstances in which a person has a reasonable expectation of privacy and a warrant would be required for law enforcement purposes;

(2) the acquisition by an electronic, mechanical, or other surveillance device of the contents of any wire communication to or from a person in the United States, without the consent of any party thereto, if such acquisition occurs in the United States, does not include the acquisition of those communications of computer trespassers that would be permissible under section 2511(2)(i) of title 18, United States Code;

(3) the intentional acquisition by an electronic, mechanical, or other surveillance device of the contents of any radio communication, under circumstances in which a person has a reasonable expectation of privacy and a warrant would be required for law enforcement purposes, and if both the sender and all intended recipients are located within the United States; or

(4) the installation or use of an electronic, mechanical, or other surveillance device in the United States for monitoring to acquire information, other than from a wire or radio communication, under circumstances in which a person has a reasonable expectation of privacy and a warrant would be required for law enforcement purposes.

(g) 'Attorney General' means the Attorney General of the United States (or Acting Attorney General) or the Deputy Attorney General, or, upon the designation of the Attorney General, the Assistant Attorney General for National Security under section 507A of title 28, United States Code.

(h) 'Minimization procedures', with respect to electronic surveillance, means–

(1) specific procedures, which shall be adopted by the Attorney General, that are reasonably designed in light of the purpose and technique of the particular surveillance, to minimize the acquisition and retention, and prohibit the dissemination, of nonpublicly available information concerning unconsenting United States persons consistent with the need of the United States to obtain, produce, and disseminate foreign intelligence information;

(2) procedures that require that nonpublicly available information, which is not foreign intelligence information, as defined in subsection (e)(1) of this section, shall not be disseminated in a manner that identifies any United States person, without such person's consent, unless such person's identity is necessary to understand foreign intelligence information or assess its importance;

(3) notwithstanding paragraphs (1) and (2), procedures that allow for the retention and dissemination of information that is evidence of a crime which has been, is being, or is about to be committed and that is to be retained or disseminated for law enforcement purposes; and

(4) notwithstanding paragraphs (1), (2), and (3), with respect to any electronic surveillance approved pursuant to section 1802(a) of this title, procedures that require that no contents of any communication to which a United States person is a party shall be disclosed, disseminated, or used for any purpose or retained for longer than 72 hours unless a court order under section 1805 of this title is obtained or unless the Attorney General determines that the information indicates a threat of death or serious bodily harm to any person.

(i) 'United States person' means a citizen of the United States, an alien lawfully admitted for permanent residence (as defined in section 1101(a)(20) of Title 8), an unincorporated association a substantial number of members of which are citizens of the United States or aliens lawfully admitted for permanent residence, or a corporation which is incorporated in the United States, but does not include a corporation or an association which is a foreign power, as defined in subsection (a)(1), (2), or (3) of this section.

(j) 'United States', when used in a geographic sense, means all areas under the territorial sovereignty of the United States and the Trust Territory of the Pacific Islands.

(k) 'Aggrieved person' means a person who is the target of an electronic surveillance or any other person whose communications or activities were subject to electronic surveillance.

(l) 'Wire communication' means any communication while it is being carried by a wire, cable, or other like connection furnished or operated by any person engaged as a common carrier in providing or operating such facilities for the transmission of interstate or foreign communications.

(m) 'Person' means any individual, including any officer or employee of the Federal Government, or any group, entity, association, corporation, or foreign power.

(n) 'Contents', when used with respect to a communication, includes any information concerning the identity of the parties to such communication or the existence, substance, purport, or meaning of that communication.

(o) 'State' means any State of the United States, the District of Columbia, the Commonwealth of Puerto Rico, the Trust Territory of the Pacific Islands, and any territory or possession of the United States.

[Sec. 110(a)(4)] (p) 'Weapon of mass destruction' means.–

(1) any explosive, incendiary, or poison gas device that is designed, intended, or has the capability to cause a mass casualty incident;

(2) any weapon that is designed, intended, or has the capability to cause death or serious bodily injury to a significant number of persons through the release, dissemination, or impact of toxic or poisonous chemicals or their precursors;

(3) any weapon involving a biological agent, toxin, or vector (as such terms are defined in section 178 of title 18, United States Code) that is designed, intended, or has the capability to cause death, illness, or serious bodily injury to a significant number of persons; or

(4) any weapon that is designed, intended, or has the capability to release radiation or radioactivity causing death, illness, or serious bodily injury to a significant number of persons.

[Sec. 401] **50 U.S.C. 1801 note [P.L. 110-261, §401] Severability.**

If any provision of this Act [P.L. 110-261], any amendment made by this Act, or the application thereof to any person or circumstances is held invalid, the validity of the remainder of the Act, of any such amendments, and of the application of such provisions to other persons and circumstances shall not be affected thereby.

50 U.S.C. 1802. Electronic Surveillance Authorization Without Court Order; Certification by Attorney General; Reports to Congressional Committees; Transmittal Under Seal; Duties and Compensation of Communication Common Carrier; Applications; Jurisdiction of Court

(a) (1) Notwithstanding any other law, the President, through the Attorney General, may authorize electronic surveillance without a court order under this subchapter to acquire foreign intelligence information for periods of up to one year if the Attorney General certifies in writing under oath that-

(A) the electronic surveillance is solely directed at-

(i) the acquisition of the contents of communications transmitted by means of communications used exclusively between or among foreign powers, as defined in section 1801(a)(1), (2), or (3) of this title; or

(ii) the acquisition of technical intelligence, other than the spoken communications of individuals, from property or premises under the open and exclusive control of a foreign power, as defined in section 1801(a)(1), (2), or (3) of this title;

(B) there is no substantial likelihood that the surveillance will acquire the contents of any communication to which a United States person is a party; and

(C) the proposed minimization procedures with respect to such surveillance meet the definition of minimization procedures under section 1801(h) of this title;

and if the Attorney General reports such minimization procedures and any changes thereto to the House Permanent Select Committee on Intelligence and the Senate Select Committee on Intelligence at least thirty days prior to their effective date, unless the Attorney General determines immediate action is required and notifies the committees immediately of such minimization procedures and the reason for their becoming effective immediately.

(2) An electronic surveillance authorized by this subsection may be conducted only in accordance with the Attorney General's certification and the minimization procedures adopted by him. The Attorney General shall assess compliance with such procedures and shall report such assessments to the House Permanent Select Committee on Intelligence and the Senate Select Committee on Intelligence under the provisions of section 1808(a) of this title.

(3) The Attorney General shall immediately transmit under seal to the court established under section 1803(a) of this title a copy of his certification. Such certification shall be maintained under security measures established by the Chief Justice with the

concurrence of the Attorney General, in consultation with the Director of National Intelligence, and shall remain sealed unless–

(A) an application for a court order with respect to the surveillance is made under sections 1801(h)(4) and 1804 of this title; or

(B) the certification is necessary to determine the legality of the surveillance under section 1806(f) of this title.

(4) With respect to electronic surveillance authorized by this subsection, the Attorney General may direct a specified communication common carrier to-

(A) furnish all information, facilities, or technical assistance necessary to accomplish the electronic surveillance in such a manner as will protect its secrecy and produce a minimum of interference with the services that such carrier is providing its customers; and

(B) maintain under security procedures approved by the Attorney General and the Director of National Intelligence any records concerning the surveillance or the aid furnished which such carrier wishes to retain.

The Government shall compensate, at the prevailing rate, such carrier for furnishing such aid.

(b) Applications for a court order under this subchapter are authorized if the President has, by written authorization, empowered the Attorney General to approve applications to the court having jurisdiction under section 1803 of this title, and a judge to whom an application is made may, notwithstanding any other law, grant an order, in conformity with section 1805 of this title, approving electronic surveillance of a foreign power or an agent of a foreign power for the purpose of obtaining foreign intelligence information, except that the court shall not have jurisdiction to grant any order approving electronic surveillance directed solely as described in paragraph (1)(A) of subsection (a) of this section unless such surveillance may involve the acquisition of communications of any United States person.

50 U.S.C. 1803. DESIGNATION OF JUDGES

(a) (1) *Court to hear applications and grant orders; record of denial; transmittal to court of review*

[Sec. 109(a)] The Chief Justice of the United States shall publicly designate 11 district court judges from at least seven of the United States judicial circuits of whom no fewer than 3 shall reside within 20 miles of the District of Columbia who shall constitute a court which shall have jurisdiction to hear applications for and grant orders approving electronic surveillance anywhere within the United States under the procedures set forth in this chapter, except that no judge designated under this subsection (except when sitting en banc under paragraph (2) shall hear the same application for electronic surveillance under this chapter which has been denied previously by another judge designated under this subsection. If any judge so designated denies an application for an order authorizing electronic surveillance under this chapter, such judge shall provide immediately for the record a written statement of each reason for his decision and, on motion of the United States, the record shall be transmitted, under seal, to the court of review established in subsection (b) of this section.

[Sec. 109(b)(1)] (2)(A) The court established under this subsection may, on its own initiative, or upon the request of the Government in any proceeding or a party under section 501(f)[50 U.S.C. 1861(f)] or paragraph (4) or (5) of section 702(h)[50 U.S.C. 1881a(h)], hold a hearing or rehearing, en banc, when ordered by a majority of the judges that constitute such court upon a determination that–

(i) en banc consideration is necessary to secure or maintain uniformity of the court's decisions; or

(ii) the proceeding involves a question of exceptional importance.

(B) Any authority granted by this Act to a judge of the court established under this subsection may be exercised by the court en banc. When exercising such authority, the court en banc shall comply with any requirements of this Act on the exercise of such authority.

(C) For purposes of this paragraph, the court en banc shall consist of all judges who constitute the court established under this subsection..

(b) *Court of review; record, transmittal to Supreme Court*

The Chief Justice shall publicly designate three judges, one of whom shall be publicly designated as the presiding judge, from the United States district courts or courts of appeals who together shall comprise a court of review which shall have jurisdiction to review the denial of any application made under this chapter. If such court determines that the application was properly denied, the court shall immediately provide for the record a written statement of each reason for its decision and, on petition of the United States for a writ of certiorari, the record shall be transmitted under seal to the Supreme Court, which shall have jurisdiction to review such decision.

(c) *Expeditious conduct of proceedings; security measures for maintenance of records*

Proceedings under this chapter shall be conducted as expeditiously as possible. The record of proceedings under this chapter, including applications made and orders granted, shall be maintained under security measures established by the Chief Justice in consultation with the Attorney General and the Director of National Intelligence.

(d) *Tenure*

Each judge designated under this section shall so serve for a maximum of seven years and shall not be eligible for redesignation, except that the judges first designated under subsection (a) of this section shall be designated for terms of from one to seven years so that one term expires each year, and that judges first designated under subsection (b) of this section shall be designated for terms of three, five, and seven years.

[Sec. 403(a)(1)(B)(ii)(I)](e)(1) Three judges designated under subsection (a) of this section who reside within 20 miles of the District of Columbia, or, if all of such judges are unavailable, other judges of the court established under subsection (a) of this section as may be designated by the presiding judge of such court, shall comprise a petition review pool which shall have jurisdiction to review petitions filed pursuant to section 1861(f)(1) or 702(h)(4)[50 U.S.C. 1881a(h)(4)]of this title.

[Sec. 403(a)(1)(B)(ii)(II)](2) Not later than 60 days after March 9, 2006, the court established under subsection (a) of this section shall adopt and, consistent with the protection of national security, publish procedures for the review of petitions filed pursuant to section 1861(f)(1) or 702(h)(4)[50 U.S.C. 1881a(h)(4)]of this title by the panel established under paragraph (1). Such procedures shall provide that review of a petition shall be conducted in camera and shall also provide for the designation of an acting presiding judge.

[Sec. 404(b)(3)] *Challenge of directives; protection from liability; use of information* – Notwithstanding any other provision of this Act or of the Foreign Intelligence Surveillance Act of 1978 (50 U.S.C. 1801 et seq.)– (A) section 103(e) of such Act, as amended by section 403(a)(1)(B)(ii), shall continue to apply with respect to any directive issued pursuant to section 702(h) of such Act, as added by section 101(a);

[Sec. 109(c)(2)] (f)(1) A judge of the court established under subsection (a), the court established under subsection (b) or a judge of that court, or the Supreme Court of the United States or a justice of that court, may, in accordance with the rules of their respective courts, enter a stay of an order or an order modifying an order of the court established under subsection (a) or the court established under subsection (b) entered under any title of this Act, while the court established under subsection

(a) conducts a rehearing, while an appeal is pending to the court established under subsection (b), or while a petition of certiorari is pending in the Supreme Court of the United States, or during the pendency of any review by that court.

(2) The authority described in paragraph (1) shall apply to an order entered under any provision of this Act.

(g) ~~(f)~~ (1) The courts established pursuant to subsections (a) and (b) of this section may establish such rules and procedures, and take such actions, as are reasonably necessary to administer their responsibilities under this chapter.

(2) The rules and procedures established under paragraph (1), and any modifications of such rules and procedures, shall be recorded, and shall be transmitted to the following:

(A) All of the judges on the court established pursuant to subsection (a) of this section.

(B) All of the judges on the court of review established pursuant to subsection (b) of this section.

(C) The Chief Justice of the United States.

(D) The Committee on the Judiciary of the Senate.

(E) The Select Committee on Intelligence of the Senate.

(F) The Committee on the Judiciary of the House of Representatives.

(G) The Permanent Select Committee on Intelligence of the House of Representatives.

(3) The transmissions required by paragraph (2) shall be submitted in unclassified form, but may include a classified annex.

[Sec. 109(d)] (i) Nothing in this Act shall be construed to reduce or contravene the inherent authority of the court established under subsection (a) to determine or enforce compliance with an order or a rule of such court or with a procedure approved by such court.

[Sec. 404(a)(5)] *Jurisdiction of foreign intelligence surveillance court.*– Notwithstanding any other provision of this Act or of the Foreign Intelligence Surveillance Act of 1978 (50 U.S.C. 1801 et seq.), section 103(e) of the Foreign Intelligence Surveillance Act (50 U.S.C. 1803(e)), as amended by section 5(a) of the Protect America Act of 2007 (Public Law 110-55; 121 Stat. 556), shall continue to apply with respect to a directive issued pursuant to section 105B of the Foreign Intelligence Surveillance Act of 1978, as added by section 2 of the Protect America Act of 2007, until the later of–

(A) the expiration of all orders, authorizations, or directives referred to in paragraph (1); or (B) the date on which final judgment is entered for any petition or other litigation relating to such order, authorization, or directive.
[Sec. 404(a)(8)] *Effective date*.– Paragraphs (1) through (7) shall take effect as if enacted on August 5, 2007.

50 U.S.C. 1804. Applications for Court Orders

(a) *Submission by Federal officer; approval of Attorney General; contents*
Each application for an order approving electronic surveillance under this subchapter shall be made by a Federal officer in writing upon oath or affirmation to a judge having jurisdiction under section 1803 of this title. Each application shall require the approval of the Attorney General based upon his finding that it satisfies the criteria and requirements of such application as set forth in this subchapter. It shall include-

(1) the identity of the Federal officer making the application;
[Sec. 104(a)(1)(A)]

(2) the identity, if known, or a description of the specific target of the electronic surveillance;

(3) a statement of the facts and circumstances relied upon by the applicant to justify his belief that-
   (A) the target of the electronic surveillance is a foreign power or an agent of a foreign power; and
   (B) each of the facilities or places at which the electronic surveillance is directed is being used, or is about to be used, by a foreign power or an agent of a foreign power;

(4) a statement of the proposed minimization procedures; [Sec. 104(a)(1)(C)]

(5) a description of the nature of the information sought and the type of communications or activities to be subjected to the surveillance;
[Sec. 104(a)(1)(D)]

(6) a certification or certifications by the Assistant to the President for National Security Affairs, ~~or~~ an executive branch official or officials designated by the President from among those executive officers employed in the area of national security or defense and appointed by the President with the advice and consent of the Senate, or the Deputy Director of the Federal Bureau of Investigation, if designated by the President as a certifying official–
   (A) that the certifying official deems the information sought to be foreign intelligence information;
   (B) that a significant purpose of the surveillance is to obtain foreign intelligence information;
   (C) that such information cannot reasonably be obtained by normal investigative techniques;
   (D) that designates the type of foreign intelligence information being sought according to the categories described in section 1801(e) of this title; and

(E) including a statement of the basis for the certification that-
(i) the information sought is the type of foreign intelligence information designated; and
(ii) such information cannot reasonably be obtained by normal investigative techniques; [Sec. 104(a)(1)(E)]

(7) a summary statement of the means by which the surveillance will be effected and a statement whether physical entry is required to effect the surveillance;

(8) a statement of the facts concerning all previous applications that have been made to any judge under this subchapter involving any of the persons, facilities, or places specified in the application, and the action taken on each previous application; and

(9) a statement of the period of time for which the electronic surveillance is required to be maintained, and if the nature of the intelligence gathering is such that the approval of the use of electronic surveillance under this subchapter should not automatically terminate when the described type of information has first been obtained,

(10)a description of facts supporting the belief that additional information of the same type will be obtained thereafter. ; and-[Sec. 104(a)(1)(A)]. -[Sec. 104(a)(2)]

Additional affidavits or certifications

The Attorney General may require any other affidavit or certification from any other officer in connection with the application.

Additional information

The judge may require the applicant to furnish such other information as may be necessary to make the determinations required by section 1805 of this title.

Requirements regarding certain application [Sec. 104(a)(1)(4)](1)

(A) Upon written request of the Director of the Federal Bureau of Investigation, the Secretary of Defense, the Secretary of State, the Director of National Intelligence, or the Director of the Central Intelligence Agency, the Attorney General shall personally review under subsection (a) an application under that subsection for a target described in section 1801(b)(2) of this title.

(B) Except when disabled or otherwise unavailable to make a request referred to in subparagraph (A), an official referred to in that subparagraph may not delegate the authority to make a request referred to in that subparagraph.

(C) Each official referred to in subparagraph (A) with authority to make a request under that subparagraph shall take appropriate actions in advance to ensure that delegation of such authority is clearly established in the event such official is disabled or otherwise unavailable to make such request.

(2) (A) If as a result of a request under paragraph (1) the Attorney General determines not to approve an application under the second sentence of subsection (a) for purposes of making the application under this section, the Attorney General shall provide written notice of the determination to the official making the request for the review of the application under that paragraph. Except when disabled or otherwise unavailable to make a determination under the preceding sentence, the Attorney General may not delegate the responsibility to make a determination under that sentence. The Attorney General shall take appropriate actions in advance to ensure that delegation of such responsibility is clearly established in the event the Attorney General is disabled or otherwise unavailable to make such determination.

(B) Notice with respect to an application under subparagraph (A) shall set forth the modifications, if any, of the application that are necessary in order for the Attorney General to approve the application under the second sentence of subsection (a) for purposes of making the application under this section.

(C) Upon review of any modifications of an application set forth under subparagraph (B), the official notified of the modifications under this paragraph shall modify the application if such official determines that such modification is warranted. Such official shall supervise the making of any modification under this subparagraph. Except when disabled or otherwise unavailable to supervise the making of any modification under the preceding sentence, such official may not delegate the responsibility to supervise the making of any modification under that preceding sentence. Each such official shall take appropriate actions in advance to ensure that delegation of such responsibility is clearly established in the event such official is disabled or otherwise unavailable to supervise the making of such modification.

50 U.S.C. 1805. Issuance of Order

(a) *Necessary findings* Upon an application made pursuant to section 1804 of this title, the judge shall enter an ex parte order as requested or as modified approving the electronic surveillance if he finds that-

[Sec. 105(a)(1)(A)

(1)–the application has been made by a Federal officer and approved by the Attorney General;

(2)–on the basis of the facts submitted by the applicant there is probable cause to believe that–

(A) the target of the electronic surveillance is a foreign power or an agent of a foreign power: Provided, That no United States person may be considered a foreign power or an agent of a foreign power solely upon the basis of activities protected by the first amendment to the Constitution of the United States; and

(B) each of the facilities or places at which the electronic surveillance is directed is being used, or is about to be used, by a foreign power or an agent of a foreign power;

(3) the proposed minimization procedures meet the definition of minimization procedures under section 1801(h) of this title; and

(4) the application which has been filed contains all statements and certifications required by section 1804 of this title and, if the target is a United States person, the certification or certifications are not clearly erroneous on the basis of the statement made under section 1804(a)(7)(E) of this title and any other information furnished under section 1804(d) of this title.[Sec. 105(a)(2)]

(b) *Determination of probable cause*

In determining whether or not probable cause exists for purposes of an order under subsection (a)(2)of this section, a judge may consider past activities of the target, as well as facts and circumstances relating to current or future activities of the target.

(c) *Specifications and directions of orders*

(1) Specifications

An order approving an electronic surveillance under this section shall specify–

(A) the identity, if known, or a description of the specific target of the electronic surveillance identified or described in the application pursuant to section 1804(a)(3) of this title;

(B) the nature and location of each of the facilities or places at which the electronic surveillance will be directed, if known;

(C) the type of information sought to be acquired and the type of communications or activities to be subjected to the surveillance;

(D) the means by which the electronic surveillance will be effected and whether physical entry will be used to effect the surveillance;

(E) the period of time during which the electronic surveillance is approved. [Sec. 105(a)(3

(2) Directions

An order approving an electronic surveillance under this section shall direct–

(A) that the minimization procedures be followed;

(B) that, upon the request of the applicant, a specified communication or other common carrier, landlord, custodian, or other specified person, or in circumstances where the Court finds, based upon specific facts provided in the application, that the actions of the target of the application may have the effect of thwarting the identification of a specified person, such other persons, furnish the applicant forthwith all information, facilities, or technical assistance necessary to accomplish the electronic surveillance in such a manner as will protect its secrecy and produce a minimum of interference with the services that such carrier, landlord, custodian, or other person is providing that target of electronic surveillance;

(C) that such carrier, landlord, custodian, or other person maintain under security procedures approved by the Attorney General and the Director of National Intelligence any records concerning the surveillance or the aid furnished that such person wishes to retain; and

(D) that the applicant compensate, at the prevailing rate, such carrier, landlord, custodian, or other person for furnishing such aid.

(3) Special directions for certain orders

An order approving an electronic surveillance under this section in circumstances where the nature and location of each of the facilities or places at which the surveillance will be directed is unknown shall direct the applicant to provide notice to the court within ten days after the date on which surveillance begins to be directed at any new facility or place, unless the court finds good cause to justify a longer period of up to 60 days, of–

(A) the nature and location of each new facility or place at which the electronic surveillance is directed;

(B) the facts and circumstances relied upon by the applicant to justify the applicant's belief that each new facility or place at which the electronic surveillance is directed is or was being used, or is about to be used, by the target of the surveillance;

(C) a statement of any proposed minimization procedures that differ from those contained in the original application or order, that may be necessitated by a change in the facility or place at which the electronic surveillance is directed; and

(D) the total number of electronic surveillances that have been or are being conducted under the authority of the order.[Sec. 105(a)(4)

Duration of order; extensions; review of circumstances under which information was acquired, retained or disseminated

(1) An order issued under this section may approve an electronic surveillance for the period necessary to achieve its purpose, or for ninety days, whichever is less, except that (A) an order under this section shall approve an electronic surveillance targeted against a foreign power, as defined in section 1801(a)(1), (2), or (3) of this title, for the period specified in the application or for one year, whichever is less, and (B) an order under this chapter for a surveillance targeted against an agent of a foreign power who is not a United States person may be for the period specified in the application or for 120 days, whichever is less.

[Sec. 110(c)(1)] (2) Extensions of an order issued under this subchapter may be granted on the same basis as an original order upon an application for an extension and new findings made in the same manner as required for an original order, except that (A) an extension of an order under this chapter for a surveillance targeted against a foreign power, as defined in of this title, or against a foreign power as defined in section 1801(a)(4) of this title that is not a United States person, may be for a period not to exceed one year if the judge finds probable cause to believe that no communication of any individual United States person will be acquired during the period, and (B) an extension of an order under this chapter for a surveillance targeted against an agent of a foreign power who is not a United States person may be for a period not to exceed 1 year.

(3) At or before the end of the period of time for which electronic surveillance is approved by an order or an extension, the judge may assess compliance with the minimization procedures by reviewing the circumstances under which information concerning United States persons was acquired, retained, or disseminated. [Sec. 105(a)(6)](e)

(1) Notwithstanding any other provision of this title, the Attorney General may authorize the emergency employment of electronic surveillance if the Attorney General-

(A) reasonably determines that an emergency situation exists with respect to the employment of electronic surveillance to obtain foreign intelligence information before an order authorizing such surveillance can with due diligence be obtained;

(B) reasonably determines that the factual basis for the issuance of an order under this title to approve such electronic surveillance exists;

(C) informs, either personally or through a designee, a judge having jurisdiction under section 103 at the time of such authorization that the decision has been made to employ emergency electronic surveillance; and

(D) makes an application in accordance with this title to a judge having jurisdiction under section 103 as soon as practicable, but not later than 7 days after the Attorney General authorizes such surveillance.

(2) If the Attorney General authorizes the emergency employment of electronic surveillance under paragraph (1), the Attorney General shall require that the minimization procedures required by this title for the issuance of a judicial order be followed.

(3) In the absence of a judicial order approving such electronic surveillance, the surveillance shall terminate when the information sought is obtained, when the application for the order is denied, or after the expiration of 7 days from the time of authorization by the Attorney General, whichever is earliest.

(4) A denial of the application made under this subsection may be reviewed as provided in section 103.

(5) In the event that such application for approval is denied, or in any other case where the electronic surveillance is terminated and no order is issued approving the surveillance, no information obtained or evidence derived from such surveillance shall be received in evidence or otherwise disclosed in any trial, hearing, or other proceeding in or before any court, grand jury, department, office, agency, regulatory body, legislative committee, or other authority of the United States, a State, or political subdivision thereof, and no information concerning any United States person acquired from such surveillance shall subsequently be used or disclosed in any other manner by Federal officers or employees without the consent of such person, except with the approval of the Attorney General if the information indicates a threat of death or serious bodily harm to any person.

(6) The Attorney General shall assess compliance with the requirements of paragraph (5).

Testing of electronic equipment; discovering unauthorized electronic surveillance; training of intelligence personnel

Notwithstanding any other provision of this subchapter, officers, employees, or agents of the United States are authorized in the normal course of their official duties to conduct electronic surveillance not targeted against the communications of any particular person or persons, under procedures approved by the Attorney General, solely to–

(1) test the capability of electronic equipment, if-

(A) it is not reasonable to obtain the consent of the persons incidentally subjected to the surveillance;

(B) the test is limited in extent and duration to that necessary to determine the capability of the equipment;

(C) the contents of any communication acquired are retained and used only for the purpose of determining the capability of the equipment, are disclosed only to test personnel, and are destroyed before or immediately upon completion of the test; and:

(D) Provided, That the test may exceed ninety days only with the prior approval of the Attorney General;

(2) determine the existence and capability of electronic surveillance equipment being used by persons not authorized to conduct electronic surveillance, if–

(A) it is not reasonable to obtain the consent of persons incidentally subjected to the surveillance;

(B) such electronic surveillance is limited in extent and duration to that necessary to determine the existence and capability of such equipment; and

(C) any information acquired by such surveillance is used only to enforce chapter 119 of Title 18, or section 605 of Title 47, or to protect information from unauthorized surveillance; or

(3) train intelligence personnel in the use of electronic surveillance equipment, if–
   (A) it is not reasonable to–
   (i) obtain the consent of the persons incidentally subjected to the surveillance;
   (ii) train persons in the course of surveillances otherwise authorized by this subchapter; or
   (iii) train persons in the use of such equipment without engaging in electronic surveillance;
   (B) such electronic surveillance is limited in extent and duration to that necessary to train the personnel in the use of the equipment; and
   (C) no contents of any communication acquired are retained or disseminated for any purpose, but are destroyed as soon as reasonably possible.

   Retention of certifications, applications and orders

   Certifications made by the Attorney General pursuant to section 1802(a) of this title and applications made and orders granted under this subchapter shall be retained for a period of at least ten years from the date of the certification or application.

   No cause of action shall lie in any court against any provider of a wire or electronic communication service, landlord, custodian, or other person (including any officer, employee, agent, or other specified person thereof) that furnishes any information, facilities, or technical assistance in accordance with a court order or request for emergency assistance under this chapter for electronic surveillance or physical search.

   [Sec. 105(a)(7)] (i) In any case in which the Government makes an application to a judge under this title to conduct electronic surveillance involving communications and the judge grants such application, upon the request of the applicant, the judge shall also authorize the installation and use of pen registers and trap and trace devices, and direct the disclosure of the information set forth in section 402(d)(2)[50 U.S.C. 1842(d)(2)].

50 U.S.C. 1805A. CLARIFICATION OF ELECTRONIC SURVEILLANCE OF PERSONS OUTSIDE THE UNITED STATES [EXPIRED]

Nothing in the definition of electronic surveillance under section 101(f) shall be construed to encompass surveillance directed at a person reasonably believed to be located outside of the United States.

[Sec. 403(a)(1)(A)]. Except as provided in section 404, sections 105A, 105B, and 105C of the Foreign Intelligence Surveillance Act of 1978 (50 U.S.C. 1805a, 1805b, and 1805c) are repealed.

[Sec. 404(a)(2) *Applicability of Protect America Act of 2007 to continued orders, authorizations, directives.*– Notwithstanding any other provision of this Act, any amendment made by this Act, or the Foreign Intelligence Surveillance Act of 1978 (50 U.S.C. 1801 et seq.)– (A) subject to paragraph (3), section 105A of such Act, as added by section 2 of the Protect America Act of 2007 (Public Law 110-55; 121 Stat. 552), shall continue to apply to any acquisition conducted pursuant to an order, authorization, or directive referred to in paragraph (1)

[Sec. 404(a)(8)] *Effective date.*– Paragraphs (1) through (7) shall take effect as if enacted on August 5, 2007.

50 U.S.C. 1805B. Additional Procedure for Authorizing Certain Acquisitions Concerning Persons Located Outside The United States [Expired]

(a) Notwithstanding any other law, the Director of National Intelligence and the Attorney General, may for periods of up to one year authorize the acquisition of foreign intelligence information concerning persons reasonably believed to be outside the United States if the Director of National Intelligence and the Attorney General determine, based on the information provided to them, that-

(1) there are reasonable procedures in place for determining that the acquisition of foreign intelligence information under this section concerns persons reasonably believed to be located outside the United States, and such procedures will be subject to review of the Court pursuant to section 105C of this Act;

(2) the acquisition does not constitute electronic surveillance;

(3) the acquisition involves obtaining the foreign intelligence information from or with the assistance of a communications service provider, custodian, or other person (including any officer, employee, agent, or other specified person of such service provider, custodian, or other person) who has access *553 to communications, either as they are transmitted or while they are stored, or equipment that is being or may be used to transmit or store such communications;

(4) a significant purpose of the acquisition is to obtain foreign intelligence information; and

(5) the minimization procedures to be used with respect to such acquisition activity meet the definition of minimization procedures under section 101(h).

This determination shall be in the form of a written certification, under oath, supported as appropriate by affidavit of appropriate officials in the national security field occupying positions appointed by the President, by and with the consent of the Senate, or the Head of any Agency of the Intelligence Community, unless immediate action by the Government is required and time does not permit the preparation of a certification. In such a case, the determination of the Director of National Intelligence and the Attorney General shall be reduced to a certification as soon as possible but in no event more than 72 hours after the determination is made.

(b) A certification under subsection (a) is not required to identify the specific facilities, places, premises, or property at which the acquisition of foreign intelligence information will be directed.

(c) The Attorney General shall transmit as soon as practicable under seal to the court established under section 103(a) a copy of a certification made under subsection (a). Such certification shall be maintained under security measures established by the Chief Justice of the United States and the Attorney General, in consultation with the

Director of National Intelligence, and shall remain sealed unless the certification is necessary to determine the legality of the acquisition under section 105B.

(d) An acquisition under this section may be conducted only in accordance with the certification of the Director of National Intelligence and the Attorney General, or their oral instructions if time does not permit the preparation of a certification, and the minimization procedures adopted by the Attorney General. The Director of National Intelligence and the Attorney General shall assess compliance with such procedures and shall report such assessments to the Permanent Select Committee on Intelligence of the House of Representatives and the Select Committee on Intelligence of the Senate under section 108(a).

(e) With respect to an authorization of an acquisition under section 105B, the Director of National Intelligence and Attorney General may direct a person to-

  (1) immediately provide the Government with all information, facilities, and assistance necessary to accomplish the acquisition in such a manner as will protect the secrecy of the acquisition and produce a minimum of interference with the services that such person is providing to the target; and

  (2) maintain under security procedures approved by the Attorney General and the Director of National Intelligence any records concerning the acquisition or the aid furnished that such person wishes to maintain.

(f) The Government shall compensate, at the prevailing rate, a person for providing information, facilities, or assistance pursuant to subsection (e).

(g) In the case of a failure to comply with a directive issued pursuant to subsection (e), the Attorney General may invoke the aid of the court established under section 103(a) to compel compliance with the directive. The court shall issue an order requiring the person to comply with the directive if it finds that the directive was issued in accordance with subsection (e) and is otherwise lawful. Failure to obey an order of the court may be punished by the court as contempt of court. Any process under this section may be served in any judicial district in which the person may be found.

(h) (1)(A) A person receiving a directive issued pursuant to subsection (e) may challenge the legality of that directive by filing a petition with the pool established under section 103(e)(1).

  (B) The presiding judge designated pursuant to section 103(b) shall assign a petition filed under subparagraph (A) to one of the judges serving in the pool established by section 103(e)(1). Not later than 48 hours after the assignment of such petition, the assigned judge shall conduct an initial review of the directive. If the assigned judge determines that the petition is frivolous, the assigned judge shall immediately deny the petition and affirm the directive or any part of the directive that is the subject of the petition. If the assigned judge determines the petition is not frivolous, the assigned judge shall, within 72 hours, consider the petition in accordance with the procedures established under section 103(e)(2) and provide a written statement for the record of the reasons for any determination under this subsection.

  (2) A judge considering a petition to modify or set aside a directive may grant such petition only if the judge finds that such directive does not meet the requirements of this section or is otherwise unlawful. If the judge does not modify or set aside

the directive, the judge shall immediately affirm such directive, and order the recipient to comply with such directive.

(3) Any directive not explicitly modified or set aside under this subsection shall remain in full effect.

(i) The Government or a person receiving a directive reviewed pursuant to subsection (h) may file a petition with the Court of Review established under section 103(b) for review of the decision issued pursuant to subsection (h) not later than 7 days after the issuance of such decision. Such court of review shall have jurisdiction to consider such petitions and shall provide for the record a written statement of the reasons for its decision. On petition for a writ of certiorari by the Government or any person receiving such directive, the record shall be transmitted under seal to the Supreme Court, which shall have jurisdiction to review such decision.

(j) Judicial proceedings under this section shall be concluded as expeditiously as possible. The record of proceedings, including petitions filed, orders granted, and statements of reasons for decision, shall be maintained under security measures established by the Chief Justice of the United States, in consultation with the Attorney General and the Director of National Intelligence.

(k) All petitions under this section shall be filed under seal. In any proceedings under this section, the court shall, upon request of the Government, review ex parte and in camera any Government submission, or portions of a submission, which may include classified information.

(l) Notwithstanding any other law, no cause of action shall lie in any court against any person for providing any information, facilities, or assistance in accordance with a directive under this section.

(m) A directive made or an order granted under this section shall be retained for a period of not less than 10 years from the date on which such directive or such order is made.

[Sec. 403(a)(1)(A)]. Except as provided in section 404, sections 105A, 105B, and 105C of the Foreign Intelligence Surveillance Act of 1978 (50 U.S.C. 1805a, 1805b, and 1805c) are repealed.

[Sec. 404(a)(1)] *Continued effect or orders, authorizations, directives*.– Except as provided in paragraph (7), notwithstanding anyother provision of law, any order, authorization, or directive issued or made pursuant to section 105B of the Foreign Intelligence Surveillance Act of 1978, as added by section 2 of the Protect America Act of 2007 (Public Law 110-55; 121 Stat. 552), shall continue in effect until the expiration of such order, authorization, or directive.

[Sec. 404(a)(2) *Applicability of Protect America Act of 2007 to continued orders, authorizations, directives*.– Notwithstanding any other provision of this Act, any amendment made by this Act, or the Foreign Intelligence Surveillance Act of 1978 (50 U.S.C. 1801 et seq.)– . . . (B) sections 105b and 105c of the Foreign Intelligence Surveillance Act of 1978, as added by sections 2 and 3, respectively, of the Protect America Act of 2007, shall continue to apply with respect to an order, authorization, or directive referred to in paragraph (1) until the later of– (i) the expiration of such order, authorization, or directive; or (ii) the date on which final judgment is entered for any petition or other litigation relating to such order, authorization, or directive.

[Sec. 404(a)(4)] *Protection from liability*.– Subsection (l) of section 105B of the Foreign Intelligence Surveillance Act of 1978, as added by section 2 of the Protect

America Act of 2007, shall continue to apply with respect to any directives issued pursuant to such section 105B.

[Sec. 404(a)(7)] *Replacement of orders, authorizations, and directives*.–

(A) *In general*.– If the Attorney General and the Director of National Intelligence seek to replace an authorization issued pursuant to section 105B of the Foreign Intelligence Surveillance Act of 1978, as added by section 2 of the Protect America Act of 2007 (Public Law 110-55), with an authorization under section 702 of the Foreign Intelligence Surveillance Act of 1978 (as added by section 101(a) of this Act), the Attorney General and the Director of National Intelligence shall, to the extent practicable, submit to the Foreign Intelligence Surveillance Court (as such term is defined in section 701(b)(2) of such Act (as so added)) a certification prepared in accordance with subsection (g) of such section 702 and the procedures adopted in accordance with subsections (d) and (e) of such section 702 at least 30 days before the expiration of such authorization.

(B) *Continuation of existing orders*.– If the Attorney General and the Director of National Intelligence seek to replace an authorization made pursuant to section 105B of the Foreign Intelligence Surveillance Act of 1978, as added by section 2 of the Protect America Act of 2007 (Public Law 110-55; 121 Stat. 522), by filing a certification in accordance with subparagraph (A), that authorization, and any directives issued thereunder and any order related thereto, shall remain in effect, notwithstanding the expiration provided for in subsection (a) of such section 105B, until the Foreign Intelligence Surveillance Court (as such term is defined in section 701(b)(2) of the Foreign Intelligence Surveillance Act of 1978 (as so added)) issues an order with respect to that certification under section 702(i)(3) of such Act (as so added) at which time the provisions of that section and of section 702(i)(4) of such Act (as so added) shall apply.

[Sec. 404(a)(8)] *Effective date*.– Paragraphs (1) through (7) shall take effect as if enacted on August 5, 2007.

50 U.S.C. 1805c. Submission to Court of Review of Procedures [Expired]

(a) No later than 120 days after the effective date of this Act, the Attorney General shall submit to the Court established under section 103(a), the procedures by which the Government determines that acquisitions conducted pursuant to section 105B do not constitute electronic surveillance. The procedures submitted pursuant to this section shall be updated and submitted to the Court on an annual basis.

(b) No later than 180 days after the effective date of this Act, the court established under section 103(a) shall assess the Government's determination under section 105B(a)(1) that those procedures are reasonably designed to ensure that acquisitions conducted pursuant to section 105B do not constitute electronic surveillance. The court's review shall be limited to whether the Government's determination is clearly erroneous.

(c) If the court concludes that the determination is not clearly erroneous, it shall enter an order approving the continued use of such procedures. If the court concludes that the determination is clearly erroneous, it shall issue an order directing the Government to submit new procedures within 30 days or cease any acquisitions under section 105B that are implicated by the court's order.

(d) The Government may appeal any order issued under subsection (c) to the court established under section 103(b). If such court determines that the order was properly entered, the court shall immediately provide for the record a written statement of each reason for its decision, and, on petition of the United States for a writ of certiorari, the record shall be transmitted under seal to the Supreme Court of the United States, which shall have jurisdiction to review such decision. Any acquisitions affected by the order issued under subsection (c) of this section may continue during the pendency of any appeal, the period during which a petition for writ of certiorari may be pending, and any review by the Supreme Court of the United States.

[Sec. 403(a)(1)(A)]. Except as provided in section 404, sections 105A, 105B, and 105C of the Foreign Intelligence Surveillance Act of 1978 (50 U.S.C. 1805a, 1805b, and 1805c) are repealed.

[Sec. 404(a)(2) *Applicability of Protect America Act of 2007 to continued orders, authorizations, directives*.– Notwithstanding any other provision of this Act, any amendment made by this Act, or the Foreign Intelligence Surveillance Act of 1978 (50 U.S.C. 1801 et seq.)– . . . (B) sections 105b and 105c of the Foreign Intelligence Surveillance Act of 1978, as added by sections 2 and 3, respectively, of the Protect America Act of 2007, shall continue to apply with respect to an order, authorization, or directive referred to in paragraph (1) until the later of– (i) the expiration of such order, authorization, or directive; or (ii) the date on which final judgment is entered for any petition or other litigation relating to such order, authorization, or directive.

[Sec. 404(a)(6)] *Reporting requirements* –

(A) *Continued applicability*.– Notwithstanding any other provision of this Act, any amendment made by this Act, the Protect America Act of 2007 (Public Law 110-55), or the Foreign Intelligence Surveillance Act of 1978 (50 U.S.C. 1801 et seq.), section 4 of the Protect America Act of 2007 shall continue to apply until the date that the certification described in subparagraph (B) is submitted.

(B) *Certification*.– The certification described in this subparagraph is a certification-- (i) made by the Attorney General; (ii) submitted as part of a semi-annual report required by section 4 of the Protect America Act of 2007; (iii) that states that there will be no further acquisitions carried out under section 105B of the Foreign Intelligence Surveillance Act of 1978, as added by section 2 of the Protect America Act of 2007, after the date of such certification; and (iv) that states that the information required to be included under such section 4 relating to any acquisition conducted under such section 105B has been included in a semi-annual report required by such section 4.

[Sec. 404(a)(8)] *Effective date*.– Paragraphs (1) through (7) shall take effect as if enacted on August 5, 2007.

50 U.S.C. 1806. Use of Information

(a) *Compliance with minimization procedures; privileged communications; lawful purposes*

Information acquired from an electronic surveillance conducted pursuant to this subchapter concerning any United States person may be used and disclosed by Federal officers and employees without the consent of the United States person only in accordance with the minimization procedures required by this subchapter. No otherwise privileged communication obtained in accordance with, or in violation of, the provisions of this subchapter shall lose its privileged character. No information acquired from an electronic surveillance pursuant to this subchapter may be used or disclosed by Federal officers or employees except for lawful purposes.

(b) *Statement for disclosure*

No information acquired pursuant to this subchapter shall be disclosed for law enforcement purposes unless such disclosure is accompanied by a statement that such information, or any information derived therefrom, may only be used in a criminal proceeding with the advance authorization of the Attorney General.

(c) *Notification by United States*

Whenever the Government intends to enter into evidence or otherwise use or disclose in any trial, hearing, or other proceeding in or before any court, department, officer, agency, regulatory body, or other authority of the United States, against an aggrieved person, any information obtained or derived from an electronic surveillance of that aggrieved person pursuant to the authority of this subchapter, the Government shall, prior to the trial, hearing, or other proceeding or at a reasonable time prior to an effort to so disclose or so use that information or submit it in evidence, notify the aggrieved person and the court or other authority in which the information is to be disclosed or used that the Government intends to so disclose or so use such information.

(d) *Notification by States or political subdivisions*

Whenever any State or political subdivision thereof intends to enter into evidence or otherwise use or disclose in any trial, hearing, or other proceeding in or before any court, department, officer, agency, regulatory body, or other authority of a State or a political subdivision thereof, against an aggrieved person any information obtained or derived from an electronic surveillance of that aggrieved person pursuant to the authority of this subchapter, the State or political subdivision thereof shall notify the aggrieved person, the court or other authority in which the information is to be disclosed or used, and the Attorney General that the State or political subdivision thereof intends to so disclose or so use such information.

(e) *Motion to suppress*

Any person against whom evidence obtained or derived from an electronic surveillance to which he is an aggrieved person is to be, or has been, introduced or otherwise used or disclosed in any trial, hearing, or other proceeding in or before any court, department, officer, agency, regulatory body, or other authority of the United States, a State, or a political subdivision thereof, may move to suppress the evidence obtained or derived from such electronic surveillance on the grounds that-

(1) the information was unlawfully acquired; or

(2) the surveillance was not made in conformity with an order of authorization or approval. Such a motion shall be made before the trial, hearing, or other proceeding unless there was no opportunity to make such a motion or the person was not aware of the grounds of the motion.

(f) *In camera and ex parte review by district court*

Whenever a court or other authority is notified pursuant to subsection (c) or (d) of this section, or whenever a motion is made pursuant to subsection (e) of this section, or whenever any motion or request is made by an aggrieved person pursuant to any other statute or rule of the United States or any State before any court or other authority of the United States or any State to discover or obtain applications or orders or other materials relating to electronic surveillance or to discover, obtain, or suppress evidence or information obtained or derived from electronic surveillance under this chapter, the United States district court or, where the motion is made before another authority, the United States district court in the same district as the authority, shall, notwithstanding any other law, if the Attorney General files an affidavit under oath that disclosure or an adversary hearing would harm the national security of the United States, review in camera and ex parte the application, order, and such other materials relating to the surveillance as may be necessary to determine whether the surveillance of the aggrieved person was lawfully authorized and conducted. In making this determination, the court may disclose to the aggrieved person, under appropriate security procedures and protective orders, portions of the application, order, or other materials relating to the surveillance only where such disclosure is necessary to make an accurate determination of the legality of the surveillance.

(g) *Suppression of evidence; denial of motion*

If the United States district court pursuant to subsection (f) of this section determines that the surveillance was not lawfully authorized or conducted, it shall, in accordance with the requirements of law, suppress the evidence which was unlawfully obtained or derived from electronic surveillance of the aggrieved person or otherwise grant the motion of the aggrieved person. If the court determines that the surveillance was lawfully authorized and conducted, it shall deny the motion of the aggrieved person except to the extent that due process requires discovery or disclosure.

(h) *Finality of orders*

Orders granting motions or requests under subsection (g) of this section, decisions under this section that electronic surveillance was not lawfully authorized or conducted, and orders of the United States district court requiring review or granting disclosure of applications, orders, or other materials relating to a surveillance shall be final orders and binding upon all courts of the United States and the several States except a United States court of appeals and the Supreme Court.

(i) *Destruction of unintentionally acquired information*
[Sec. 106] In circumstances involving the unintentional acquisition by an electronic, mechanical, or other surveillance device of the contents of any ~~radio~~ communication, under circumstances in which a person has a reasonable expectation of privacy and a warrant would be required for law enforcement purposes, and if both the sender and all intended recipients are located within the United States, such contents shall be destroyed upon recognition, unless the Attorney General determines that the contents indicate a threat of death or serious bodily harm to any person.

(j) *Notification of emergency employment of electronic surveillance; contents; postponement, suspension or elimination*
If an emergency employment of electronic surveillance is authorized under section 1805(e) of this title and a subsequent order approving the surveillance is not obtained, the judge shall cause to be served on any United States person named in the application and on such other United States persons subject to electronic surveillance as the judge may determine in his discretion it is in the interest of justice to serve, notice of-
(1) the fact of the application;
(2) the period of the surveillance; and
(3) the fact that during the period information was or was not obtained. On an ex parte showing of good cause to the judge the serving of the notice required by this subsection may be postponed or suspended for a period not to exceed ninety days. Thereafter, on a further ex parte showing of good cause, the court shall forego ordering the serving of the notice required under this subsection.

(k) *Consultation with Federal law enforcement officer*
(1) Federal officers who conduct electronic surveillance to acquire foreign intelligence information under this title may consult with Federal law enforcement officers or law enforcement personnel of a State or political subdivision of a State (including the chief executive officer of that State or political subdivision who has the authority to appoint or direct the chief law enforcement officer of that State or political subdivision to coordinate efforts to investigate or protect against–
(A) actual or potential attack or other grave hostile acts of a foreign power or an agent of a foreign power;
[Sec. 110(b)(2)]
(B) sabotage, international terrorism, or the international proliferation of weapons of mass destruction by a foreign power or an agent of a foreign power; or
(C) clandestine intelligence activities by an intelligence service or network of a foreign power or by an agent of a foreign power.
(2) Coordination authorized under paragraph (1) shall not preclude the certification required by section 104(a)(7)(B) or the entry of an order under section 105.

[Sec. 404(a)(3)] *Use of information.*– Information acquired from an acquisition conducted pursuant to an order, authorization, or directive referred to in paragraph (1)[relating to 50 U.S.C. 1805b] shall be deemed to be information acquired from an electronic surveillance pursuant to title I of the Foreign Intelligence Surveillance Act of 1978 (50 U.S.C. 1801 et seq.) for purposes of section 106 of such Act (50 U.S.C. 1806), except for purposes of subsection (j) of such section.

[Sec. 404(a)(8)] *Effective date.*– Paragraphs (1) through (7) shall take effect as if enacted on August 5, 2007.

50 U.S.C. 1807. Report to Administrative Office of the United States Courts and to Congress

In April of each year, the Attorney General shall transmit to the Administrative Office of the United States Court and to Congress a report setting forth with respect to the preceding calendar year-

(a) the total number of applications made for orders and extensions of orders approving electronic surveillance under this subchapter; and

(b) the total number of such orders and extensions either granted, modified, or denied.

50 U.S.C. 1808. Report of Attorney General to Congressional Committees; Limitation on Authority or Responsibility of Information Gather Activities of Congressional Committees; Report of Congressional Committees to Congress

(a) (1) On a semiannual basis the Attorney General shall fully inform the House Permanent Select Committee on Intelligence and the Senate Select Committee on Intelligence, and the Committee on the Judiciary of the Senate, concerning all electronic surveillance under this subchapter. Nothing in this subchapter shall be deemed to limit the authority and responsibility of the appropriate committees of each House of Congress to obtain such information as they may need to carry out their respective functions and duties.

(2) Each report under the first sentence of paragraph (1) shall include a description of–

(A) the total number of applications made for orders and extensions of orders approving electronic surveillance under this subchapter where the nature and location of each facility or place at which the electronic surveillance will be directed is unknown;

(B) each criminal case in which information acquired under this chapter has been authorized for use at trial during the period covered by such report; and

[Sec. 105(b)] (C) the total number of emergency employments of electronic surveillance under section 1805(e)—of this title and the total number of subsequent orders approving or denying such electronic surveillance.

(b) On or before one year after October 25, 1978, and on the same day each year for four years thereafter, the Permanent Select Committee on Intelligence and the Senate Select Committee on Intelligence shall report respectively to the House of Representatives and the Senate, concerning the implementation of this chapter. Said reports shall include but not be limited to an analysis and recommendations concerning whether this chapter should be (1) amended, (2) repealed, or (3) permitted to continue in effect without amendment.

50 U.S.C. 1809. Criminal Sanctions

[Sec. 102(b)]

(a) *Prohibited activities* A person is guilty of an offense if he intentionally-

   (1) engages in electronic surveillance under color of law except as authorized by this Act, chapter 119, 121, or 206 of title 18, United States Code, or any express statutory authorization that is an additional exclusive means for conducting electronic surveillance under section 112; or

   (2) discloses or uses information obtained under color of law by electronic surveillance, knowing or having reason to know that the information was obtained through electronic surveillance not authorized by this Act, chapter 119, 121, or 206 of title 18, United States Code, or any express statutory authorization that is an additional exclusive means for conducting electronic surveillance under section 112.

(b) *Defense*

It is a defense to a prosecution under subsection (a) of this section that the defendant was a law enforcement or investigative officer engaged in the course of his official duties and the electronic surveillance was authorized by and conducted pursuant to a search warrant or court order of a court of competent jurisdiction.

(c) *Penalties*

An offense described in this section is punishable by a fine of not more than $10,000 or imprisonment for not more than five years, or both.

(d) *Federal jurisdiction*

There is Federal jurisdiction over an offense under this section if the person committing the offense was an officer or employee of the United States at the time the offense was committed.

50 U.S.C. 1810. Civil Liability

An aggrieved person, other than a foreign power or an agent of a foreign power, as defined in section 1801(a) or (b)(1)(A) of this title, respectively, who has been subjected to an electronic surveillance or about whom information obtained by electronic surveillance of such person has been disclosed or used in violation of section 1809 of this title shall have a cause of action against any person who committed such violation and shall be entitled to recover-

(a) actual damages, but not less than liquidated damages of $1,000 or $100 per day for each day of violation, whichever is greater;
(b) punitive damages; and
(c) reasonable attorney's fees and other investigation and litigation costs reasonably incurred.

50 U.S.C. 1811. Authorization During Time of War

Notwithstanding any other law, the President, through the Attorney General, may authorize electronic surveillance without a court order under this subchapter to acquire foreign intelligence information for a period not to exceed fifteen calendar days following a declaration of war by the Congress.

[Sec. 102(a)] 50 U.S.C. 1812. Statement of Exclusive Means by Which Electronic Surveillance and Interception of Certain Communications May Be Conducted.

(a) Except as provided in subsection (b), the procedures of chapters 119, 121, and 206 of title 18, United States Code, and this Act shall be the exclusive means by which electronic surveillance and the interception of domestic wire, oral, or electronic communications may be conducted.
(b) Only an express statutory authorization for electronic surveillance or the interception of domestic wire, oral, or electronic communications, other than as an amendment to this Act or chapters 119, 121, or 206 of title 18, United States Code, shall constitute an additional exclusive means for the purpose of subsection (a)

1821. Definitions

As used in this subchapter:
[Sec. 110(c)(2)]
(1) The terms "foreign power", "agent of a foreign power", "'international terrorism", "sabotage", "foreign intelligence information", "Attorney General", "United States person", "United States", "person", “weapon of mass destruction”, and "State" shall have the same meanings as in section 1801 of this title, except as specifically provided by this subchapter.
(2) "Aggrieved person" means a person whose premises, property, information, or material is the target of physical search or any other person whose premises, property, information, or material was subject to physical search.
(3) "Foreign Intelligence Surveillance Court" means the court established by section 1803(a) of this title.
(4) "Minimization procedures" with respect to physical search, means-
(A) specific procedures, which shall be adopted by the Attorney General, that are reasonably designed in light of the purposes and technique of the particular physical search, to minimize the acquisition and retention, and prohibit the

dissemination, of nonpublicly available information concerning unconsenting United States persons consistent with the need of the United States to obtain, produce, and disseminate foreign intelligence information;

(B) procedures that require that nonpublicly available information, which is not foreign intelligence information, as defined in section 1801(e)(1) of this title, shall not be disseminated in a manner that identifies any United States person, without such person's consent, unless such person's identity is necessary to understand such foreign intelligence information or assess its importance;

(C) notwithstanding subparagraphs (A) and (B), procedures that allow for the retention and dissemination of information that is evidence of a crime which has been, is being, or is about to be committed and that is to be retained or disseminated for law enforcement purposes; and

(D) notwithstanding subparagraphs (A), (B), and (C), with respect to any physical search approved pursuant to section 1822(a) of this title, procedures that require that no information, material, or property of a United States person shall be disclosed, disseminated, or used for any purpose or retained for longer than 72 hours unless a court order under section 1824 of this title is obtained or unless the Attorney General determines that the information indicates a threat of death or serious bodily harm to any person.

(5) "Physical search" means any physical intrusion within the United States into premises or property (including examination of the interior of property by technical means) that is intended to result in a seizure, reproduction, inspection, or alteration of information, material, or property, under circumstances in which a person has a reasonable expectation of privacy and a warrant would be required for law enforcement purposes, but does not include (A) "electronic surveillance", as defined in section 1801(f) of this title, or (B) the acquisition by the United States Government of foreign intelligence information from international or foreign communications, or foreign intelligence activities conducted in accordance with otherwise applicable Federal law involving a foreign electronic communications system, utilizing a means other than electronic surveillance as defined in section 1801(f) of this title.

50 U.S.C. 1822. Authorization of Physical Searches for Foreign Intelligence Purposes

(a) *Presidential authorization*

(1) Notwithstanding any other provision of law, the President, acting through the Attorney General, may authorize physical searches without a court order under this subchapter to acquire foreign intelligence information for periods of up to one year if-

(A) the Attorney General certifies in writing under oath that-

(i) the physical search is solely directed at premises, information, material, or property used exclusively by, or under the open and exclusive control of, a foreign power or powers (as defined in section 1801(a)(1), (2), or (3) of this title);

(ii) there is no substantial likelihood that the physical search will involve the premises, information, material, or property of a United States person; and

(iii) the proposed minimization procedures with respect to such physical search meet the definition of minimization procedures under paragraphs (1) through (4) of section 1821(4) of this title; and

(B) the Attorney General reports such minimization procedures and any changes thereto to the Permanent Select Committee on Intelligence of the House of Representatives and the Select Committee on Intelligence of the Senate at least 30 days before their effective date, unless the Attorney General determines that immediate action is required and notifies the committees immediately of such minimization procedures and the reason for their becoming effective immediately.

(2) A physical search authorized by this subsection may be conducted only in accordance with the certification and minimization procedures adopted by the Attorney General. The Attorney General shall assess compliance with such procedures and shall report such assessments to the Permanent Select Committee on Intelligence of the House of Representatives and the Select Committee on Intelligence of the Senate under the provisions of section 1826 of this title.

(3) The Attorney General shall immediately transmit under seal to the Foreign Intelligence Surveillance Court a copy of the certification. Such certification shall be maintained under security measures established by the Chief Justice of the United States with the concurrence of the Attorney General, in consultation with the Director of Central Intelligence, and shall remain sealed unless-

(A) an application for a court order with respect to the physical search is made under section 1821(4) of this title and section 1823 of this title; or

(B) the certification is necessary to determine the legality of the physical search under section 1825(g) of this title.

(4) (A) With respect to physical searches authorized by this subsection, the Attorney General may direct a specified landlord, custodian, or other specified person to-

(i) furnish all information, facilities, or assistance necessary to accomplish the physical search in such a manner as will protect its secrecy and produce a minimum of interference with the services that such landlord, custodian, or other person is providing the target of the physical search; and

(ii) maintain under security procedures approved by the Attorney General and the Director of Central Intelligence any records concerning the search or the aid furnished that such person wishes to retain.

(B) The Government shall compensate, at the prevailing rate, such landlord, custodian, or other person for furnishing such aid.

(b) *Application for order; authorization*

Applications for a court order under this subchapter are authorized if the President has, by written authorization, empowered the Attorney General to approve applications to the Foreign Intelligence Surveillance Court. Notwithstanding any other provision of law, a judge of the court to whom application is made may grant an order in accordance with section 1824 of this title approving a physical search in the United States of the premises, property, information, or material of a foreign

power or an agent of a foreign power for the purpose of collecting foreign intelligence information.

(c) *Jurisdiction of Foreign Intelligence Surveillance Court*
[Sec. 109(b)(2)(B)]The Foreign Intelligence Surveillance Court shall have jurisdiction to hear applications for and grant orders approving a physical search for the purpose of obtaining foreign intelligence information anywhere within the United States under the procedures set forth in this subchapter, except that no judge (except when sitting en banc) shall hear the same application which has been denied previously by another judge designated under section 1803(a) of this title. If any judge so designated denies an application for an order authorizing a physical search under this subchapter, such judge shall provide immediately for the record a written statement of each reason for such decision and, on motion of the United States, the record shall be transmitted, under seal, to the court of review established under section 1803(b) of this title.

(d) *Court of review; record; transmittal to Supreme Court*
The court of review established under section 1803(b) of this title shall have jurisdiction to review the denial of any application made under this subchapter. If such court determines that the application was properly denied, the court shall immediately provide for the record a written statement of each reason for its decision and, on petition of the United States for a writ of certiorari, the record shall be transmitted under seal to the Supreme Court, which shall have jurisdiction to review such decision.

(e) *Expeditious conduct of proceedings; security measures for maintenance of records*
Judicial proceedings under this subchapter shall be concluded as expeditiously as possible. The record of proceedings under this subchapter, including applications made and orders granted, shall be maintained under security measures established by the Chief Justice of the United States in consultation with the Attorney General and the Director of Central Intelligence.

50 U.S.C. 1823. APPLICATION FOR AN ORDER

(a) *Submission by Federal officer; approval of Attorney General; contents*
Each application for an order approving a physical search under this subchapter shall be made by a Federal officer in writing upon oath or affirmation to a judge of the Foreign Intelligence Surveillance Court. Each application shall require the approval of the Attorney General based upon the Attorney General's finding that it satisfies the criteria and requirements for such application as set forth in this subchapter. Each application shall include-

(1) the identity of the Federal officer making the application;
[Sec. 107(a)(1)(A)]
[Sec. 107(a)(1)(C)]

(2) the identity, if known, or a description of the target of the search, and a detailed description of the premises or property to be searched and of the information, material, or property to be seized, reproduced, or altered;

(3) a statement of the facts and circumstances relied upon by the applicant to justify the applicant's belief that-

(A) the target of the physical search is a foreign power or an agent of a foreign power;

(B) the premises or property to be searched contains foreign intelligence information; and [Sec. 107(a)(1)(D)] (C) the premises or property to be searched is or is about to be owned, used, possessed by, or is in transit to or from a foreign power or an agent of a foreign power;

(4) a statement of the proposed minimization procedures;

(5) a statement of the nature of the foreign intelligence sought and the manner in which the physical search is to be conducted;

[Sec. 107(a)(1)(E)]

(6) a certification or certifications by the Assistant to the President for National Security Affairs ~~or~~ an executive branch official or officials designated by the President from among those executive branch officers employed in the area of national security or defense and appointed by the President, by and with the advice and consent of the Senate, or the Deputy Director of the Federal Bureau of Investigation, if designated by the President as a certifying official –

(A) that the certifying official deems the information sought to be foreign intelligence information;

(B) that a significant purpose of the search is to obtain foreign intelligence information;

(C) that such information cannot reasonably be obtained by normal investigative techniques;

(D) that designates the type of foreign intelligence information being sought according to the categories described in section 1801(e) of this title; and

(E) includes a statement explaining the basis for the certifications required by subparagraphs (C) and (D);

(7)– where the physical search involves a search of the residence of a United States person, the Attorney General shall state what investigative techniques have previously been utilized to obtain the foreign intelligence information concerned and the degree to which these techniques resulted in acquiring such information; and

(8) a statement of the facts concerning all previous applications that have been made to any judge under this subchapter involving any of the persons, premises, or property specified in the application, and the action taken on each previous application.

(b) *Additional affidavits or certifications*

The Attorney General may require any other affidavit or certification from any other officer in connection with the application.

(c) *Additional information*

The judge may require the applicant to furnish such other information as may be necessary to make the determinations required by section 1824 of this title.

(d) *Requirements regarding certain applications*

[Sec. 107(a)(2)] (1)(A) Upon written request of the Director of the Federal Bureau of Investigation, the Secretary of Defense, the Secretary of State, or the Director of National Intelligence, or the Director of the Central Intelligence Agency, the

Attorney General shall personally review under subsection (a) an application under that subsection for a target described in section 1801(b)(2) of this title.

(B) Except when disabled or otherwise unavailable to make a request referred to in subparagraph (A), an official referred to in that subparagraph may not delegate the authority to make a request referred to in that subparagraph.

(C) Each official referred to in subparagraph (A) with authority to make a request under that subparagraph shall take appropriate actions in advance to ensure that delegation of such authority is clearly established in the event such official is disabled or otherwise unavailable to make such request.

(2) (A) If as a result of a request under paragraph (1) the Attorney General determines not to approve an application under the second sentence of subsection (a) for purposes of making the application under this section, the Attorney General shall provide written notice of the determination to the official making the request for the review of the application under that paragraph. Except when disabled or otherwise unavailable to make a determination under the preceding sentence, the Attorney General may not delegate the responsibility to make a determination under that sentence. The Attorney General shall take appropriate actions in advance to ensure that delegation of such responsibility is clearly established in the event the Attorney General is disabled or otherwise unavailable to make such determination.

(B) Notice with respect to an application under subparagraph (A) shall set forth the modifications, if any, of the application that are necessary in order for the Attorney General to approve the application under the second sentence of subsection (a) for purposes of making the application under this section.

(C) Upon review of any modifications of an application set forth under subparagraph (B), the official notified of the modifications under this paragraph shall modify the application if such official determines that such modification is warranted. Such official shall supervise the making of any modification under this subparagraph. Except when disabled or otherwise unavailable to supervise the making of any modification under the preceding sentence, such official may not delegate the responsibility to supervise the making of any modification under that preceding sentence. Each such official shall take appropriate actions in advance to ensure that delegation of such responsibility is clearly established in the event such official is disabled or otherwise unavailable to supervise the making of such modification.

50 U.S.C. 1824. Issuance of an Order

(a) *Necessary findings* Upon an application made pursuant to section 1823 of this title, the judge shall enter an ex parte order as requested or as modified approving the physical search if the judge finds that-

[Sec.107(b)(1)(A)]

(1)–the application has been made by a Federal officer and approved by the Attorney General;

(2)– on the basis of the facts submitted by the applicant there is probable cause to believe that-

(A) the target of the physical search is a foreign power or an agent of a foreign power, except that no United States person may be considered an agent of a foreign power solely upon the basis of activities protected by the first amendment to the Constitution of the United States; and

[Sec. 107(b)(1)(C)] (B) the premises or property to be searched is or is about to be owned, used, possessed by, or is in transit to or from an agent of a foreign power or a foreign power;

(3)—the proposed minimization procedures meet the definition of minimization contained in this subchapter; and

[Sec. 107(c)(1)]

(4) the application which has been filed contains all statements and certifications required by section 1823 of this title, and, if the target is a United States person, the certification or certifications are not clearly erroneous on the basis of the statement made under section 1823(a)(6)(e) of this title and any other information furnished under section 1823(c) of this title.

(b) *Probable cause*

In determining whether or not probable cause exists for purposes of an order under subsection (a)(3), a judge may consider past activities of the target, as well as facts and circumstances relating to current or future activities of the target.

(c) *Specifications and directions of orders* An order approving a physical search under this section shall-

(1) specify-

(A) the identity, if known, or a description of the target of the physical search;

(B) the nature and location of each of the premises or property to be searched;

(C) the type of information, material, or property to be seized, altered, or reproduced;

(D) a statement of the manner in which the physical search is to be conducted and, whenever more than one physical search is authorized under the order, the authorized scope of each search and what minimization procedures shall apply to the information acquired by each search; and

(E) the period of time during which physical searches are approved; and

(2) direct-

(A) that the minimization procedures be followed;

(B) that, upon the request of the applicant, a specified landlord, custodian, or other specified person furnish the applicant forthwith all information, facilities, or assistance necessary to accomplish the physical search in such a manner as will protect its secrecy and produce a minimum of interference with the services that such landlord, custodian, or other person is providing the target of the physical search;

(C) that such landlord, custodian, or other person maintain under security procedures approved by the Attorney General and the Director of Central Intelligence any records concerning the search or the aid furnished that such person wishes to retain;

(D) that the applicant compensate, at the prevailing rate, such landlord, custodian, or other person for furnishing such aid; and

(E) that the Federal officer conducting the physical search promptly report to the court the circumstances and results of the physical search.

(d) *Duration of order; extensions; review of circumstances under which information was acquired, retained, or disseminated*

(1) An order issued under this section may approve a physical search for the period necessary to achieve its purpose, or for 90 days, whichever is less, except that (A) an order under this section shall approve a physical search targeted against a foreign power, as defined in paragraph (1), (2), or (3) of section 1801(a) of this title, for the period specified in the application or for one year, whichever is less, and (B) an order under this Act for a surveillance targeted against an agent of a foreign power, who is not a United States person may be for the period specified in the application or for 120 days, whichever is less.
[Sec. 110(c)(3)]

(2) Extensions of an order issued under this subchapter may be granted on the same basis as the original order upon an application for an extension and new findings made in the same manner as required for the original order, except that an extension of an order under this chapter for a physical search targeted against a foreign power, as defined in (5), (6), or (7) of section 101(a)[50 U.S.C. 1801(a)] of this title, or against a foreign power, as defined in section 1801(a)(4) of this title, that is not a United States person, or an agent of as foreign power, who is not a United States person, may be for a period not to exceed one year if the judge finds probable cause to believe that no property of any individual United States person will be acquired during the period.

(3) At or before the end of the period of time for which a physical search is approved by an order or an extension, or at any time after a physical search is carried out, the judge may assess compliance with the minimization procedures by reviewing the circumstances under which information concerning United States persons was acquired, retained, or disseminated.

(e) [Sec. 107(b)(2))] (1) Notwithstanding any other provision of this title, the Attorney General may authorize the emergency employment of a physical search if the attorney general–

(A) reasonably determines that an emergency situation exists with respect to the employment of a physical search to obtain foreign intelligence information before an order authorizing such physical search can with due diligence be obtained;

(B) reasonably determines that the factual basis for issuance of an order under this title to approve such physical search exists;

(C) informs, either personally or through a designee, a judge of the Foreign Intelligence Surveillance Court at the time of such authorization that the decision has been made to employ an emergency physical search; and

(D) makes an application in accordance with this title to a judge of the Foreign Intelligence Surveillance Court as soon as practicable, but not more than 7 days after the Attorney General authorizes such physical search.

(2) If the Attorney General authorizes the emergency employment of a physical search under paragraph (1), the Attorney General shall require that the minimization procedures required by this title for the issuance of a judicial order be followed.

(3) In the absence of a judicial order approving such physical search, the physical search shall terminate when the information sought is obtained,

when the application for the order is denied, or after the expiration of 7 days from the time of authorization by the Attorney General, whichever is earliest.

(4) A denial of the application made under this subsection may be reviewed as provided in section 103 [50 U.S.C. 1803].

(5) In the event that such application for approval is denied, or in any other case where the physical search is terminated and no order is issued approving the physical search, no information obtained or evidence derived from such physical search shall be received in evidence or otherwise disclosed in any trial, hearing, or other proceeding in or before any court, grand jury, department, office, agency, regulatory body, legislative committee, or other authority of the United States, a State, or political subdivision thereof, and no information concerning any United States person acquired from such physical search shall subsequently be used or disclosed in any other manner by Federal officers or employees without the consent of such person, except with the approval of the Attorney General if the information indicates a threat of death or serious bodily harm to any person.

(6) The Attorney General shall assess compliance with the requirements of paragraph (5).

(f) *Retention of applications and orders*
Applications made and orders granted under this subchapter shall be retained for a period of at least 10 years from the date of the application.

50 U.S.C. 1825. USE OF INFORMATION

(a) *Compliance with minimization procedures; lawful purposes*
Information acquired from a physical search conducted pursuant to this subchapter concerning any United States person maybe used and disclosed by Federal officers and employees without the consent of the United States person only in accordance with the minimization procedures required by this subchapter. No information acquired from a physical search pursuant to this subchapter may be used or disclosed by Federal officers or employees except for lawful purposes.

(b) *Notice of search and identification of property seized, altered, or reproduced*
Where a physical search authorized and conducted pursuant to section 1824 of this title involves the residence of a United States person, and, at any time after the search the Attorney General determines there is no national security interest in continuing to maintain the secrecy of the search, the Attorney shall provide notice to the United States person whose residence was searched of the fact of the search conducted pursuant to this chapter and shall identify any property of such person seized, altered, or reproduced during such search.

(c) *Statement for disclosure*
No information acquired pursuant to this subchapter shall be disclosed for law enforcement purposes unless such disclosure is accompanied by a statement that such information, or any information derived therefrom, may only be used in a criminal proceeding with the advance authorization of the Attorney General.

(d) *Notification by United States*
Whenever the United States intends to enter into evidence or otherwise use or disclose in any trial, hearing, or other proceeding in or before any court, department, officer, agency, regulatory body, or other authority of the United States, against an aggrieved person, any information obtained or derived from a physical search pursuant to the authority of this subchapter, the United States shall, prior to the trial, hearing, or the other proceeding or at a reasonable time prior to an effort to so disclose or so use that information or submit it in evidence, notify the aggrieved person and the court or other authority in which the information is to be disclosed or used that the United States intends to so disclose or so use such information.

(e) *Notification by States or political subdivisions*
Whenever any State or political subdivision thereof intends to enter into evidence or otherwise use or disclose in any trial, hearing, or other proceeding in or before any court, department, officer, agency, regulatory body, or other authority of a State or a political subdivision thereof against an aggrieved person any information obtained or derived from a physical search pursuant to the authority of this subchapter, the State or political subdivision thereof shall notify the aggrieved person, the court or other authority in which the information is to be disclosed or used, and the Attorney General that the State or political subdivision thereof intends to so disclose or so use such information.

(f) *Motion to suppress*
(1) Any person against whom evidence obtained or derived from a physical search to which he is an aggrieved person is to be, or has been, introduced or otherwise used or disclosed in any trial, hearing, or other proceeding in or before any court, department, officer, agency, regulatory body, or other authority of the United States, a State, or a political subdivision thereof, may move to suppress the evidence obtained or derived from such search on the grounds that-
(A) the information was unlawfully acquired; or
(B) the physical search was not made in conformity with an order of authorization or approval.
(2) Such a motion shall be made before the trial, hearing, or other proceeding unless there was no opportunity to make such a motion or the person was not aware of the grounds of the motion.

(g) *In camera and ex parte review by district court*
Whenever a court or other authority is notified pursuant to subsection (d) or (e) of this section, or whenever a motion is made pursuant to subsection (f) of this section, or whenever any motion or request is made by an aggrieved person pursuant to any

other statute or rule of the United States or any State before any court or other authority of the United States or any State to discover or obtain applications or orders or other materials relating to a physical search authorized by this subchapter or to discover, obtain, or suppress evidence or information obtained or derived from a physical search authorized by this subchapter, the United States district court or, where the motion is made before another authority, the United States district court in the same district as the authority shall, notwithstanding any other provision of law, if the Attorney General files an affidavit under oath that disclosure or any adversary hearing would harm the national security of the United States, review in camera and ex parte the application, order, and such other materials relating to the physical search as may be necessary to determine whether the physical search of the aggrieved person was lawfully authorized and conducted. In making this determination, the court may disclose to the aggrieved person, under appropriate security procedures and protective orders, portions of the application, order, or other materials relating to the physical search, or may require the Attorney General to provide to the aggrieved person a summary of such materials, only where such disclosure is necessary to make an accurate determination of the legality of the physical search.

(h) *Suppression of evidence; denial of motion*

If the United States district court pursuant to subsection (g) of this section determines that the physical search was not lawfully authorized or conducted, it shall, in accordance with the requirements of law, suppress the evidence which was unlawfully obtained or derived from the physical search of the aggrieved person or otherwise grant the motion of the aggrieved person. If the court determines that the physical search was lawfully authorized or conducted, it shall deny the motion of the aggrieved person except to the extent that due process requires discovery or disclosure.

(i) *Finality of orders*

Orders granting motions or requests under subsection (h) of this section, decisions under this section that a physical search was not lawfully authorized or conducted, and orders of the United States district court requiring review or granting disclosure of applications, orders, or other materials relating to the physical search shall be final orders and binding upon all courts of the United States and the several States except a United States Court of Appeals or the Supreme Court.

(j) *Notification of emergency execution of physical search; contents; postponement, suspension or elimination*

(1) If an emergency execution of a physical search is authorized under section 1824(d) of this title and a subsequent order approving the search is not obtained, the judge shall cause to be served on any United States person named in the application and on such other United States persons subject to the search as the judge may determine in his discretion it is in the interests of justice to serve, notice of-

(A) the fact of the application;
(B) the period of the search; and
(C) the fact that during the period information was or was not obtained.

(2) On an ex parte showing of good cause to the judge, the serving of the notice required by this subsection may be postponed or suspended for a period not to exceed 90 days. Thereafter, on a further ex parte showing of good cause, the court shall forego ordering the serving of the notice required under this subsection.

(k) (1) Federal officers who conduct electronic surveillance to acquire foreign intelligence information under this title may consult with Federal law enforcement officers or law enforcement personnel of a State or political subdivision of a State (including the chief executive officer of that State or political subdivision who has the authority to appoint or direct the chief law enforcement officer of that State or political subdivision to coordinate efforts to investigate or protect against–

(A) actual or potential attack or other grave hostile acts of a foreign power or an agent of a foreign power;

[Sec. 110(b)(2)]

(B) sabotage, international terrorism, or the international proliferation of weapons of mass destruction by a foreign power or an agent of a foreign power; or

(C) clandestine intelligence activities by an intelligence service or network of a foreign power or by an agent of a foreign power.

[Sec. 107(c)(2)] (2) Coordination authorized under paragraph (1) shall not preclude the certification required by section 303(a)(6) [50 U.S.C. 1803(a)(6)] or the entry of an order under section 304 [50 U.S.C. 1804].

50 U.S.C. 1826. Congressional Oversight

On a semiannual basis the Attorney General shall fully inform the Permanent Select Committee on Intelligence of the House of Representatives and the Select Committee on Intelligence of the Senate, and the Committee on the Judiciary of the Senate, concerning all physical searches conducted pursuant to this subchapter. On a semiannual basis the Attorney General shall also provide to those committees and the Committee on the Judiciary of the House of Representatives a report setting forth with respect to the preceding six-month period-

(1) the total number of applications made for orders approving physical searches under this subchapter;
(2) the total number of such orders either granted, modified, or denied;
(3) the number of physical searches which involved searches of the residences, offices, or personal property of United States persons, and the number of occasions, if any, where the Attorney General provided notice pursuant to section 1825(b) of this title; and
(4) the total number of emergency physical searches authorized by the Attorney General under section 1824(e) of this title and the total number of subsequent orders approving or denying such physical searches.

50 U.S.C. 1827. Penalties

(a) *Prohibited activities* A person is guilty of an offense if he intentionally-

(1) under color of law for the purpose of obtaining foreign intelligence information, executes a physical search within the United States except as authorized by statute; or

(2) discloses or uses information obtained under color of law by physical search within the United States, knowing or having reason to know that the information was obtained through physical search not authorized by statute, for the purpose of obtaining intelligence information.

(b) *Defense*

It is a defense to a prosecution under subsection (a) of this section that the defendant was a law enforcement or investigative officer engaged in the course of his official duties and the physical search was authorized by and conducted pursuant to a search warrant or court order of a court of competent jurisdiction.

(c) *Fine or imprisonment*

An offense described in this section is punishable by a fine of not more than $10,000 or imprisonment for not more than five years, or both.

(d) *Federal jurisdiction*

There is Federal jurisdiction over an offense under this section if the person committing the offense was an officer or employee of the United States at the time the offense was committed.

50 U.S.C. 1828. Civil Liability

An aggrieved person, other than a foreign power or an agent of a foreign power, as defined in section 1801(a) or (b)(1)(A), respectively, of this title, whose premises, property, information, or material has been subjected to a physical search within the United States or about whom information obtained by such a physical search has been disclosed or used in violation of section 1827 of this title shall have a cause of action against any person who committed such violation and shall be entitled to recover-

(1) actual damages, but not less than liquidated damages of $1,000 or $100 per day for each day of violation, whichever is greater;

(2) punitive damages; and

(3) reasonable attorney's fees and other investigative and litigation costs reasonably incurred.

50 U.S.C. 1829. Authorization During Time of War

Notwithstanding any other provision of law, the President, through the Attorney General, may authorize physical searches without a court order under this subchapter to acquire foreign intelligence information for a period not to exceed 15 calendar days following a declaration of war by the Congress.

50 U.S.C. 1841. Definitions

As used in this subchapter:

(1) The terms "foreign power", "agent of a foreign power", "international terrorism", "foreign intelligence information", "Attorney General", "United States person", "United States', "person", and "State" shall have the same meanings as in section 1801 of this title.
(2) The terms 'pen register' and 'trap and trace device' have the meanings given such terms in section 3127 of Title 18.
(3) The term 'aggrieved person' means any person-
    (A) whose telephone line was subject to the installation or use of a pen register or trap and trace device authorized by this subchapter of this chapter; or
    (B) whose communication instrument or device was subject to the use of a pen register or trap and trace device authorized by this subchapter to capture incoming electronic or other communications impulses.

50 U.S.C. 1842. Pen Registers and Trap and Trace Devices for Foreign Intelligence and International Terrorism Investigations

(a) *Application for authorization or approval*
    (1) Notwithstanding any other provision of law, the Attorney General or a designated attorney for the Government may make an application for an order or an extension of an order authorizing or approving the installation and use of a pen register or trap and trace device for any investigation to obtain foreign intelligence information not concerning a United States person or to protect against international terrorism or clandestine intelligence activities, provided that such investigation of a United States person is not conducted solely upon the basis of activities protected by the first amendment to the Constitution which is being conducted by the Federal Bureau of Investigation under such guidelines as the Attorney General approves pursuant to Executive Order No. 12333, or a successor order.
    (2) The authority under paragraph (1) is in addition to the authority under subchapter I of this chapter to conduct the electronic surveillance referred to in that paragraph.

(b) *Form of application; recipient*
Each application under this section shall be in writing under oath or affirmation to-
(1) a judge of the court established by section 1803(a) of this title; or
(2) a United States Magistrate Judge under chapter 43 of Title 28, who is publicly designated by the Chief Justice of the United States to have the power to hear applications for and grant orders approving the installation and use of a pen register or trap and trace device on behalf of a judge of that court.

(c) *Executive approval; contents of application*
Each application under this section shall require the approval of the Attorney General, or a designated attorney for the Government, and shall include-
(1) the identity of the Federal officer seeking to use the pen register or trap and trace device covered by the application; and
(2) a certification by the applicant that the information likely to be obtained is foreign intelligence information not concerning a United States person or is relevant to an ongoing investigation to protect against international terrorism or clandestine intelligence activities, provided that such investigation of a United States person is not conducted solely upon the basis of activities protected by the first amendment to the Constitution.
(3) Repealed. Publ. 107-56, Title II, § 214(a)(3), Oct. 26, 2001, 115 Stat. 286

(d) *Ex parte judicial order of approval*
(1) Upon an application made pursuant to this section, the judge shall enter an ex parte order as requested, or as modified, approving the installation and use of a pen register or trap and trace device if the judge finds that the application satisfies the requirements of this section.
(2) An order issued under this section-
(A) shall specify-
(i) the identity, if known, of the person who is the subject of the investigation;
(ii) the identity, if known, of the person to whom is leased or in whose name is listed the telephone line or other facility to which the pen register or trap and trace device is to be attached or applied; and
(iii) the attributes of the communications to which the order applies, such as the number or other identifier, and, if known, the location of the telephone line or other facility to which the pen register or trap and trace device is to be attached or applied and, in the case of a trap and trace device, the geographic limits of the trap and trace order;
(B) shall direct that–
(i) upon request of the applicant, the provider of a wire or electronic communication service, landlord, custodian, or other person shall furnish any information, facilities, or technical assistance necessary to accomplish the installation and operation of the pen register or trap and trace device in such a manner as will protect its secrecy and produce a minimum amount of interference with the services that such provider, landlord, custodian, or other person is providing the person concerned;
(ii) such provider, landlord, custodian, or other person-

(I) shall not disclose the existence of the investigation or of the pen register or trap and trace device to any person unless or until ordered by the court; and

(II) shall maintain, under security procedures approved by the Attorney General and the Director of National Intelligence pursuant to section 1805(b)(2)(C) of this title, any records concerning the pen register or trap and trace device or the aid furnished; and

(iii) the applicant shall compensate such provider, landlord, custodian, or other person for reasonable expenses incurred by such provider, landlord, custodian, or other person in providing such information, facilities, or technical assistance; and

(C) shall direct that, upon the request of the applicant, the provider of a wire or electronic communication service shall disclose to the Federal officer using the pen register or trap and trace device covered by the order-

(i) in the case of the customer or subscriber using the service covered by the order (for the period specified by the order)-

(I) the name of the customer or subscriber;

(II) the address of the customer or subscriber;

(III) the telephone or instrument number, or other subscriber number or identifier, of the customer or subscriber, including any temporarily assigned network address or associated routing or transmission information;

(IV) the length of the provision of service by such provider to the customer or subscriber and the types of services utilized by the customer or subscriber;

(V) in the case of a provider of local or long distance telephone service, any local or long distance telephone records of the customer or subscriber;

(VI) if applicable, any records reflecting period of usage (or sessions) by the customer or subscriber; and

(VII) any mechanisms and sources of payment for such service, including the number of any credit card or bank account utilized for payment for such service; and

(ii) if available, with respect to any customer or subscriber of incoming or outgoing communications to or from the service covered by the order-

(I) the name of such customer or subscriber;

(II) the address of such customer or subscriber;

(III) the telephone or instrument number, or other subscriber number or identifier, of such customer or subscriber, including any temporarily assigned network address or associated routing or transmission information; and

(IV) the length of the provision of service by such provider to such customer or subscriber and the types of services utilized by such customer or subscriber.

(e) *Time limitation*

(1) Except as provided in paragraph (2), an order issued under this section shall authorize the installation and use of a pen register or trap and trace device for a period not to exceed 90 days. Extensions of such an order may be granted, but only upon an application for an order under this section and upon the judicial finding required by subsection (d) of this section. The period of extension shall be for a period not to exceed 90 days.

(2) In the case of an application under subsection (c) of this section where the applicant has certified that the information likely to be obtained is foreign intelligence information not concerning a United States person, an order, or an extension of an order, under this section may be for a period not to exceed one year.

(f) *Cause of action barred*

No cause of action shall lie in any court against any provider of a wire or electronic communication service, landlord, custodian, or other person (including any officer, employee, agent, or other specified person thereof) that furnishes any information, facilities, or technical assistance under subsection (d) of this section in accordance with the terms of an order issued under this section.

(g) *Furnishing of results*

Unless otherwise ordered by the judge, the results of a pen register or trap and trace device shall be furnished at reasonable intervals during regular business hours for the duration of the order to the authorized Government official or officials.

50 U.S.C. 1843. Authorization During Emergencies

(a) Notwithstanding any other provision of this subchapter, when the Attorney General makes a determination described in subsection (b), the Attorney General may authorize the installation and use of a pen register or trap and trace device on an emergency basis to gather foreign intelligence information not concerning a United States person or information to protect against international terrorism or clandestine intelligence activities, provided that such investigation of a United States person is not conducted solely upon the basis of activities protected by the first amendment to the Constitution if –

(1) a judge referred to in section 1842(b) of this title is informed by the Attorney General or his designee at the time of such authorization that the decision has been made to install and use the pen register or trap and trace device, as the case may be, on an emergency basis; and

[Sec. 108(1)] (2) an application in accordance with section 1842(a)(1) of this title is made to such judge as soon as practicable, but not more than 7 days after the Attorney General authorizes the installation and use of the pen register or trap and trace device, as the case may be, under this section.

(b) A determination under this subsection is a reasonable determination by the Attorney General that-

(1) an emergency requires the installation and use of a pen register or trap and trace device to obtain foreign intelligence information not concerning a United States

person or information to protect against international terrorism or clandestine intelligence activities, provided that such investigation of a United States person is not conducted solely upon the basis of activities protected by the first amendment to the Constitution before an order authorizing the installation and use of the pen register or trap and trace device, as the case may be, can with due diligence be obtained under section 1842 of this title; and

(2) the factual basis for issuance of an order under such section 1842(c) of this title to approve the installation and use of the pen register or trap and trace device, as the case may be, exists.

(c) (1) In the absence of an order applied for under subsection (a)(2) approving the installation and use of a pen register or trap and trace device authorized under this section, the installation and use of the pen register or trap and trace device, as the case may be, shall terminate at the earlier of-

(A) when the information sought is obtained;

(B) when the application for the order is denied under section 1842 of this title; or [Sec. 108(2)] (C) 7 days after the time of the authorization by the Attorney General.

(2) In the event that an application for an order applied for under subsection (a)(2) is denied, or in any other case where the installation and use of a pen register or trap and trace device under this section is terminated and no order under section 1842(b)(2) of this title is issued approving the installation and use of the pen register or trap and trace device, as the case may be, no information obtained or evidence derived from the use of the pen register or trap and trace device, as the case may be, shall be received in evidence or otherwise disclosed in any trial, hearing, or other proceeding in or before any court, grand jury, department, office, agency, regulatory body, legislative committee, or other authority of the United States, a State, or political subdivision thereof, and no information concerning any United States person acquired from the use of the pen register or trap and trace device, as the case may be, shall subsequently be used or disclosed in any other manner by Federal officers or employees without the consent of such person, except with the approval of the Attorney General if the information indicates a threat of death or serious bodily harm to any person.

50 U.S.C. 1844. Authorization During Time of War

Notwithstanding any other provision of law, the President, through the Attorney General, may authorize the use of a pen register or trap and trace device without a court order under this subchapter [50 U.S.C.A. s 1841 et seq.] to acquire foreign intelligence information for a period not to exceed 15 calendar days following a declaration of war by Congress.

50 U.S.C. 1845. Use of Information

(a) (1) Information acquired from the use of a pen register or trap and trace device installed pursuant to this subchapter concerning any United States person may be used and disclosed by Federal officers and employees without the consent of the United States person only in accordance with the provisions of this section.

(2) No information acquired from a pen register or trap and trace device installed and used pursuant to this subchapter may be used or disclosed by Federal officers or employees except for lawful purposes.

(b) No information acquired pursuant to this subchapter shall be disclosed for law enforcement purposes unless such disclosure is accompanied by a statement that such information, or any information derived therefrom, may only be used in a criminal proceeding with the advance authorization of the Attorney General.

(c) Whenever the United States intends to enter into evidence or otherwise use or disclose in any trial, hearing, or other proceeding in or before any court, department, officer, agency, regulatory body, or other authority of the United States against an aggrieved person any information obtained or derived from the use of a pen register or trap and trace device pursuant to this subchapter, effort to so disclose or so use that information or submit it in evidence, notify the aggrieved person and the court or other authority in which the information is to be disclosed or used that the United States intends to so disclose or so use such information.

(d) Whenever any State or political subdivision thereof intends to enter into evidence or otherwise use or disclose in any trial, hearing, or other proceeding in or before any court, department, officer, agency, regulatory body, or other authority of the State or political subdivision thereof against an aggrieved person any information obtained or derived from the use of a pen register or trap and trace device pursuant to this subchapter, the State or political subdivision thereof shall notify the aggrieved person, the court or other authority in which the information is to be disclosed or used, and the Attorney General that the State or political subdivision thereof intends to so disclose or so use such information.

(e) (1) Any aggrieved person against whom evidence obtained or derived from the use of a pen register or trap and trace device is to be, or has been, introduced or otherwise used or disclosed in any trial, hearing, or other proceeding in or before any court, department, officer, agency, regulatory body, or other authority of the United States, or a State or political subdivision thereof, may move to suppress the evidence obtained or derived from the use of the pen register or trap and trace device, as the case may be, on the grounds that-

(A) the information was unlawfully acquired; or

(B) the use of the pen register or trap and trace device, as the case may be, was not made in conformity with an order of authorization or approval under this subchapter.

(2) A motion under paragraph (1) shall be made before the trial, hearing, or other proceeding unless there was no opportunity to make such a motion or the aggrieved person concerned was not aware of the grounds of the motion.

(f) (1) Whenever a court or other authority is notified pursuant to subsection (c) or (d), whenever a motion is made pursuant to subsection (e), or whenever any motion or request is made by an aggrieved person pursuant to any other statute or rule of the United States or any State before any court or other authority of the United States or any State to discover or obtain applications or orders or other materials relating to the use of a pen register or trap and trace device authorized by this subchapter or to discover, obtain, or suppress evidence or information obtained or derived from the use of a pen register or trap and trace device authorized by this subchapter, the

United States district court or, where the motion is made before another authority, the United States district court in the same district as the authority shall, notwithstanding any other provision of law and if the Attorney General files an affidavit under oath that disclosure or any adversary hearing would harm the national security of the United States, review in camera and ex parte the application, order, and such other materials relating to the use of the pen register or trap and trace device, as the case may be, as may be necessary to determine whether the use of the pen register or trap and trace device, as the case may be, was lawfully authorized and conducted.

(2) In making a determination under paragraph (1), the court may disclose to the aggrieved person, under appropriate security procedures and protective orders, portions of the application, order, or other materials relating to the use of the pen register or trap and trace device, as the case may be, or may require the Attorney General to provide to the aggrieved person a summary of such materials, only where such disclosure is necessary to make an accurate determination of the legality of the use of the pen register or trap and trace device, as the case may be.

(g) (1) If the United States district court determines pursuant to subsection (f) that the use of a pen register or trap and trace device was not lawfully authorized or conducted, the court may, in accordance with the requirements of law, suppress the evidence which was unlawfully obtained or derived from the use of the pen register or trap and trace device, as the case may be, or otherwise grant the motion of the aggrieved person.

(2) If the court determines that the use of the pen register or trap and trace device, as the case may be, was lawfully authorized or conducted, it may deny the motion of the aggrieved person except to the extent that due process requires discovery or disclosure.

(h) Orders granting motions or requests under subsection (g), decisions under this section that the use of a pen register or trap and trace device was not lawfully authorized or conducted, and orders of the United States district court requiring review or granting disclosure of applications, orders, or other materials relating to the installation and use of a pen register or trap and trace device shall be final orders and binding upon all courts of the United States and the several States except a United States Court of Appeals or the Supreme Court.

50 U.S.C. 1846. Congressional Oversight

(a) On a semiannual basis, the Attorney General shall fully inform the Permanent Select Committee on Intelligence of the House of Representatives and the Select Committee on Intelligence of the Senate, and the Committee on the Judiciary of the House of Representatives and the Committee on the Judiciary of the Senate, concerning all uses of pen registers and trap and trace devices pursuant to this subchapter.

(b) On a semiannual basis, the Attorney General shall also provide to the committees referred to in subsection (a) of this section and to the Committees on the Judiciary of the House of Representatives and the Senate a report setting forth with respect to the preceding 6-month period-

(1) the total number of applications made for orders approving the use of pen registers or trap and trace devices under this subchapter;
(2) the total number of such orders either granted, modified, or denied; and
(3) the total number of pen registers and trap and trace devices whose installation and use was authorized by the Attorney General on an emergency basis under section 1843 of this title, and the total number of subsequent orders approving or denying the installation and use of such pen registers and trap and trace devices.

50 U.S.C. 1861. Access to Certain Business Records for Foreign Intelligence and International Terrorism Investigations

(a) (1) Subject to paragraph (3), the Director of the Federal Bureau of Investigation or a designee of the Director (whose rank shall be no lower than Assistant Special Agent in Charge) may make an application for an order requiring the production of any tangible things (including books, records, papers, documents, and other items) for an investigation to obtain foreign intelligence information not concerning a United States person or to protect against international terrorism or clandestine intelligence activities, provided that such investigation of a United States person is not conducted solely upon the basis of activities protected by the first amendment to the Constitution.

(2) An investigation conducted under this section shall

(A) be conducted under guidelines approved by the Attorney General under Executive Order 12333 (or a successor order); and
(B) not be conducted of a United States person solely upon the basis of activities protected by the first amendment to the Constitution of the United States.

(3) In the case of an application for an order requiring the production of library circulation records, library patron lists, book sales records, book customer lists, firearms sales records, tax return records, educational records, or medical records containing information that would identify a person, the Director of the Federal Bureau of Investigation may delegate the authority to make such application to either the Deputy Director of the Federal Bureau of Investigation or the Executive Assistant Director for National Security (or any successor position). The Deputy Director or the Executive Assistant Director may not further delegate such authority.

(b) Each application under this section
  (1) shall be made to-
    (A) a judge of the court established by section 1803(a) of this title; or
    (B) a United States Magistrate Judge under chapter 43 of Title 28, who is publicly designated by the Chief Justice of the United States to have the power to hear applications and grant orders for the production of tangible things under this section on behalf of a judge of that court; and
  (2) shall include-
    (A) a statement of facts showing that there are reasonable grounds to believe that the tangible things sought are relevant to an authorized investigation (other than a threat assessment) conducted in accordance with subsection (a)(2) of

this section to obtain foreign intelligence information not concerning a United States person or to protect against international terrorism or clandestine intelligence activities, such things being presumptively relevant to an authorized investigation if the applicant shows in the statement of the facts that they pertain to-

(i) a foreign power or an agent of a foreign power;

(ii) the activities of a suspected agent of a foreign power who is the subject of such authorized investigation; or

(iii) an individual in contact with, or known to, a suspected agent of a foreign power who is the subject of such authorized investigation; and

(B) an enumeration of the minimization procedures adopted by the Attorney General under subsection (g) of this section that are applicable to the retention and dissemination by the Federal Bureau of Investigation of any tangible things to be made available to the Federal Bureau of Investigation based on the order requested in such application.

(c)(1) Upon an application made pursuant to this section, if the judge finds that the application meets the requirements of subsections (a) and (b) of this section, the judge shall enter an ex parte order as requested, or as modified, approving the release of tangible things. Such order shall direct that minimization procedures adopted pursuant to subsection (g) of this section be followed.

(2) An order under this subsection-

(A) shall describe the tangible things that are ordered to be produced with sufficient particularity to permit them to be fairly identified;

(B) shall include the date on which the tangible things must be provided, which shall allow a reasonable period of time within which the tangible things can be assembled and made available;

(C) shall provide clear and conspicuous notice of the principles and procedures described in subsection (d) of this section;

(D) may only require the production of a tangible thing if such thing can be obtained with a subpoena duces tecum issued by a court of the United States in aid of a grand jury investigation or with any other order issued by a court of the United States directing the production of records or tangible things; and

(E) shall not disclose that such order is issued for purposes of an investigation described in subsection (a) of this section.

(d) (1) No person shall disclose to any other person that the Federal bureau of investigation has sought or obtained tangible things pursuant to an order under this section, other than to

(A) those persons to whom disclosure is necessary to comply with such order;

(B) an attorney to obtain legal advice or assistance with respect to the production of things in response to the order; or

(C) other persons as permitted by the Director of the Federal Bureau of Investigation or the designee of the Director.

(2) (A) A person to whom disclosure is made pursuant to paragraph (1) shall be subject to the nondisclosure requirements applicable to a person to whom an order is directed under this section in the same manner as such person.

(B) Any person who discloses to a person described in subparagraph (A), (B), or (C) of paragraph (1) that the Federal Bureau of Investigation has sought or obtained tangible things pursuant to an order under this section shall notify such person of the nondisclosure requirements of this subsection.

(C) At the request of the Director of the Federal Bureau of Investigation or the designee of the Director, any person making or intending to make a disclosure under subparagraph (A) or (C) of paragraph (1) shall identify to the Director or such designee the person to whom such disclosure will be made or to whom such disclosure was made prior to the request.

(e) A person who, in good faith, produces tangible things under an order pursuant to this section shall not be liable to any other person for such production. Such production shall not be deemed to constitute a waiver of any privilege in any other proceeding or context.

(f) (1) In this subsection-

(A) the term "production order" means an order to produce any tangible thing under this section; and

(B) the term "nondisclosure order" means an order imposed under subsection (d) of this section.

(2) (A)(i) A person receiving a production order may challenge the legality of that order by filing a petition with the pool established by section 1803(e)(1) of this title. Not less than 1 year after the date of the issuance of the production order, the recipient of a production order may challenge the nondisclosure order imposed in connection with such production order by filing a petition to modify or set aside such nondisclosure order, consistent with the requirements of subparagraph (c), with the pool established by section 1803(e)(1) of this title.

(ii) The presiding judge shall immediately assign a petition under clause (i) to 1 of the judges serving in the pool established by section 1803(e)(1) of this title. Not later than 72 hours after the assignment of such petition, the assigned judge shall conduct an initial review of the petition. If the assigned judge determines that the petition is frivolous, the assigned judge shall immediately deny the petition and affirm the production order or nondisclosure order. If the assigned judge determines the petition is not frivolous, the assigned judge shall promptly consider the petition in accordance with the procedures established under section 1803(e)(2) of this title.

(iii) The assigned judge shall promptly provide a written statement for the record of the reasons for any determination under this subsection. Upon the request of the Government, any order setting aside a nondisclosure order shall be stayed pending review pursuant to paragraph (3).

(B) A judge considering a petition to modify or set aside a production order may grant such petition only if the judge finds that such order does not meet the requirements of this section or is otherwise unlawful. If the judge does not modify or set aside the production order, the judge shall immediately affirm such order, and order the recipient to comply therewith.

(C) (i) A judge considering a petition to modify or set aside a nondisclosure order may grant such petition only if the judge finds that there is no reason to believe that disclosure may endanger the national security of the United States, interfere with a criminal, counter terrorism, or counterintelligence investigation, interfere with diplomatic relations, or endanger the life or physical safety of any person.

(ii) If, upon filing of such a petition, the Attorney General, Deputy Attorney General, an Assistant Attorney General, or the Director of the Federal Bureau of

Investigation certifies that disclosure may endanger the national security of the United States or interfere with diplomatic relations, such certification shall be treated as conclusive, unless the judge finds that the certification was made in bad faith.

(iii) If the judge denies a petition to modify or set aside a nondisclosure order, the recipient of such order shall be precluded for a period of 1 year from filing another such petition with respect to such nondisclosure order.

(D) Any production or nondisclosure order not explicitly modified or set aside consistent with this subsection shall remain in full effect.

(3) A petition for review of a decision under paragraph (2) to affirm, modify, or set aside an order by the Government or any person receiving such order shall be made to the court of review established under section 1803(b) of this title, which shall have jurisdiction to consider such petitions. The court of review shall provide for the record a written statement of the reasons for its decision and, on petition by the Government or any person receiving such order for writ of certiorari, the record shall be transmitted under seal to the Supreme Court of the United States, which shall have jurisdiction to review such decision.

(4) Judicial proceedings under this subsection shall be concluded as expeditiously as possible. The record of proceedings, including petitions filed, orders granted, and statements of reasons for decision, shall be maintained under security measures established by the Chief Justice of the United States, in consultation with the Attorney General and the Director of National Intelligence.

(5) All petitions under this subsection shall be filed under seal. In any proceedings under this subsection, the court shall, upon request of the Government, review ex parte and in camera any Government submission, or portions thereof, which may include classified information.

(g) *Minimization procedures*

(1) In general

Not later than 180 days after March 9, 2006, the Attorney General shall adopt specific minimization procedures governing the retention and dissemination by the Federal Bureau of Investigation of any tangible things, or information therein, received by the Federal Bureau of Investigation in response to an order under this subchapter.

(2) Defined

In this section, the term "minimization procedures" means-

(A) specific procedures that are reasonably designed in light of the purpose and technique of an order for the production of tangible things, to minimize the retention, and prohibit the dissemination, of nonpublicly available information concerning unconsenting United States persons consistent with the need of the United States to obtain, produce, and disseminate foreign intelligence information;

(B) procedures that require that nonpublicly available information, which is not foreign intelligence information, as defined in section 1801(e)(1) of this title, shall not be disseminated in a manner that identifies any United States person, without such person's consent, unless such person's identity is necessary to understand foreign intelligence information or assess its importance; and

(C) notwithstanding subparagraphs (A) and (B), procedures that allow for the retention and dissemination of information that is evidence of a crime which has been, is being, or is about to be committed and that is to be retained or disseminated for law enforcement purposes.

(h) *Use of information*

Information acquired from tangible things received by the Federal Bureau of Investigation in response to an order under this subchapter concerning any United States person may be used and disclosed by Federal officers and employees without the consent of the United States person only in accordance with the minimization procedures adopted pursuant to subsection (g) of this section. No otherwise privileged information acquired from tangible things received by the Federal Bureau of Investigation in accordance with the provisions of this subchapter shall lose its privileged character. No information acquired from tangible things received by the Federal Bureau of Investigation in response to an order under this subchapter may be used or disclosed by Federal officers or employees except for lawful purposes.

50 U.S.C. 1862. Congressional Oversight

(a) On a annual basis, the Attorney General shall fully inform the Permanent Select Committee on Intelligence of the House of Representatives and the Select Committee on Intelligence and the Committee on the Judiciary of the Senate concerning all requests for the production of tangible things under section 1861 of this title.

(b) In April of each year, the Attorney General shall submit to the House and Senate Committees on the Judiciary and the House Permanent Select Committee on Intelligence and the Senate Select Committee on Intelligence a report setting forth with respect to the preceding calendar year-

(1) the total number of applications made for orders approving requests for the production of tangible things under section 1861 of this title;

(2) the total number of such orders either granted, modified, or denied; and

(3) the number of such orders either granted, modified, or denied for the production of each of the following:

(A) Library circulation records, library patron lists, book sales records, or book customer lists.

(B) Firearms sales records.

(C) Tax return records.

(D) Educational records.

(E) Medical records containing information that would identify a person.

(c) (1) In April of each year, the Attorney General shall submit to Congress a report setting forth with respect to the preceding year–

(A) the total number of applications made for orders approving requests for the production of tangible things under section 1861 of this title; and

(B) the total number of such orders either granted, modified, or denied.

(2) Each report under this subsection shall be submitted in unclassified form.

[Sec. 403(b)(2)(B)] Effective December 31, 2012 . . .(B) except as provided in section 404, section 601(a)(1) of such Act (50 U.S.C. 1871(a)(1)) is amended to read as such section read on the day before the date of the enactment of this Act .

50 U.S.C. 1871. Semiannual Report of The Attorney General

(a) Report

On a semiannual basis, the Attorney General shall submit to the Permanent Select Committee on Intelligence of the House of Representatives, the Select Committee on Intelligence of the Senate, and the Committees on the Judiciary of the House of Representatives and the Senate, in a manner consistent with the protection of the national security, a report setting forth with respect to the preceding 6-month period-

[Sec. 101(c)(2)](1) the aggregate number of persons targeted for orders issued under this chapter, including a breakdown of those targeted for-

(A) electronic surveillance under section 1805 of this title;
(B) physical searches under section 1824 of this title;
(C) pen registers under section 1842 of this title; ~~and~~
(D) access to records under section 1861 of this title;
(E) acquisitions under section 703; and
(F) acquisitions under section 704.

(2) the number of individuals covered by an order issued pursuant to section 1801(b)(1)(c) of this title;

(3) the number of times that the Attorney General has authorized that information obtained under this chapter may be used in a criminal proceeding or any information derived therefrom may be used in a criminal proceeding;

(4) a summary of significant legal interpretations of this chapter involving matters before the Foreign Intelligence Surveillance Court or the Foreign Intelligence Surveillance Court of Review, including interpretations presented in applications or pleadings filed with the Foreign Intelligence Surveillance Court or the Foreign Intelligence Surveillance Court of Review by the Department of Justice; and

[Sec. 103(a)] (5) copies of all decisions, orders or opinions of the Foreign Intelligence Surveillance Court or Foreign Intelligence Surveillance Court of Review that include significant construction or interpretation of the provisions of this chapter.

(b) Frequency

The first report under this section shall be submitted not later than 6 months after December 17, 2004. Subsequent reports under this section shall be submitted semi-annually thereafter.

[Sec. 103(b)] (c) Submissions to Congress.– The Attorney General shall submit to the committees of Congress referred to in subsection (a)–

(1) a copy of any decision, order, or opinion issued by the Foreign Intelligence Surveillance Court or the Foreign Intelligence Surveillance Court of Review that includes significant construction or interpretation of any provision of this Act,

and any pleadings, applications, or memoranda of law associated with such decision, order, or opinion, not later than 45 days after such decision, order, or opinion is issued; and

(2) a copy of each such decision, order, or opinion, and any pleadings, applications, or memoranda of law associated with such decision, order, or opinion, that was issued during the 5-year period ending on the date of the enactment of the FISA Amendments Act of 2008 and not previously submitted in a report under subsection (a).

(d) Protection of national security.– The Attorney General, in consultation with the Director of National Intelligence, may authorize redactions of materials described in subsection (c) that are provided to the committees of Congress referred to in subsection (a), if such redactions are necessary to protect the national security of the United States and are limited to sensitive sources and methods information or the identities of targets.

[Sec. 104] (e) Definitions.– In this section:

(1) Foreign intelligence surveillance court.– The term 'Foreign Intelligence Surveillance Court' means the court established under section 103(a).

(2) Foreign intelligence surveillance court of review.– The term 'Foreign Intelligence Surveillance Court of Review' means the court established under section 103(b).

[Sec. 404(b)(4)] *Reporting requirements*.–

(A) *Continued applicability*.– Notwithstanding any other provision of this Act or of the Foreign Intelligence Surveillance Act of 1978 (50 U.S.C. 1801 et seq.), section 601(a) of such Act (50 U.S.C. 1871(a)), as amended by section 101(c)(2), and sections 702(l) and 707 of such Act, as added by section 101(a), shall continue to apply until the date that the certification described in subparagraph (B) is submitted.

(B) *Certification*.– The certification described in this subparagraph is a certification–

(i) made by the Attorney General;

(ii) submitted to the Select Committee on Intelligence of the Senate, the Permanent Select Committee on Intelligence of the House of Representatives, and the Committees on the Judiciary of the Senate and the House of Representatives;

(iii) that states that there will be no further acquisitions carried out under title VII of the Foreign Intelligence Surveillance Act of 1978, as amended by section 101(a), after the date of such certification; and

(iv) that states that the information required to be included in a review, assessment, or report under section 601 of such Act, as amended by section 101(c), or section 702(l) or 707 of such Act, as added by section 101(a), relating to any acquisition conducted under title VII of such Act, as amended by section 101(a), has been included in a review, assessment, or report under such section 601, 702(l), or 707.

[Sec. 101(a)(2)]**50 U.S.C. 1881. Definitions.**

(a) *In General*.– The terms "agent of a foreign power", "Attorney General", "contents", "electronic surveillance", "foreign intelligence information", "foreign power", "person", "United States", and "United States person" have the meanings given such terms in section 101, except as specifically provided in this title.

(b) *Additional Definitions.–*

(1) *Congressional Intelligence Committees.*--The term "congressional intelligence committees" means–

(A) the Select Committee on Intelligence of the Senate; and

(B) the Permanent Select Committee on Intelligence of the House of Representatives.

(2) *Foreign Intelligence Surveillance Court; Court.–* The terms "Foreign Intelligence Surveillance Court" and "Court" mean the court established under section 103(a).

(3) *Foreign Intelligence Surveillance Court of Review; Court of Review.*-- The terms "Foreign Intelligence Surveillance Court of Review" and "Court of Review" mean the court established under section 103(b).

(4) Electronic Communication Service Provider.--The term "electronic communication service provider" means–

(A) a telecommunications carrier, as that term is defined in section 3 of the Communications Act of 1934 (47 U.S.C. 153);

(B) a provider of electronic communication service, as that term is defined in section 2510 of title 18, United States Code;

(C) a provider of a remote computing service, as that term is defined in section 2711 of title 18, United States Code;

(D) any other communication service provider who has access to wire or electronic communications either as such communications are transmitted or as such communications are stored; or

(E) an officer, employee, or agent of an entity described in subparagraph (A), (B), (c), or (D).

(5) Intelligence Community.– The term "intelligence community" has the meaning given the term in section 3(4) of the National Security Act of 1947 (50 U.S.C. 401a(4)).

[Sec. 403(b)(1)] Except as provided in section 404, effective December 31, 2012, title VII of the Foreign Intelligence Surveillance Act of 1978, as amended by section 101(a), [50 U.S.C. 1881 to 1881g]]is repealed.

[Sec. 404(b)] *Transition procedures for FISA Amendments Act of 2008 Provisions.–*

(1) *Orders in effect on December 31, 2012.* – Notwithstanding any other provision of this Act, any amendment made by this Act, or the Foreign Intelligence Surveillance Act of 1978 (50 U.S.C. 1801 et seq.), any order, authorization, or directive issued or made under title VII of the Foreign Intelligence Surveillance Act of 1978, as amended by section 101(a) [50 U.S.C. 1881-1881g], shall continue in effect until the date of the expiration of such order, authorization, or directive.

(2) *Applicability of Title VII of FISA to continued orders, authorizations, directives.–* Notwithstanding any other provision of this Act, any amendment made by this Act, or the Foreign Intelligence Surveillance Act of 1978 (50 U.S.C. 1801 et seq.), with respect to any order, authorization, or directive referred to in paragraph (1), title VII of such Act, as amended by

section 101(a) [50 U.S.C. 1881-1881g], shall continue to apply until the later of– (A) the expiration of such order, authorization, or directive; or (B) the date on which final judgment is entered for any petition or other litigation relating to such order, authorization, or directive.

50 U.S.C. 1881A. Procedures for Targeting Certain Persons Outside The United States Other than United States Persons

(a) *Authorization.*– Notwithstanding any other provision of law, upon the issuance of an order in accordance with subsection (i)(3) or a determination under subsection (c)(2), the Attorney General and the Director of National Intelligence may authorize jointly, for a period of up to 1 year from the effective date of the authorization, the targeting of persons reasonably believed to be located outside the United States to acquire foreign intelligence information.

(b) *Limitations.*– An acquisition authorized under subsection (a)–

(1) may not intentionally target any person known at the time of acquisition to be located in the United States;

(2) may not intentionally target a person reasonably believed to be located outside the United States if the purpose of such acquisition is to target a particular, known person reasonably believed to be in the United States;

(3) may not intentionally target a United States person reasonably believed to be located outside the United States;

(4) may not intentionally acquire any communication as to which the sender and all intended recipients are known at the time of the acquisition to be located in the United States; and

(5) shall be conducted in a manner consistent with the fourth amendment to the Constitution of the United States.

(c) *Conduct of acquisition.*–

(1) *In General.*--An acquisition authorized under subsection (a) shall be conducted only in accordance with –

(A) the targeting and minimization procedures adopted in accordance with subsections (d) and (e); and

(B) upon submission of a certification in accordance with subsection (g), such certification.

(2) *Determination.*--A determination under this paragraph and for purposes of subsection (a) is a determination by the Attorney General and the Director of National Intelligence that exigent circumstances exist because, without immediate implementation of an authorization under subsection (a), intelligence important to the national security of the United States may be lost or not timely acquired and time does not permit the issuance of an order pursuant to subsection (i)(3) prior to the implementation of such authorization.

(3) *Timing of determination.*--The Attorney General and the Director of National Intelligence may make the determination under paragraph (2)-

(A) before the submission of a certification in accordance with subsection (g); or

(B) by amending a certification pursuant to subsection (i)(1)(c) at any time during which judicial review under subsection (i) of such certification is pending.

(4) *Construction.*- Nothing in title I shall be construed to require an application for a court order under such title for an acquisition that is targeted in accordance with this section at a person reasonably believed to be located outside the United States.

(d) *Targeting Procedures.–*

(1) *Requirement to adopt.*--The Attorney General, in consultation with the Director of National Intelligence, shall adopt targeting procedures that are reasonably designed to-

(A) ensure that any acquisition authorized under subsection (a) is limited to targeting persons reasonably believed to be located outside the United States; and

(B) prevent the intentional acquisition of any communication as to which the sender and all intended recipients are known at the time of the acquisition to be located in the United States.

(2) *Judicial review.–* The procedures adopted in accordance with paragraph (1) shall be subject to judicial review pursuant to subsection (i).

(e) *Minimization Procedures.–*

(1) *Requirement to adopt.–* The Attorney General, in consultation with the Director of National Intelligence, shall adopt minimization procedures that meet the definition of minimization procedures under section 101(h) or 301(4), as appropriate, for acquisitions authorized under subsection (a).

(2) *Judicial review.–* The minimization procedures adopted in accordance with paragraph (1) shall be subject to judicial review pursuant to subsection (i).

(f) *Guidelines for compliance with limitations.–*

(1) *Requirement to adopt.*--The Attorney General, in consultation with the Director of National Intelligence, shall adopt guidelines to ensure–

(A) compliance with the limitations in subsection (b); and

(B) that an application for a court order is filed as required by this Act.

(2) *Submission of guidelines.*--The Attorney General shall provide the guidelines adopted in accordance with paragraph (1) to–

(A) the congressional intelligence committees;

(B) the Committees on the Judiciary of the Senate and the House of Representatives; and

(C) the Foreign Intelligence Surveillance Court.

(g) *Certification.–*

(1) *In General.–*

(A) *Requirement.*--Subject to subparagraph (B), prior to the implementation of an authorization under subsection (a), the Attorney General and the Director of National Intelligence shall provide to the Foreign Intelligence Surveillance Court a written certification and any supporting affidavit, under oath and under seal, in accordance with this subsection.

(B) *Exception.–* If the Attorney General and the Director of National Intelligence make a determination under subsection (c)(2) and time does not permit the submission of a certification under this subsection prior to the implementation of an authorization under subsection (a), the Attorney General and the Director of National Intelligence shall submit to the Court a certification for such authorization as soon as practicable but in no event later than 7 days after such determination is made.

(2) *Requirements*.--A certification made under this subsection shall-

(A) attest that–

(i) there are procedures in place that have been approved, have been submitted for approval, or will be submitted with the certification for approval by the Foreign Intelligence Surveillance Court that are reasonably designed to–

(I) ensure that an acquisition authorized under subsection (a) is limited to targeting persons reasonably believed to be located outside the United States; and

(II) prevent the intentional acquisition of any communication as to which the sender and all intended recipients are known at the time of the acquisition to be located in the United States;

(ii) the minimization procedures to be used with respect to such acquisition-

(I) meet the definition of minimization procedures under section 101(h) or 301(4), as appropriate; and

(II) have been approved, have been submitted for approval, or will be submitted with the certification for approval by the Foreign Intelligence Surveillance Court;

(iii) guidelines have been adopted in accordance with subsection (f) to ensure compliance with the limitations in subsection (b) and to ensure that an application for a court order is filed as required by this Act;

(iv) the procedures and guidelines referred to in clauses (i), (ii), and (iii) are consistent with the requirements of the fourth amendment to the Constitution of the United States;

(v) a significant purpose of the acquisition is to obtain foreign intelligence information;

(vi) the acquisition involves obtaining foreign intelligence information from or with the assistance of an electronic communication service provider; and

(vii)the acquisition complies with the limitations in subsection (b);

(B) include the procedures adopted in accordance with subsections (d) and (e);

(C) be supported, as appropriate, by the affidavit of any appropriate official in the area of national security who is–

(i) appointed by the President, by and with the advice and consent of the Senate; or

(ii) the head of an element of the intelligence community;

(D) include–

(i) an effective date for the authorization that is at least 30 days after the submission of the written certification to the court; or

(ii) if the acquisition has begun or the effective date is less than 30 days after the submission of the written certification to the court, the date the acquisition began or the effective date for the acquisition; and

(E) if the Attorney General and the Director of National Intelligence make a determination under subsection (c)(2), include a statement that such determination has been made.

(3) *Change in effective date*.--The Attorney General and the Director of National Intelligence may advance or delay the effective date referred to in paragraph (2)(D) by submitting an amended certification in accordance with subsection (i)(1)(c) to the Foreign Intelligence Surveillance Court for review pursuant to subsection (i).

(4) *Limitation* --A certification made under this subsection is not required to identify the specific facilities, places, premises, or property at which an acquisition authorized under subsection (a) will be directed or conducted.

(5) *Maintenance of certification*.--The Attorney General or a designee of the Attorney General shall maintain a copy of a certification made under this subsection.

(6) *Review*.--A certification submitted in accordance with this subsection shall be subject to judicial review pursuant to subsection (i).

(h) *Directives and judicial review of directives*.–

(1) *Authority*.--With respect to an acquisition authorized under subsection (a), the Attorney General and the Director of National Intelligence may direct, in writing, an electronic communication service provider to-

(A) immediately provide the Government with all information, facilities, or assistance necessary to accomplish the acquisition in a manner that will protect the secrecy of the acquisition and produce a minimum of interference with the services that such electronic communication service provider is providing to the target of the acquisition; and

(B) maintain under security procedures approved by the Attorney General and the Director of National Intelligence any records concerning the acquisition or the aid furnished that such electronic communication service provider wishes to maintain.

(2) *Compensation*.--The Government shall compensate, at the prevailing rate, an electronic communication service provider for providing information, facilities, or assistance in accordance with a directive issued pursuant to paragraph (1).

(3) *Release from liability*.– No cause of action shall lie in any court against any electronic communication service provider for providing any information, facilities, or assistance in accordance with a directive issued pursuant to paragraph (1).

(4) *Challenging of directives*.-

(A) *Authority to Challenge*.– An electronic communication service provider receiving a directive issued pursuant to paragraph (1) may file a petition to modify or set aside such directive with the Foreign Intelligence Surveillance Court, which shall have jurisdiction to review such petition.

(B) *Assignment*.--The presiding judge of the Court shall assign a petition filed under subparagraph (A) to 1 of the judges serving in the pool established under section 103(e)(1) not later than 24 hours after the filing of such petition.

(C) *Standards for review*.– A judge considering a petition filed under subparagraph (A) may grant such petition only if the judge finds that the directive does not meet the requirements of this section, or is otherwise unlawful.

(D) *Procedures for initial review.*– A judge shall conduct an initial review of a petition filed under subparagraph (A) not later than 5 days after being assigned such petition. If the judge determines that such petition does not consist of claims, defenses, or other legal contentions that are warranted by existing law or by a nonfrivolous argument for extending, modifying, or reversing existing law or for establishing new law, the judge shall immediately deny such petition and affirm the directive or any part of the directive that is the subject of such petition and order the recipient to comply with the directive or any part of it. Upon making a determination under this subparagraph or promptly thereafter, the judge shall provide a written statement for the record of the reasons for such determination.

(E) *Procedures for plenary review.*– If a judge determines that a petition filed under subparagraph (A) requires plenary review, the judge shall affirm, modify, or set aside the directive that is the subject of such petition not later than 30 days after being assigned such petition. If the judge does not set aside the directive, thc judge shall immediately affirm or affirm with modifications the directive, and order the recipient to comply with the directive in its entirety or as modified. The judge shall provide a written statement for the record of the reasons for a determination under this subparagraph.

(F) *Continued effect.*– Any directive not explicitly modified or set aside under this paragraph shall remain in full effect.

(G) *Contempt of court.*– Failure to obey an order issued under this paragraph may be punished by the Court as contempt of court.

(5) *Enforcement of directives.*–

(A) *Order to compel.*--If an electronic communication service provider fails to comply with a directive issued pursuant to paragraph (1), the Attorney General may file a petition for an order to compel the electronic communication service provider to comply with the directive with the Foreign Intelligence Surveillance Court, which shall have jurisdiction to review such petition.

(B) *Assignment.*– The presiding judge of the Court shall assign a petition filed under subparagraph (A) to 1 of the judges serving in the pool established under section 103(e)(1) not later than 24 hours after the filing of such petition.

(C) *Procedures for review.*– judge considering a petition filed under subparagraph (A) shall, not later than 30 days after being assigned such petition, issue an order requiring the electronic communication service provider to comply with the directive or any part of it, as issued or as modified, if the judge finds that the directive meets the requirements of this section and is otherwise lawful. The judge shall provide a written statement for the record of the reasons for a determination under this paragraph.

(D) *Contempt of court.*– Failure to obey an order issued under this paragraph may be punished by the Court as contempt of court.

(E) *Process.*– Any process under this paragraph may be served in any judicial district in which the electronic communication service provider may be found.

(6) *Appeal.*–

(A) *Appeal to the court of review.*--The Government or an electronic communication service provider receiving a directive issued pursuant to paragraph (1) may file a petition with the Foreign Intelligence Surveillance Court of Review for review of a decision issued pursuant to paragraph (4) or (5). The Court of Review shall have jurisdiction to consider such petition and shall provide a written statement for the record of the reasons for a decision under this subparagraph.

(B) *Certiorari to the Supreme Court.*– The Government or an electronic communication service provider receiving a directive issued pursuant to paragraph (1) may file a petition for a writ of certiorari for review of a decision of the Court of Review issued under subparagraph (A). The record for such review shall be transmitted under seal to the Supreme Court of the United States, which shall have jurisdiction to review such decision.

[[Sec. 404(b)(3)] *Challenge of directives; protection from liability; use of information* – Notwithstanding any other provision of this Act or of the Foreign Intelligence Surveillance Act of 1978 (50 U.S.C. 1801 et seq.) . . . (B) section 702(h)(3) of such Act (as so added) shall continue to apply with respect to any directive issued pursuant to section 702(h) of such Act (as so added);]

(i) *Judicial review of certifications and procedures.*–

(1) *In General.*–

(A) *Review by the Foreign Intelligence Surveillance Court.*– The Foreign Intelligence Surveillance Court shall have jurisdiction to review a certification submitted in accordance with subsection (g) and the targeting and minimization procedures adopted in accordance with subsections (d) and (e), and amendments to such certification or such procedures.

(B) *Time period for review.*– The Court shall review a certification submitted in accordance with subsection (g) and the targeting and minimization procedures adopted in accordance with subsections (d) and (e) and shall complete such review and issue an order under paragraph (3) not later than 30 days after the date on which such certification and such procedures are submitted.

(C) *Amendments.*– The Attorney General and the Director of National Intelligence may amend a certification submitted in accordance with subsection (g) or the targeting and minimization procedures adopted in accordance with subsections (d) and (e) as necessary at any time, including if the Court is conducting or has completed review of such certification or such procedures, and shall submit the amended certification or amended procedures to the Court not later than 7 days after amending such certification or such procedures. The Court shall review any amendment under this subparagraph under the procedures set forth in this subsection. The Attorney General and the Director of National Intelligence may authorize the use of an amended certification or amended procedures pending the Court's review of such amended certification or amended procedures.

(2) *Review.*– The Court shall review the following:

(A) *Certification.*– A certification submitted in accordance with subsection (g) to determine whether the certification contains all the required elements.

(B) *Targeting procedures.*– The targeting procedures adopted in accordance with subsection (d) to assess whether the procedures are reasonably designed to-

(i) ensure that an acquisition authorized under subsection (a) is limited to targeting persons reasonably believed to be located outside the United States; and

(ii) prevent the intentional acquisition of any communication as to which the sender and all intended recipients are known at the time of the acquisition to be located in the United States.

(C) *Minimization procedures.*– The minimization procedures adopted in accordance with subsection (e) to assess whether such procedures meet the definition of minimization procedures under section 101(h) or section 301(4), as appropriate.

(3) *Orders.*–

(A) *Approval.*– If the Court finds that a certification submitted in accordance with subsection (g) contains all the required elements and that the targeting and minimization procedures adopted in accordance with subsections (d) and (e) are consistent with the requirements of those subsections and with the fourth amendment to the Constitution of the United States, the Court shall enter an order approving the certification and the use, or continued use in the case of an acquisition authorized pursuant to a determination under subsection (c)(2), of the procedures for the acquisition.

(B) *Correction of deficiencies.*– If the Court finds that a certification submitted in accordance with subsection (g) does not contain all the required elements, or that the procedures adopted in accordance with subsections (d) and (e) are not consistent with the requirements of those subsections or the fourth amendment to the Constitution of the United States, the Court shall issue an order directing the Government to, at the Government's election and to the extent required by the Court's order–

(i) correct any deficiency identified by the Court's order not later than 30 days after the date on which the Court issues the order; or

(ii) cease, or not begin, the implementation of the authorization for which such certification was submitted.

(C) *Requirement for written statement.*– In support of an order under this subsection, the Court shall provide, simultaneously with the order, for the record a written statement of the reasons for the order.

(4) *Appeal.*–

(A) *Appeal to the court of review.*– The Government may file a petition with the Foreign Intelligence Surveillance Court of Review for review of an order under this subsection. The Court of Review shall have jurisdiction to consider such petition. For any decision under this subparagraph affirming, reversing, or modifying an order of the Foreign Intelligence Surveillance Court, the Court of Review shall provide for the record a written statement of the reasons for the decision.

(B) *Continuation of acquisition pending rehearing or appeal.–* Any acquisition affected by an order under paragraph (3)(B) may continue–

(i) during the pendency of any rehearing of the order by the Court en banc; and

(ii) if the Government files a petition for review of an order under this section, until the Court of Review enters an order under subparagraph (c).

(C) *Implementation pending appeal.–* Not later than 60 days after the filing of a petition for review of an order under paragraph (3)(B) directing the correction of a deficiency, the Court of Review shall determine, and enter a corresponding order regarding, whether all or any part of the correction order, as issued or modified, shall be implemented during the pendency of the review.

(D) *Certiorari to the Supreme Court –* The Government may file a petition for a writ of certiorari for review of a decision of the Court of Review issued under subparagraph (A). The record for such review shall be transmitted under seal to the Supreme Court of the United States, which shall have jurisdiction to review such decision.

(5) *Schedule.–*

(A) *Reauthorization of authorizations in effect.–* If the Attorney General and the Director of National Intelligence seek to reauthorize or replace an authorization issued under subsection (a), the Attorney General and the Director of National Intelligence shall, to the extent practicable, submit to the Court the certification prepared in accordance with subsection (g) and the procedures adopted in accordance with subsections (d) and (e) at least 30 days prior to the expiration of such authorization.

(B) *Reauthorization of orders, authorizations , and directives.–* If the Attorney General and the Director of National Intelligence seek to reauthorize or replace an authorization issued under subsection (a) by filing a certification pursuant to subparagraph (A), that authorization, and any directives issued thereunder and any order related thereto, shall remain in effect, notwithstanding the expiration provided for in subsection (a), until the Court issues an order with respect to such certification under paragraph (3) at which time the provisions of that paragraph and paragraph (4) shall apply with respect to such certification.

(j) *Judicial proceedings.–*

(1) *Expedited judicial proceedings.–* Judicial proceedings under this section shall be conducted as expeditiously as possible.

(2) *Time limits.–* A time limit for a judicial decision in this section shall apply unless the Court, the Court of Review, or any judge of either the Court or the Court of Review, by order for reasons stated, extends that time as necessary for good cause in a manner consistent with national security.

(k) *Maintenance and security of records and proceedings.–*

(1) *Standards.–* he Foreign Intelligence Surveillance Court shall maintain a record of a proceeding under this section, including petitions, appeals, orders, and statements of reasons for a decision, under security measures adopted by the Chief Justice of the United States, in consultation with the Attorney General and the Director of National Intelligence.

(2) *Filing and review.*--All petitions under this section shall be filed under seal. In any proceedings under this section, the Court shall, upon request of the Government, review ex parte and in camera any Government submission, or portions of a submission, which may include classified information.

(3) *Retention of records.–* The Attorney General and the Director of National Intelligence shall retain a directive or an order issued under this section for a period of not less than 10 years from the date on which such directive or such order is issued.

(l) *Assessments and reviews.–*

(1) *Semiannual assessment.–* Not less frequently than once every 6 months, the Attorney General and Director of National Intelligence shall assess compliance with the targeting and minimization procedures adopted in accordance with subsections (d) and (e) and the guidelines adopted in accordance with subsection (f) and shall submit each assessment to-

(A) the Foreign Intelligence Surveillance Court; and

(B) consistent with the Rules of the House of Representatives, the Standing Rules of the Senate, and Senate Resolution 400 of the 94th Congress or any successor Senate resolution-

(i) the congressional intelligence committees; and

(ii) the Committees on the Judiciary of the House of Representatives and the Senate.

(2) *Agency assessment.–* The Inspector General of the Department of Justice and the Inspector General of each element of the intelligence community authorized to acquire foreign intelligence information under subsection (a), with respect to the department or element of such Inspector General–

(A) are authorized to review compliance with the targeting and minimization procedures adopted in accordance with subsections (d) and (e) and the guidelines adopted in accordance with subsection (f);

(B) with respect to acquisitions authorized under subsection (a), shall review the number of disseminated intelligence reports containing a reference to a United States-person identity and the number of United States-person identities subsequently disseminated by the element concerned in response to requests for identities that were not referred to by name or title in the original reporting;

(C) with respect to acquisitions authorized under subsection (a), shall review the number of targets that were later determined to be located in the United States and, to the extent possible, whether communications of such targets were reviewed; and

(D) shall provide each such review to-

(i) the Attorney General;

(ii) the Director of National Intelligence; and

(iii) consistent with the Rules of the House of Representatives, the Standing Rules of the Senate, and Senate Resolution 400 of the 94th Congress or any successor Senate resolution–
(I) the congressional intelligence committees; and
(II) the Committees on the Judiciary of the House of Representatives and the Senate.

(3) *Annual review.–*
(A) *Requirement to conduct.–* The head of each element of the intelligence community conducting an acquisition authorized under subsection (a) shall conduct an annual review to determine whether there is reason to believe that foreign intelligence information has been or will be obtained from the acquisition. The annual review shall provide, with respect to acquisitions authorized under subsection (a)-
(i) an accounting of the number of disseminated intelligence reports containing a reference to a United States-person identity;
(ii) an accounting of the number of United States-person identities subsequently disseminated by that element in response to requests for identities that were not referred to by name or title in the original reporting;
(iii) the number of targets that were later determined to be located in the United States and, to the extent possible, whether communications of such targets were reviewed; and
(iv) a description of any procedures developed by the head of such element of the intelligence community and approved by the Director of National Intelligence to assess, in a manner consistent with national security, operational requirements and the privacy interests of United States persons, the extent to which the acquisitions authorized under subsection (a) acquire the communications of United States persons, and the results of any such assessment.
(B) *Use of review.–* The head of each element of the intelligence community that conducts an annual review under subparagraph (A) shall use each such review to evaluate the adequacy of the minimization procedures utilized by such element and, as appropriate, the application of the minimization procedures to a particular acquisition authorized under subsection (a).
(C) *Provision of review.–* The head of each element of the intelligence community that conducts an annual review under subparagraph (A) shall provide such review to-
(i) the Foreign Intelligence Surveillance Court;
(ii) the Attorney General;
(iii) the Director of National Intelligence; and
(iv) consistent with the Rules of the House of Representatives, the Standing Rules of the Senate, and Senate Resolution 400 of the 94th Congress or any successor Senate resolution–
(I) the congressional intelligence committees; and
(II) the Committees on the Judiciary of the House of Representatives and the Senate.

[Sec. 403(b)(1)] Except as provided in section 404, effective December 31, 2012, title VII of the Foreign Intelligence Surveillance Act of 1978, as amended by section 101(a), [50 U.S.C. 1881 to 1881g]]is repealed.

[Sec. 404(b)] *Transition procedures for FISA Amendments Act of 2008 Provisions.–*

(1) *Orders in effect on December 31, 2012.* – Notwithstanding any other provision of this Act, any amendment made by this Act, or the Foreign Intelligence Surveillance Act of 1978 (50 U.S.C. 1801 et seq.), any order, authorization, or directive issued or made under title VII of the Foreign Intelligence Surveillance Act of 1978, as amended by section 101(a) [50 U.S.C. 1881-1881g], shall continue in effect until the date of the expiration of such order, authorization, or directive.

(2) *Applicability of Title VII of FISA to continued orders, authorizations, directives.–* Notwithstanding any other provision of this Act, any amendment made by this Act, or the Foreign Intelligence Surveillance Act of 1978 (50 U.S.C. 1801 et seq.), with respect to any order, authorization, or directive referred to in paragraph (1), title VII of such Act, as amended by section 101(a) [50 U.S.C. 1881-1881g], shall continue to apply until the later of– (A) the expiration of such order, authorization, or directive; or (B) the date on which final judgment is entered for any petition or other litigation relating to such order, authorization, or directive.

50 U.S.C. 1881B. Certain Acquisitions Inside The United States Targeting United States Persons Outside The United States

(a) *Jurisdiction of the foreign intelligence surveillance court.–*

(1) *In general.–* The Foreign Intelligence Surveillance Court shall have jurisdiction to review an application and to enter an order approving the targeting of a United States person reasonably believed to be located outside the United States to acquire foreign intelligence information, if the acquisition constitutes electronic surveillance or the acquisition of stored electronic communications or stored electronic data that requires an order under this Act, and such acquisition is conducted within the United States.

(2) *Limitation.–* If a United States person targeted under this subsection is reasonably believed to be located in the United States during the effective period of an order issued pursuant to subsection (c), an acquisition targeting such United States person under this section shall cease unless the targeted United States person is again reasonably believed to be located outside the United States while an order issued pursuant to subsection (c) is in effect. Nothing in this section shall be construed to limit the authority of the Government to seek an order or authorization under, or otherwise engage in any activity that is authorized under, any other title of this Act.

(b) *Application.–*

(1) *In general.–* each application for an order under this section shall be made by a Federal officer in writing upon oath or affirmation to a judge having jurisdiction under subsection (a)(1). Each application shall require the approval of the Attorney General based upon the Attorney General's finding that it satisfies the

criteria and requirements of such application, as set forth in this section, and shall include–

(A) the identity of the Federal officer making the application;

(B) the identity, if known, or a description of the United States person who is the target of the acquisition;

(C) a statement of the facts and circumstances relied upon to justify the applicant's belief that the United States person who is the target of the acquisition is–

(i) a person reasonably believed to be located outside the United States; and

(ii) a foreign power, an agent of a foreign power, or an officer or employee of a foreign power;

(D) a statement of proposed minimization procedures that meet the definition of minimization procedures under section 101(h) or 301(4), as appropriate;

(E) a description of the nature of the information sought and the type of communications or activities to be subjected to acquisition;

(F) a certification made by the Attorney General or an official specified in section 104(a)(6) that-

(i) the certifying official deems the information sought to be foreign intelligence information;

(ii) a significant purpose of the acquisition is to obtain foreign intelligence information;

(iii) such information cannot reasonably be obtained by normal investigative techniques;

(iv) designates the type of foreign intelligence information being sought according to the categories described in section 101(e); and

(v) includes a statement of the basis for the certification that–

(I) the information sought is the type of foreign intelligence information designated; and

(II) such information cannot reasonably be obtained by normal investigative techniques;

(G) a summary statement of the means by which the acquisition will be conducted and whether physical entry is required to effect the acquisition;

(H) the identity of any electronic communication service provider necessary to effect the acquisition, provided that the application is not required to identify the specific facilities, places, premises, or property at which the acquisition authorized under this section will be directed or conducted;

(I) a statement of the facts concerning any previous applications that have been made to any judge of the Foreign Intelligence Surveillance Court involving the United States person specified in the application and the action taken on each previous application; and

(J) a statement of the period of time for which the acquisition is required to be maintained, provided that such period of time shall not exceed 90 days per application.

(2) *Other requirements of the attorney general.–* The Attorney General may require any other affidavit or certification from any other officer in connection with the application.

(3) *Other requirements of the judge.–* he judge may require the applicant to furnish such other information as may be necessary to make the findings required by subsection (c)(1).

(c) *Order.–*

(1) *Findings.–* Upon an application made pursuant to subsection (b), the Foreign Intelligence Surveillance Court shall enter an ex parte order as requested or as modified by the Court approving the acquisition if the Court finds that-

(A) the application has been made by a Federal officer and approved by the Attorney General;

(B) on the basis of the facts submitted by the applicant, for the United States person who is the target of the acquisition, there is probable cause to believe that the target is-

(i) a person reasonably believed to be located outside the United States; and

(ii) a foreign power, an agent of a foreign power, or an officer or employee of a foreign power;

(C) the proposed minimization procedures meet the definition of minimization procedures under section 101(h) or 301(4), as appropriate; and

(D) the application that has been filed contains all statements and certifications required by subsection (b) and the certification or certifications are not clearly erroneous on the basis of the statement made under subsection (b)(1)(F)(v) and any other information furnished under subsection (b)(3).

(2) *Probable cause.–* In determining whether or not probable cause exists for purposes of paragraph (1)(B), a judge having jurisdiction under subsection (a)(1) may consider past activities of the target and facts and circumstances relating to current or future activities of the target. No United States person may be considered a foreign power, agent of a foreign power, or officer or employee of a foreign power solely upon the basis of activities protected by the first amendment to the Constitution of the United States.

(3) *Review.–*

(A) Limitation of review.– Review by a judge having jurisdiction under subsection (a)(1) shall be limited to that required to make the findings described in paragraph (1).

(B) *Review of probable cause.–* If the judge determines that the facts submitted under subsection (b) are insufficient to establish probable cause under paragraph (1)(B), the judge shall enter an order so stating and provide a written statement for the record of the reasons for the determination. The Government may appeal an order under this subparagraph pursuant to subsection (f).

(C) *Review of minimization procedures* – If the judge determines that the proposed minimization procedures referred to in paragraph (1)(c) do not meet the definition of minimization procedures under section 101(h) or 301(4), as appropriate, the judge shall enter an order so stating and provide a written statement for the record of the reasons for the determination. The

Government may appeal an order under this subparagraph pursuant to subsection (f).

(D) *Review of certification* – If the judge determines that an application pursuant to subsection (b) does not contain all of the required elements, or that the certification or certifications are clearly erroneous on the basis of the statement made under subsection (b)(1)(F)(v) and any other information furnished under subsection (b)(3), the judge shall enter an order so stating and provide a written statement for the record of the reasons for the determination. The Government may appeal an order under this subparagraph pursuant to subsection (f).

(4) *Specifications.*– An order approving an acquisition under this subsection shall specify-

(A) the identity, if known, or a description of the United States person who is the target of the acquisition identified or described in the application pursuant to subsection (b)(1)(B);

(B) if provided in the application pursuant to subsection (b)(1)(H), the nature and location of each of the facilities or places at which the acquisition will be directed;

(C) the nature of the information sought to be acquired and the type of communications or activities to be subjected to acquisition;

(D) a summary of the means by which the acquisition will be conducted and whether physical entry is required to effect the acquisition; and

(E) the period of time during which the acquisition is approved.

(5) *Directives* – An order approving an acquisition under this subsection shall direct-

(A) that the minimization procedures referred to in paragraph (1)(c), as approved or modified by the Court, be followed;

(B) if applicable, an electronic communication service provider to provide to the Government forthwith all information, facilities, or assistance necessary to accomplish the acquisition authorized under such order in a manner that will protect the secrecy of the acquisition and produce a minimum of interference with the services that such electronic communication service provider is providing to the target of the acquisition;

(C) if applicable, an electronic communication service provider to maintain under security procedures approved by the Attorney General any records concerning the acquisition or the aid furnished that such electronic communication service provider wishes to maintain; and

(D) if applicable, that the Government compensate, at the prevailing rate, such electronic communication service provider for providing such information, facilities, or assistance.

(6) *Duration.*– An order approved under this subsection shall be effective for a period not to exceed 90 days and such order may be renewed for additional 90-day periods upon submission of renewal applications meeting the requirements of subsection (b).

(7) *Compliance.*– At or prior to the end of the period of time for which an acquisition is approved by an order or extension under this section, the judge may assess compliance with the minimization procedures referred to in

paragraph (1)(c) by reviewing the circumstances under which information concerning United States persons was acquired, retained, or disseminated.

(d) *Emergency authorization.–*

(1) *Authority for emergency authorization.–* notwithstanding any other provision of this Act, if the Attorney General reasonably determines that–

(A) an emergency situation exists with respect to the acquisition of foreign intelligence information for which an order may be obtained under subsection (c) before an order authorizing such acquisition can with due diligence be obtained, and

(B) the factual basis for issuance of an order under this subsection to approve such acquisition exists, the Attorney General may authorize such acquisition if a judge having jurisdiction under subsection (a)(1) is informed by the Attorney General, or a designee of the Attorney General, at the time of such authorization that the decision has been made to conduct such acquisition and if an application in accordance with this section is made to a judge of the Foreign Intelligence Surveillance Court as soon as practicable, but not more than 7 days after the Attorney General authorizes such acquisition.

(2) *Minimization procedures.–* If the Attorney General authorizes an acquisition under paragraph (1), the Attorney General shall require that the minimization procedures referred to in subsection (c)(1)(C) for the issuance of a judicial order be followed.

(3) *Termination of emergency authorization.*--In the absence of a judicial order approving an acquisition under paragraph (1), such acquisition shall terminate when the information sought is obtained, when the application for the order is denied, or after the expiration of 7 days from the time of authorization by the Attorney General, whichever is earliest.

(4) *Use of information.–* If an application for approval submitted pursuant to paragraph (1) is denied, or in any other case where the acquisition is terminated and no order is issued approving the acquisition, no information obtained or evidence derived from such acquisition, except under circumstances in which the target of the acquisition is determined not to be a United States person, shall be received in evidence or otherwise disclosed in any trial, hearing, or other proceeding in or before any court, grand jury, department, office, agency, regulatory body, legislative committee, or other authority of the United States, a State, or political subdivision thereof, and no information concerning any United States person acquired from such acquisition shall subsequently be used or disclosed in any other manner by Federal officers or employees without the consent of such person, except with the approval of the Attorney General if the information indicates a threat of death or serious bodily harm to any person.

(e) *Release from liability.–* No cause of action shall lie in any court against any electronic communication service provider for providing any information, facilities, or assistance in accordance with an order or request for emergency assistance issued pursuant to subsection (c) or (d), respectively.

[[Sec. 404(b)(3)] *Challenge of directives; protection from liability; use of information* – Notwithstanding any other provision of this Act or of the Foreign Intelligence Surveillance Act of 1978 (50 U.S.C. 1801 et seq.) . . (c) section 703(e) of such Act (as so added) shall continue to apply with respect to an order or request for emergency assistance under that section;]

(f) *Appeal.–*

(1) *Appeal to the foreign intelligence surveillance court of review.–* The Government may file a petition with the Foreign Intelligence Surveillance Court of Review for review of an order issued pursuant to subsection (c). The Court of Review shall have jurisdiction to consider such petition and shall provide a written statement for the record of the reasons for a decision under this paragraph.

(2) *Certiorari to the Supreme Court.–* The Government may file a petition for a writ of certiorari for review of a decision of the Court of Review issued under paragraph (1). The record for such review shall be transmitted under seal to the Supreme Court of the United States, which shall have jurisdiction to review such decision.

(g) *Construction.–* Except as provided in this section, nothing in this Act shall be construed to require an application for a court order for an acquisition that is targeted in accordance with this section at a United States person reasonably believed to be located outside the United States.

[Sec. 403(b)(1)] Except as provided in section 404, effective December 31, 2012, title VII of the Foreign Intelligence Surveillance Act of 1978, as amended by section 101(a), [50 U.S.C. 1881 to 1881g]]is repealed.

[404(b)] *Transition procedures for FISA Amendments Act of 2008 Provisions.–*

(1) *Orders in effect on December 31, 2012.* – Notwithstanding any other provision of this Act, any amendment made by this Act, or the Foreign Intelligence Surveillance Act of 1978 (50 U.S.C. 1801 et seq.), any order, authorization, or directive issued or made under title VII of the Foreign Intelligence Surveillance Act of 1978, as amended by section 101(a) [50 U.S.C. 1881-1881g], shall continue in effect until the date of the expiration of such order, authorization, or directive.

(2) *Applicability of Title VII of FISA to continued orders, authorizations, directives.–* Notwithstanding any other provision of this Act, any amendment made by this Act, or the Foreign Intelligence Surveillance Act of 1978 (50 U.S.C. 1801 et seq.), with respect to any order, authorization, or directive referred to in paragraph (1), title VII of such Act, as amended by section 101(a) [50 U.S.C. 1881-1881g], shall continue to apply until the later of– (A) the expiration of such order, authorization, or directive; or (B) the date on which final judgment is entered for any petition or other litigation relating to such order, authorization, or directive.

50 U.S.C. 1881C. OTHER ACQUISITIONS TARGETING UNITED STATES PERSONS OUTSIDE THE UNITED STATES

(a) *Jurisdiction and scope.–*

(1) *Jurisdiction.–* The Foreign Intelligence Surveillance Court shall have jurisdiction to enter an order pursuant to subsection (c).

(2) *Scope.–* No element of the intelligence community may intentionally target, for the purpose of acquiring foreign intelligence information, a United States person reasonably believed to be located outside the United States under circumstances in which the targeted United States person has a reasonable expectation of

privacy and a warrant would be required if the acquisition were conducted inside the United States for law enforcement purposes, unless a judge of the Foreign Intelligence Surveillance Court has entered an order with respect to such targeted United States person or the Attorney General has authorized an emergency acquisition pursuant to subsection (c) or (d), respectively, or any other provision of this Act.

(3) *Limitations.–*

(A) *Moving or misidentified targets.–* If a United States person targeted under this subsection is reasonably believed to be located in the United States during the effective period of an order issued pursuant to subsection (c), an acquisition targeting such United States person under this section shall cease unless the targeted United States person is again reasonably believed to be located outside the United States during the effective period of such order.

(B) *Applicability.–* If an acquisition for foreign intelligence purposes is to be conducted inside the United States and could be authorized under section 703, the acquisition may only be conducted if authorized under section 703 or in accordance with another provision of this Act other than this section.

(C) *Construction.–* Nothing in this paragraph shall be construed to limit the authority of the Government to seek an order or authorization under, or otherwise engage in any activity that is authorized under, any other title of this Act.

(b) *Application.–* Each application for an order under this section shall be made by a Federal officer in writing upon oath or affirmation to a judge having jurisdiction under subsection (a)(1). Each application shall require the approval of the Attorney General based upon the Attorney General's finding that it satisfies the criteria and requirements of such application as set forth in this section and shall include-

(1) the identity of the Federal officer making the application;

(2) the identity, if known, or a description of the specific United States person who is the target of the acquisition;

(3) a statement of the facts and circumstances relied upon to justify the applicant's belief that the United States person who is the target of the acquisition is-

(A) a person reasonably believed to be located outside the United States; and

(B) a foreign power, an agent of a foreign power, or an officer or employee of a foreign power;

(4) a statement of proposed minimization procedures that meet the definition of minimization procedures under section 101(h) or 301(4), as appropriate;

(5) a certification made by the Attorney General, an official specified in section 104(a)(6), or the head of an element of the intelligence community that-

(A) the certifying official deems the information sought to be foreign intelligence information; and

(B) a significant purpose of the acquisition is to obtain foreign intelligence information;

(6) a statement of the facts concerning any previous applications that have been made to any judge of the Foreign Intelligence Surveillance Court involving the United States person specified in the application and the action taken on each previous application; and

(7) a statement of the period of time for which the acquisition is required to be maintained, provided that such period of time shall not exceed 90 days per application.

(c) *Order–*

(1) *Findings.–* Upon an application made pursuant to subsection (b), the Foreign Intelligence Surveillance Court shall enter an ex parte order as requested or as modified by the Court if the Court finds that-

(A) the application has been made by a Federal officer and approved by the Attorney General;

(B) on the basis of the facts submitted by the applicant, for the United States person who is the target of the acquisition, there is probable cause to believe that the target is-

(i) a person reasonably believed to be located outside the United States; and

(ii) a foreign power, an agent of a foreign power, or an officer or employee of a foreign power;

(C) the proposed minimization procedures, with respect to their dissemination provisions, meet the definition of minimization procedures under section 101(h) or 301(4), as appropriate; and

(D) the application that has been filed contains all statements and certifications required by subsection (b) and the certification provided under subsection (b)(5) is not clearly erroneous on the basis of the information furnished under subsection (b).

(2) *Probable cause* – In determining whether or not probable cause exists for purposes of paragraph (1)(B), a judge having jurisdiction under subsection (a)(1) may consider past activities of the target and facts and circumstances relating to current or future activities of the target. No United States person may be considered a foreign power, agent of a foreign power, or officer or employee of a foreign power solely upon the basis of activities protected by the first amendment to the Constitution of the United States.

(3) *Review.–*

(A) *Limitations on review.–* Review by a judge having jurisdiction under subsection (a)(1) shall be limited to that required to make the findings described in paragraph (1). The judge shall not have jurisdiction to review the means by which an acquisition under this section may be conducted.

(B) *Review of probable cause.–* If the judge determines that the facts submitted under subsection (b) are insufficient to establish probable cause to issue an order under this subsection, the judge shall enter an order so stating and provide a written statement for the record of the reasons for such determination. The Government may appeal an order under this subparagraph pursuant to subsection (e).

(C) *Review of minimization procedures.–* If the judge determines that the minimization procedures applicable to dissemination of information obtained through an acquisition under this subsection do not meet the definition of minimization procedures under section 101(h) or 301(4), as appropriate, the judge shall enter an order so stating and provide a written statement for the record of the reasons for such determination. The

Government may appeal an order under this subparagraph pursuant to subsection (e).

(D) *Scope of review of certification.*– If the judge determines that an application under subsection (b) does not contain all the required elements, or that the certification provided under subsection (b)(5) is clearly erroneous on the basis of the information furnished under subsection (b), the judge shall enter an order so stating and provide a written statement for the record of the reasons for such determination. The Government may appeal an order under this subparagraph pursuant to subsection (e).

(4) *Duration.*– An order under this paragraph shall be effective for a period not to exceed 90 days and such order may be renewed for additional 90-day periods upon submission of renewal applications meeting the requirements of subsection (b).

(5) *Compliance.*– At or prior to the end of the period of time for which an order or extension is granted under this section, the judge may assess compliance with the minimization procedures referred to in paragraph (1)(c) by reviewing the circumstances under which information concerning United States persons was disseminated, provided that the judge may not inquire into the circumstances relating to the conduct of the acquisition.

(d) *Emergency authorization.*–

(1) *Authority for emergency authorization.*– Notwithstanding any other provision of this section, if the Attorney General reasonably determines that–

(A) an emergency situation exists with respect to the acquisition of foreign intelligence information for which an order may be obtained under subsection (c) before an order under that subsection can, with due diligence, be obtained, and

(B) the factual basis for the issuance of an order under this section exists, the Attorney General may authorize the emergency acquisition if a judge having jurisdiction under subsection (a)(1) is informed by the Attorney General or a designee of the Attorney General at the time of such authorization that the decision has been made to conduct such acquisition and if an application in accordance with this section is made to a judge of the Foreign Intelligence Surveillance Court as soon as practicable, but not more than 7 days after the Attorney General authorizes such acquisition.

(2) *Minimization procedures.*– f the Attorney General authorizes an emergency acquisition under paragraph (1), the Attorney General shall require that the minimization procedures referred to in subsection (c)(1)(c) be followed.

(3) *Termination of emergency authorization.*– n the absence of an order under subsection (c), an emergency acquisition under paragraph (1) shall terminate when the information sought is obtained, if the application for the order is denied, or after the expiration of 7 days from the time of authorization by the Attorney General, whichever is earliest.

(4) *Use of information.*– If an application submitted to the Court pursuant to paragraph (1) is denied, or in any other case where the acquisition is terminated and no order with respect to the target of the acquisition is issued under subsection (c), no information obtained or evidence derived from such acquisition, except under circumstances in which the target of the acquisition is determined not to be a United States person, shall be received in evidence or

otherwise disclosed in any trial, hearing, or other proceeding in or before any court, grand jury, department, office, agency, regulatory body, legislative committee, or other authority of the United States, a State, or political subdivision thereof, and no information concerning any United States person acquired from such acquisition shall subsequently be used or disclosed in any other manner by Federal officers or employees without the consent of such person, except with the approval of the Attorney General if the information indicates a threat of death or serious bodily harm to any person.

(e) *Appeal.–*

(1) *Appeal to the court of review.–* he Government may file a petition with the Foreign Intelligence Surveillance Court of Review for review of an order issued pursuant to subsection (c). The Court of Review shall have jurisdiction to consider such petition and shall provide a written statement for the record of the reasons for a decision under this paragraph.

(2) *Certiorari to the supreme court.–* The Government may file a petition for a writ of certiorari for review of a decision of the Court of Review issued under paragraph (1). The record for such review shall be transmitted under seal to the Supreme Court of the United States, which shall have jurisdiction to review such decision.

[Sec. 403(b)(1)] Except as provided in section 404, effective December 31, 2012, title VII of the Foreign Intelligence Surveillance Act of 1978, as amended by section 101(a), [50 U.S.C. 1881 to 1881g]]is repealed.

[Sec. 404(b)] *Transition procedures for FISA Amendments Act of 2008 Provisions.–*

(1) *Orders in effect on December 31, 2012.* – Notwithstanding any other provision of this Act, any amendment made by this Act, or the Foreign Intelligence Surveillance Act of 1978 (50 U.S.C. 1801 et seq.), any order, authorization, or directive issued or made under title VII of the Foreign Intelligence Surveillance Act of 1978, as amended by section 101(a) [50 U.S.C. 1881-1881g], shall continue in effect until the date of the expiration of such order, authorization, or directive.

(2) *Applicability of Title VII of FISA to continued orders, authorizations, directives.–* Notwithstanding any other provision of this Act, any amendment made by this Act, or the Foreign Intelligence Surveillance Act of 1978 (50 U.S.C. 1801 et seq.), with respect to any order, authorization, or directive referred to in paragraph (1), title VII of such Act, as amended by section 101(a) [50 U.S.C. 1881-1881g], shall continue to apply until the later of– (A) the expiration of such order, authorization, or directive; or (B) the date on which final judgment is entered for any petition or other litigation relating to such order, authorization, or directive.

50 U.S.C. 1881D. JOINT APPLICATIONS AND CONCURRENT AUTHORIZATIONS

(a) *Joint applications and orders.–* If an acquisition targeting a United States person under section 703 or 704 is proposed to be conducted both inside and outside the United States, a judge having jurisdiction under section 703(a)(1) or 704(a)(1) may issue simultaneously, upon the request of the Government in a joint application complying with the requirements of sections 703(b) and 704(b), orders under sections 703(c) and 704(c), as appropriate.

(b) *Concurrent authorization*– If an order authorizing electronic surveillance or physical search has been obtained under section 105 or 304, the Attorney General may authorize, for the effective period of that order, without an order under section 703 or 704, the targeting of that United States person for the purpose of acquiring foreign intelligence information while such person is reasonably believed to be located outside the United States.

[Sec. 403(b)(1)] Except as provided in section 404, effective December 31, 2012, title VII of the Foreign Intelligence Surveillance Act of 1978, as amended by section 101(a), [50 U.S.C. 1881 to 1881g]]is repealed.

[Sec. 404(b)] *Transition procedures for FISA Amendments Act of 2008 Provisions.–*

(1) *Orders in effect on December 31, 2012.* – Notwithstanding any other provision of this Act, any amendment made by this Act, or the Foreign Intelligence Surveillance Act of 1978 (50 U.S.C. 1801 et seq.), any order, authorization, or directive issued or made under title VII of the Foreign Intelligence Surveillance Act of 1978, as amended by section 101(a) [50 U.S.C. 1881-1881g], shall continue in effect until the date of the expiration of such order, authorization, or directive.

(2) *Applicability of Title VII of FISA to continued orders, authorizations, directives.*– Notwithstanding any other provision of this Act, any amendment made by this Act, or the Foreign Intelligence Surveillance Act of 1978 (50 U.S.C. 1801 et seq.), with respect to any order, authorization, or directive referred to in paragraph (1), title VII of such Act, as amended by section 101(a) [50 U.S.C. 1881-1881g], shall continue to apply until the later of– (A) the expiration of such order, authorization, or directive; or (B) the date on which final judgment is entered for any petition or other litigation relating to such order, authorization, or directive. . . .

[Sec. 404(b)(5)] *Transition procedures concerning the targeting of United States persons overseas.*– Any authorization in effect on the date of enactment of this Act under section 2.5 of Executive Order 12333 to intentionally target a United States person reasonably believed to be located outside the United States shall continue in effect, and shall constitute a sufficient basis for conducting such an acquisition targeting a United States person located outside the United States until the earlier of–

(A) the date that authorization expires; or

(B) the date that is 90 days after the date of the enactment of this Act.

50 U.S.C. 1881E. USE OF INFORMATION ACQUIRED UNDER TITLE VII

(a) *Information acquired under section 702.*– Information acquired from an acquisition conducted under section 702 shall be deemed to be information acquired from an electronic surveillance pursuant to title I for purposes of section 106, except for the purposes of subsection (j) of such section.

(b) *Information acquired under section 703.*– Information acquired from an acquisition conducted under section 703 shall be deemed to be information acquired from an electronic surveillance pursuant to title I for purposes of section 106.

[Sec. 403(b)(1)] Except as provided in section 404, effective December 31, 2012, title VII of the Foreign Intelligence Surveillance Act of 1978, as amended by section 101(a), [50 U.S.C. 1881 to 1881g]]is repealed.

[Sec. 404(b)] *Transition procedures for FISA Amendments Act of 2008 Provisions.*–

(1) *Orders in effect on December 31, 2012.* – Notwithstanding any other provision of this Act, any amendment made by this Act, or the Foreign Intelligence Surveillance Act of 1978 (50 U.S.C. 1801 et seq.), any order, authorization, or directive issued or made under title VII of the Foreign Intelligence Surveillance Act of 1978, as amended by section 101(a) [50 U.S.C. 1881-1881g], shall continue in effect until the date of the expiration of such order, authorization, or directive.

(2) *Applicability of Title VII of FISA to continued orders, authorizations, directives.*– Notwithstanding any other provision of this Act, any amendment made by this Act, or the Foreign Intelligence Surveillance Act of 1978 (50 U.S.C. 1801 et seq.), with respect to any order, authorization, or directive referred to in paragraph (1), title VII of such Act, as amended by section 101(a) [50 U.S.C. 1881-1881g], shall continue to apply until the later of– (A) the expiration of such order, authorization, or directive; or (B) the date on which final judgment is entered for any petition or other litigation relating to such order, authorization, or directive.

(3) *Challenge of directives; protection from liability; use of information* – Notwithstanding any other provision of this Act or of the Foreign Intelligence Surveillance Act of 1978 (50 U.S.C. 1801 et seq.) . . (D) section 706 of such Act (as so added) shall continue to apply to an acquisition conducted under section 702 or 703 of such Act (as so added);

50 U.S.C. 1881F. CONGRESSIONAL OVERSIGHT

(a) *Semiannual report.*– Not less frequently than once every 6 months, the Attorney General shall fully inform, in a manner consistent with national security, the congressional intelligence committees and the Committees on the Judiciary of the Senate and the House of Representatives, consistent with the Rules of the House of Representatives, the Standing Rules of the Senate, and Senate Resolution 400 of the 94th Congress or any successor Senate resolution, concerning the implementation of this title.

(b) *Content.*– Each report under subsection (a) shall include-

(1) with respect to section 702–

(A) reporting period;

(B) with respect to each determination under section 702(c)(2), the reasons for exercising the authority under such section;

(C) any directives issued under section 702(h) during the reporting period;

(D) a description of the judicial review during the reporting period of such certifications and targeting and minimization procedures adopted in accordance with subsections (d) and (e) of section 702 and utilized with respect to an acquisition under such section, including a copy of an order or pleading in connection with such review that contains a significant legal interpretation of the provisions of section 702;

(E) any actions taken to challenge or enforce a directive under paragraph (4) or (5) of section 702(h);

(F) any compliance reviews conducted by the Attorney General or the Director of National Intelligence of acquisitions authorized under section 702(a);

(G) a description of any incidents of noncompliance-

(i) with a directive issued by the Attorney General and the Director of National Intelligence under section 702(h), including incidents of noncompliance by a specified person to whom the Attorney General and Director of National Intelligence issued a directive under section 702(h); and

(ii) by an element of the intelligence community with procedures and guidelines adopted in accordance with subsections (d), (e), and (f) of section 702; and

(H) any procedures implementing section 702;

(2) with respect to section 70.-

(A) the total number of applications made for orders under section 703(b);

(B) the total number of such orders-

(i) granted;

(ii) modified; and

(iii) denied; and

(c) the total number of emergency acquisitions authorized by the Attorney General under section 703(d) and the total number of subsequent orders approving or denying such acquisitions; and

(3) with respect to section 704-

(A) the total number of applications made for orders under section 704(b);

(B) the total number of such orders-

(i) granted;

(ii) modified; and

(iii) denied; and

(C) the total number of emergency acquisitions authorized by the Attorney General under section 704(d) and the total number of subsequent orders approving or denying such applications.

[Sec. 403(b)(1)] Except as provided in section 404, effective December 31, 2012, title VII of the Foreign Intelligence Surveillance Act of 1978, as amended by section 101(a), [50 U.S.C. 1881 to 1881g]]is repealed.

[Sec. 404(b)] *Transition procedures for FISA Amendments Act of 2008 Provisions.–*

(1) *Orders in effect on December 31, 2012.* – Notwithstanding any other provision of this Act, any amendment made by this Act, or the Foreign Intelligence Surveillance Act of 1978 (50 U.S.C. 1801 et seq.), any order, authorization, or directive issued or made under title VII of the Foreign Intelligence Surveillance Act of 1978, as amended by section

101(a) [50 U.S.C. 1881-1881g], shall continue in effect until the date of the expiration of such order, authorization, or directive.

(2) *Applicability of Title VII of FISA to continued orders, authorizations, directives.–* Notwithstanding any other provision of this Act, any amendment made by this Act, or the Foreign Intelligence Surveillance Act of 1978 (50 U.S.C. 1801 et seq.), with respect to any order, authorization, or directive referred to in paragraph (1), title VII of such Act, as amended by section 101(a) [50 U.S.C. 1881-1881g], shall continue to apply until the later of– (A) the expiration of such order, authorization, or directive; or (B) the date on which final judgment is entered for any petition or other litigation relating to such order, authorization, or directive.

50 U.S.C. 1881G. SAVINGS PROVISION

Nothing in this title shall be construed to limit the authority of the Government to seek an order or authorization under, or otherwise engage in any activity that is authorized under, any other title of this Act.

[Sec. 403(b)(1)] Except as provided in section 404, effective December 31, 2012, title VII of the Foreign Intelligence Surveillance Act of 1978, as amended by section 101(a), [50 U.S.C. 1881 to 1881g]]is repealed.

[Sec. 404(b)] Transition procedures for FISA Amendments Act of 2008 Provisions.–

(1) *Orders in effect on December 31, 2012.* – Notwithstanding any other provision of this Act, any amendment made by this Act, or the Foreign Intelligence Surveillance Act of 1978 (50 U.S.C. 1801 et seq.), any order, authorization, or directive issued or made under title VII of the Foreign Intelligence Surveillance Act of 1978, as amended by section 101(a) [50 U.S.C. 1881-1881g], shall continue in effect until the date of the expiration of such order, authorization, or directive.

(2) *Applicability of Title VII of FISA to continued orders, authorizations, directives.–* Notwithstanding any other provision of this Act, any amendment made by this Act, or the Foreign Intelligence Surveillance Act of 1978 (50 U.S.C. 1801 et seq.), with respect to any order, authorization, or directive referred to in paragraph (1), title VII of such Act, as amended by section 101(a) [50 U.S.C. 1881-1881g], shall continue to apply until the later of– (A) the expiration of such order, authorization, or directive; or (B) the date on which final judgment is entered for any petition or other litigation relating to such order, authorization, or directive.

[Sec. 201] **50 U.S.C. 1885. Definitions**.

In this title:

(1) Assistance.– The term "assistance" means the provision of, or the provision of access to, information (including communication contents, communications records, or other information relating to a customer or communication), facilities, or another form of assistance.

(2) Civil action.– The term "civil action" includes a covered civil action.

(3) Congressional intelligence committees.– The term "congressional intelligence committees" means–
  (A) the Select Committee on Intelligence of the Senate; and
  (B) the Permanent Select Committee on Intelligence of the House of Representatives.

(4) Contents.– The term "contents" has the meaning given that term in section 101(n).

(5) Covered civil action.– The term "covered civil action" means a civil action filed in a Federal or State court that-
  (A) alleges that an electronic communication service provider furnished assistance to an element of the intelligence community; and
  (B) seeks monetary or other relief from the electronic communication service provider related to the provision of such assistance.

(6) Electronic Communication Service Provider.– The term "electronic communication service provider"means-
  (A) a telecommunications carrier, as that term is defined in section 3 of the Communications Act of 1934 (47 U.S.C. 153);
  (B) a provider of electronic communication service, as that term is defined in section 2510 of title 18, United States Code;
  (C) a provider of a remote computing service, as that term is defined in section 2711 of title 18, United States Code;
  (D) any other communication service provider who has access to wire or electronic communications either as such communications are transmitted or as such communications are stored;
  (E) a parent, subsidiary, affiliate, successor, or assignee of an entity described in subparagraph (A), (B), (c), or (D); or
  (F) an officer, employee, or agent of an entity described in subparagraph (A), (B), (c), (D), or (E).

(7) Intelligence community.– The term "intelligence community" has the meaning given the term in section 3(4) of the National Security Act of 1947 (50 U.S.C. 401a(4)).

(8) Person– The term "person" means–
  (A) an electronic communication service provider; or
  (B) a landlord, custodian, or other person who may be authorized or required to furnish assistance pursuant to–
    (i) an order of the court established under section 103(a) directing such assistance;
    (ii) a certification in writing under section 2511(2)(a)(ii)(B) or 2709(b) of title 18, United States Code; or
    (iii) a directive under section 102(a)(4), 105B(e), as added by section 2 of the Protect America Act of 2007 (Public Law 110-55), or 702(h).

(9) State.– The term "State" means any State, political subdivision of a State, the Commonwealth of Puerto Rico, the District of Columbia, and any territory or possession of the United States, and includes any officer, public utility commission, or other body authorized to regulate an electronic communication service provider.

50 U.S.C. 1885A. Procedures for Implementing Statutory Defenses

(a) *Requirement for certification.*– Notwithstanding any other provision of law, a civil action may not lie or be maintained in a Federal or State court against any person for providing assistance to an element of the intelligence community, and shall be promptly dismissed, if the Attorney General certifies to the district court of the United States in which such action is pending that-
  (1) any assistance by that person was provided pursuant to an order of the court established under section 103(a) directing such assistance;
  (2) any assistance by that person was provided pursuant to a certification in writing under section 2511(2)(a)(ii)(B) or 2709(b) of title 18, United States Code;
  (3) any assistance by that person was provided pursuant to a directive under section 102(a)(4), 105B(e), as added by section 2 of the Protect America Act of 2007 (Public Law 110-55), or 702(h) directing such assistance;
  (4) in the case of a covered civil action, the assistance alleged to have been provided by the electronic communication service provider was-
    (A) in connection with an intelligence activity involving communications that was-
      (i) authorized by the President during the period beginning on September 11, 2001, and ending on January 17, 2007; and
      (ii) designed to detect or prevent a terrorist attack, or activities in preparation for a terrorist attack, against the United States; and
    (B) the subject of a written request or directive, or a series of written requests or directives, from the Attorney General or the head of an element of the intelligence community (or the deputy of such person) to the electronic communication service provider indicating that the activity was-
      (i) authorized by the President; and
      (ii) determined to be lawful; or
  (5) the person did not provide the alleged assistance.

(b) *Judicial review.*–
  (1) *Review of certifications.*– A certification under subsection (a) shall be given effect unless the court finds that such certification is not supported by substantial evidence provided to the court pursuant to this section.
  (2) *Supplemental materials.*– In its review of a certification under subsection (a), the court may examine the court order, certification, written request, or directive described in subsection (a) and any relevant court order, certification, written request, or directive submitted pursuant to subsection (d).

(c) *Limitations on disclosure.*– If the Attorney General files a declaration under section 1746 of title 28, United States Code, that disclosure of a certification made pursuant to subsection (a) or the supplemental materials provided pursuant to subsection (b) or (d) would harm the national security of the United States, the court shall-
  (1) review such certification and the supplemental materials in camera and ex parte; and
  (2) limit any public disclosure concerning such certification and the supplemental materials, including any public order following such in camera and ex parte review, to a statement as to whether the case is dismissed and a description of the

legal standards that govern the order, without disclosing the paragraph of subsection (a) that is the basis for the certification.

(d) *Role of the parties*.– Any plaintiff or defendant in a civil action may submit any relevant court order, certification, written request, or directive to the district court referred to in subsection (a) for review and shall be permitted to participate in the briefing or argument of any legal issue in a judicial proceeding conducted pursuant to this section, but only to the extent that such participation does not require the disclosure of classified information to such party. To the extent that classified information is relevant to the proceeding or would be revealed in the determination of an issue, the court shall review such information in camera and ex parte, and shall issue any part of the court's written order that would reveal classified information in camera and ex parte and maintain such part under seal.

(e) *Nondelegation*.– The authority and duties of the Attorney General under this section shall be performed by the Attorney General (or Acting Attorney General) or the Deputy Attorney General.

(f) *Appeal*.– The courts of appeals shall have jurisdiction of appeals from interlocutory orders of the district courts of the United States granting or denying a motion to dismiss or for summary judgment under this section.

(g) *Removal*.– A civil action against a person for providing assistance to an element of the intelligence community that is brought in a State court shall be deemed to arise under the Constitution and laws of the United States and shall be removable under section 1441 of title 28, United States Code.

(h) *Relationship to other laws*.– Nothing in this section shall be construed to limit any otherwise available immunity, privilege, or defense under any other provision of law.

(i) *Applicability*.– This section shall apply to a civil action pending on or filed after the date of the enactment of the FISA Amendments Act of 2008.

50 U.S.C. 1885B. PREEMPTION

(a) *In general*.– No State shall have authority to-

  (1) conduct an investigation into an electronic communication service provider's alleged assistance to an element of the intelligence community;

  (2) require through regulation or any other means the disclosure of information about an electronic communication service provider's alleged assistance to an element of the intelligence community;

  (3) impose any administrative sanction on an electronic communication service provider for assistance to an element of the intelligence community; or

  (4) commence or maintain a civil action or other proceeding to enforce a requirement that an electronic communication service provider disclose information concerning alleged assistance to an element of the intelligence community.

(b) *Suits by the United States*.– The United States may bring suit to enforce the provisions of this section.

(c) *Jurisdiction*.– The district courts of the United States shall have jurisdiction over any civil action brought by the United States to enforce the provisions of this section.

(d) *Application.*– This section shall apply to any investigation, action, or proceeding that is pending on or commenced after the date of the enactment of the FISA Amendments Act of 2008.

50 U.S.C. 1885c. Reporting

(a) *Semiannual report.*– Not less frequently than once every 6 months, the Attorney General shall, in a manner consistent with national security, the Rules of the House of Representatives, the Standing Rules of the Senate, and Senate Resolution 400 of the 94th Congress or any successor Senate resolution, fully inform the congressional intelligence committees, the Committee on the Judiciary of the Senate, and the Committee on the Judiciary of the House of Representatives concerning the implementation of this title.

(b) *Content.*– Each report made under subsection (a) shall include-
  (1) any certifications made under section 802;
  (2) a description of the judicial review of the certifications made under section 802; and
  (3) any actions taken to enforce the provisions of section 803.

P.L. 110-261, 122 Stat. 2436 (2008)
Title III--Review of Previous Actions

Sec. 301. Review of Previous Actions

(a) *Definitions.*– In this section:
  (1) *Appropriate Committees of Congress.*– The term “appropriate committees of Congress” means–
    (A) the Select Committee on Intelligence and the Committee on the Judiciary of the Senate; and
    (B) the Permanent Select Committee on Intelligence and the Committee on the Judiciary of the House of Representatives.
  (2) *Foreign intelligence surveillance court.*– The term “Foreign Intelligence Surveillance Court” means the court established under section 103(a) of the Foreign Intelligence Surveillance Act of 1978 (50 U.S.C. 1803(a)).
  (3) *President’s surveillance program and program.*– The terms “President’s Surveillance Program” and “Program” mean the intelligence activity involving communications that was authorized by the President during the period beginning on September 11, 2001, and ending on January 17, 2007, including the program referred to by the President in a radio address on December 17, 2005 (commonly known as the Terrorist Surveillance Program).

(b) *Reviews.*–
  (1) *Requirement to conduct.*– The Inspectors General of the Department of Justice, the Office of the Director of National Intelligence, the National Security Agency, the Department of Defense, and any other element of the intelligence community that participated in the President's Surveillance Program, shall complete a

comprehensive review of, with respect to the oversight authority and responsibility of each such Inspector General–

(A) all of the facts necessary to describe the establishment, implementation, product, and use of the product of the Program;

(B) access to legal reviews of the Program and access to information about the Program;

(C) communications with, and participation of, individuals and entities in the private sector related to the Program;

(D) interaction with the Foreign Intelligence Surveillance Court and transition to court orders related to the Program; and

(E) any other matters identified by any such Inspector General that would enable that Inspector General to complete a review of the Program, with respect to such Department or element.

(2) *Cooperation and Coordination.–*

(A) *Cooperation.–* Each Inspector General required to conduct a review under paragraph (1) shall-

(i) work in conjunction, to the extent practicable, with any other Inspector General required to conduct such a review; and

(ii) utilize, to the extent practicable, and not unnecessarily duplicate or delay, such reviews or audits that have been completed or are being undertaken by any such Inspector General or by any other office of the Executive Branch related to the Program.

(B) *Integration of other reviews.–* The Counsel of the Office of Professional Responsibility of the Department of Justice shall provide the report of any investigation conducted by such Office on matters relating to the Program, including any investigation of the process through which legal reviews of the Program were conducted and the substance of such reviews, to the Inspector General of the Department of Justice, who shall integrate the factual findings and conclusions of such investigation into its review.

(C) *Coordination.–* The Inspectors General shall designate one of the Inspectors General required to conduct a review under paragraph (1) that is appointed by the President, by and with the advice and consent of the Senate, to coordinate the conduct of the reviews and the preparation of the reports.

(c) *Reports.–*

(1) *Preliminary reports.*--Not later than 60 days after the date of the enactment of this Act, the Inspectors General of the Department of Justice, the Office of the Director of National Intelligence, the National Security Agency, the Department of Defense, and any other Inspector General required to conduct a review under subsection (b)(1), shall submit to the appropriate committees of Congress an interim report that describes the planned scope of such review.

(2) *Final report.–* Not later than 1 year after the date of the enactment of this Act, the Inspectors General of the Department of Justice, the Office of the Director of National Intelligence, the National Security Agency, the Department of Defense, and any other Inspector General required to conduct a review under subsection (b)(1), shall submit to the appropriate committees of Congress, in a manner

consistent with national security, a comprehensive report on such reviews that includes any recommendations of any such Inspectors General within the oversight authority and responsibility of any such Inspector General with respect to the reviews.

(3) *Form.–* report under this subsection shall be submitted in unclassified form, but may include a classified annex. The unclassified report shall not disclose the name or identity of any individual or entity of the private sector that participated in the Program or with whom there was communication about the Program, to the extent that information is classified.

(d) *Resources.–*

(1) *Expedited security clearance.–* The Director of National Intelligence shall ensure that the process for the investigation and adjudication of an application by an Inspector General or any appropriate staff of an Inspector General for a security clearance necessary for the conduct of the review under subsection (b)(1) is carried out as expeditiously as possible.

(2) *Additional personnel for the inspectors general.–* An Inspector General required to conduct a review under subsection (b)(1) and submit a report under subsection (c) is authorized to hire such additional personnel as may be necessary to carry out such review and prepare such report in a prompt and timely manner. Personnel authorized to be hired under this paragraph-

(A) shall perform such duties relating to such a review as the relevant Inspector General shall direct; and

(B) are in addition to any other personnel authorized by law.

(3) *Transfer of personnel.–* The Attorney General, the Secretary of Defense, the Director of National Intelligence, the Director of the National Security Agency, or the head of any other element of the intelligence community may transfer personnel to the relevant Office of the Inspector General required to conduct a review under subsection (b)(1) and submit a report under subsection (c) and, in addition to any other personnel authorized by law, are authorized to fill any vacancy caused by such a transfer. Personnel transferred under this paragraph shall perform such duties relating to such review as the relevant Inspector General shall direct.

In: Privacy: An Overview of Federal Law…
Editor: Alderic Jimenez
ISBN: 978-1-60741-654-8

INDEX

9

A

D

E

G

H

I

T

U

V

W